The Micro-politics of Microcredit

Microcredit has been seen in recent decades as having great potential for aiding development in poor developing countries, with Bangladesh being one of the countries which has pioneered microcredit and implemented it most widely. This book, based on extensive original research, explores how micro-credit works in practice, and assesses its effectiveness. It discusses how microcredit, usually channelled through women, is often passed to the men of the family, a practice disapproved of by some, but regarded as acceptable by borrowers who have a communal approach to debt, rather than viewing debt as something held by single individuals. The book demonstrates how the rules concerning microcredit are often regarded as irksome by the borrowers, how lenders often charge high rates of interest and work primarily to preserve their institutions, thereby going against the spirit of the microcredit movement, and how borrowers often end up on a downward spiral, falling deeper and deeper in debt. Overall, the book argues that although microcredit does much good, it also has many drawbacks.

Mohammad Jasim Uddin is professor of Sociology at Shahjalal University of Science & Technology, Sylhet, Bangladesh. His areas of interest include rural poverty, gender and development.

The Micro-politics of Microcredit

Gender and neoliberal development in Bangladesh

Mohammad Jasim Uddin

Routledge
Taylor & Francis Group

LONDON AND NEW YORK

First published 2015 by Routledge

2 Park Square, Milton Park, Abingdon, Oxfordshire OX14 4RN
711 Third Avenue, New York, NY 10017

Routledge is an imprint of the Taylor & Francis Group, an informa business

First issued in paperback 2017

British Library Cataloguing in Publication Data
A catalogue record for this book is available from the British Library

Library of Congress Cataloging in Publication Data
Jasim Uddin, Mohammad.
   The micro-politics of microcredit : gender and neoliberal development in Bangladesh / by Mohammad Jasim Uddin.
      pages cm. – (Asian Studies Association of Australia women in Asia series)
   1. Microfinance–Bangladesh. 2. Women–Bangladesh–Economic conditions. 3. Women–Bangladesh–Social conditions. 4. Women in development–Bangladesh. 5. Rural women–Bangladesh–Economic conditions. 6. Rural poor–Bangladesh. 7. Neoliberalism–Bangladesh. I. Title.
   HG178.33.B3J37 2015
   332–dc23
                    2014048883

ISBN: 978-1-138-90271-8 (hbk)
ISBN: 978-0-8153-6428-3 (pbk)

Typeset in Times New Roman
by Taylor & Francis Books

Dedicated to my parents, my wife Joya and son Anindya

Contents

List of illustrations

Figures

Tables

Preface

Microcredit has gained huge attention internationally as a route out of poverty and as a means to women's empowerment, and is generally upheld as a development success story, with the founder of Grameen Bank, Mohammad Yunus, receiving the Nobel Peace Prize for his work in 2006. This book is a study of how the provision of microcredit by two flagship microfinance organizations in Bangladesh - Grameen Bank (GB) and the Bangladesh Rural Advancement Committee (BRAC) - relates to the everyday lives of borrowers in rural Bangladesh. More specifically, this study delves into whether the 'group-based' micro-loans that are channelled through women can actually facilitate social capital, reconstruct gender relations and provide a way out of poverty at the village level in Bangladesh. The study looks at three aspects: the social capital paradigm, the women's empowerment paradigm, and the poverty alleviation paradigm of the microcredit programmes. Unlike any previous study on microcredit in Bangladesh all three are combined in this volume.

I address the question of how on the one hand non-governmental organizations (NGOs) use neoliberal policies and credit, and on the other hand how local people access and appropriate credit. I stress the power relations, implications of enforced *institutional discipline* of microcredit organizations, and vulnerability of microcredit borrowers. Drawing on Michel Foucault's theoretical concepts of *disciplinary power* and *governmentality*, the study illustrates processes and practices of governance, calculated means of intervention and the creation of a set of rules to govern and discipline the developmental subjects (i.e. microcredit borrowers) to achieve certain goals. By applying James Scott's notions of *hidden resistance* and the weapons of the weak, I have focused on the way in which microcredit borrowers criticize the rules of programmes and procedures out of earshot of the NGO officials. Following the *entitlement approach* outlined by Sen, I have also addressed the mechanism whereby poor people can take credit year after year, and thus become further mired in debt.

While microcredit is a fairly well-trodden area of research, relatively few qualitative studies have been carried out that are based on in-depth fieldwork and ethnography. Most of the studies and claims about the economic success and women's empowerment of microcredit in Bangladesh are based on statistical surveys, quantitative data, econometric analyses, and are donor-driven: i.e. they were sponsored by the World Bank, international organizations or the NGOs themselves. The empirical data used in the present study was collected from 151 married female microcredit borrowers involved in two project areas of GB and two project areas of BRAC in the Sylhet District, Bangladesh where both GB and BRAC have been operating micro-loans for several years. My study focuses on women but also on the part played by men, and most of my respondents are women. I also collected data from GB and BRAC micro-lending field officials in my research areas. My most important research material is qualitative and my analytical approach is interpretative. By combining personal observation with didactic themed and in-depth interviews, case studies as well as informal discussions, and bringing the perspective of both microcredit clients and the microcredit officials into the analysis, this study provides a complete and detailed description of the appropriation of credit as part of the local economic, social and cultural settings and processes of the studied villages. The study has also explored the hidden practices through which the game of microcredit is largely played out. My decision to study microcredit programmes in Bangladesh is rooted in my conviction that a qualitative study approach has much to offer to research into this global development paradigm. Qualitative research provides information in a particular but meaningful context and is increasingly used to provide evidence for policy makers.

The Micro-politics of Microcredit is aimed at development practitioners, academics and postgraduate students. My scholarship not only complements the prevailing research on GB and BRAC through the addition of another study but it also offers critical viewpoints from other research findings on microcredit policy and practices, poverty alleviation and women's empowerment. I would like to highlight a couple of findings that add nuance to established knowledge about microcredit.

The social capital school has hitherto demonstrated a direct association between organizational membership, the creation of societal engagement and cooperative behaviour. The findings of this study, however, have contested the romanticized notions of social capital, solidarity and participatory emancipation involved in the concept of microcredit membership. The study shows how group-based microcredit causes various anxieties, expectations and conflict among the members. Although social capital plays a significant role in the formation of borrowing groups, the analysis of data indicates that collectiveness, mutual support and economic exchange among borrowers are, overall, very scarce. Overall, the social collateral mechanism works as an entry route to a credit programme for borrowers, but for NGOs it is a mechanism for promoting their governance and disciplinary power over borrowers and a furtherance of capitalist gains through the collection of instalments when they are due. Although according to the microcredit rhetoric group members take joint-liability for loan repayments, there is no clear example of joint-liability arrangements whereby group members take responsibility for other members' repayment difficulties in the study areas. The package of training, meetings to discuss problems and consciousness-raising lessons that originally accompanied the microcredit programme is no longer part of the practice of microcredit organization.

The fact that credit channelled to women is frequently appropriated by male family members is a strong and consistent criticism of microcredit's ability to empower women. Some studies (e.g. Goetz and Sen Gupta, 1996; Karim, 2008; Rahman, 1999) are frequently cited by critics of microfinance as proof of its failure to improve women's economic position with their families and societies. In sharp contrast to these findings, my study argues that such criticism cannot easily be made because credit is not regarded by female borrowers as individual property but rather as a family or collective resource that is used for the welfare of all members of the household. The present study challenges the ethnocentric biases of such findings by demonstrating that to a large extent the notion of personal use and individual responsibility is not valid in rural Bangladesh. Unlike other researchers who view men's use of loans taken out by women as an indication of the subordination of women, this study asserts that women do not believe that they alone are entitled to their loans. They regard the money as a collective resource and its use by men in the family is not an issue of conflict. The fact that women pass on the loaned money to men is a reflection of the rural reality that men are more familiar with the workings of the public domain within which more lucrative activities are located. Consequently, the ethnocentric Euro-American notions of personal use and individual responsibility make it difficult to grasp how credit is controlled and channelled in families in Bangladesh. However, credit granted to women is not entirely a noble mission in Bangladesh. The research reveals a glaring ideological clash between the microfinance industry's articulation of a public transcript that supposedly encourages women to become independent economic agents whereas it actually relies upon their subordinate position in society and their being embedded in patriarchal gender relations to ensure its own survival.

The global microfinance industry (MFI) operates within a broad neoliberal agenda of diminished welfare states, drastically reduced social spending and the increased privatization and deregulation of public institutions. It has placed too much emphasis on individual responsibility to take control of his or her own situation according to market principles of 'disciplines, efficiency, and competitiveness.' The MFI has always relied on a grand narrative about its ability to alleviate poverty and empower women in order to justify its existence. The present study complicates this 'public transcript' by revealing both the logistics and the 'micro-politics' of a 'hidden transcript' that suggest that in practice microcredit does not accomplish perfectly any of the goals that are supposed to be its main *raison d'etre*. However, the MFI continues to hide behind the rhetoric of women's empowerment and poverty reduction for the purpose of self-preservation. In terms of the disadvantageous ways in which poor people are incorporated into economic and social life, this study illustrates the major disjuncture between microcredit policies, their practices and the inherent structural obstacles that the poor encounter in everyday life. Microfinance has emerged as a lucrative commercial business, operated by different organizations and pursuing a diversity of techniques, each exhibiting its power to create its own 'economic habitus' in the rural credit market. While dispelling some of these oft-repeated mythologies about microcredit, I go on to explore the reasons for which poor people continue to borrow money from these institutions and how microcredit regulates repayment behaviour and perpetuates borrower dependence on credit. During my field-work I was to hear again and again from borrowers that 'we took new loans for the payment of outstanding dues' (*amra loan deye loan mari*).

The present study argues that microcredit can be regarded as a form of governmentality that is exercised via generalized control of people's behaviour and their beliefs, which spreads the values of entrepreneurship within the 'market' as a solution for all ills. While the much-lauded microcredit organizations encourage rural borrowers to adopt neoliberal ideologies, ultimately they have failed because many borrowers cannot earn sufficient profit or use credit for the purpose for which it was originally intended. Microcredit organizations reinforce traditional kinship and gender structures, and there has been a widespread 'mission creep', which has turned micro-lending NGOs into money-lending businesses or instalment-collecting organizations.

The arguments presented in this book have been pursued over a number of years and in that time I have accumulated intellectual debts to my teachers, colleagues, friends and students. I am happy to acknowledge these debts as to my mind the pursuit of scholarship is a collective endeavour and the contribution of one is heavily dependent upon the help of others. However, all the limitations, errors and omissions are mine alone. My greatest debt is to Professor Sirpa Tenhunen at the University of Helsinki to whom I am humbly grateful. Many thanks to Professor Katy Gardner at the University of Sussex, and Professor Bipasha Baruah at the University of Western Ontario for their comments about my research which have helped to raise my work to a higher analytical level. I am grateful to Professor Karen Armstrong, who gave me the opportunity to attend and present my research at the postgraduate seminar of the Social and Cultural Anthropology Department for several years. I particularly benefited from the discussions and comments of the participants at the seminars.

I am deeply grateful to Dr Minna Säävälä who was so kind to me. I am greatly indebted to her in many ways. My cordial thanks to Professor Anssi Peräkylä, Professor Timo Kartineen and Dr Timo Kortteinen at the University of Helsinki for their valuable support and encouragement. I benefited from the assistance of Professor Huma Ahmed Ghosh at San Diego State University, who at an early stage of writing read my research proposal and gave her critical comments.

I want to thank my wife Professor Dr Laila Ashrafun Joya and my son Anindya for their unceasing love. They are my lifelong friends. Joya's help is unforgettable. She is my inspiration. I often shared my ideas, got involved in conversations with her and sought her opinion. My gratitude also goes to my teachers Professor K. A. M. Saad Uddin, Professor H. K. S. Arefeen, Professor A. I. Mahbub Uddin Ahmed, and the late Professor A. M. M. Shahidulla at Dhaka University, who inspired me in many ways to pursue my academic career.

My most profound debt of gratitude is to family members, some of whom are no longer with us, but who were and still are an inspiration to me. In particular, I remember my father the late M. Solaiman Miah, a visionary man who dreamed that his son would be awarded a doctorate. My deep gratitude goes to my mother and my brothers and sisters, who have always loved and supported me. I fondly remember my uncle, the late M. Mofizur Rahman, who made great contributions to my academic life.

This study was made possible by research funding from the Academy of Finland and a scholarship from the Jenny and Antti Wihuri Foundation. I would like to thank the funding agencies for their support. I owe especial thanks to the series editor Louise Edwards, Peter Sowden, the Routledge editorial board, Ruth Bradley and Alison Phillips for publishing my research in the form of this book. Finally, I thank the men and women in my research areas who shared their experiences, anecdotes and opinions with me and also invited me into their homes. Special thanks are also due to the microcredit officials working in my research areas.

Introduction
Development paradigms – old and new

Central conceptions through which development can be brought about in Third World countries in the quickest, most efficient and least expensive way are intrinsically linked to the modernization theories or paradigms of development. The foremost thinking of modernization theorists in the mid-1940s and 1950s was that the underdeveloped countries could facilitate development through top-down state-administered development planning. Governments in the developing world could create economic prosperity by replicating the industrial model and technology of the industrial society of the West – so the thinking went (Chamlee-Wright, 2005; Sorensen, 1993; Lerner, 1972). Sector-wide development planning and top-down financial interventions were considered state of the art during the 1950s and 1960s, and policies that favoured cumbersome control of economy persisted into 1970s. Various planning efforts were initiated to reduce poverty, and one of the most admired policies involved state-owned development institutions offering loans at heavily subsidized rates of interest to the rural poor farmers in the conviction that this would increase their incomes, multiply agricultural productivity, and thereby producing a surplus, which would in turn expedite industrialization (Chamlee-Wright, 2005; Hoff and Stiglitz, 1990).

However, in many developing countries, such policies largely failed to reduce corruption, food shortages or mass starvation, substantially decrease global poverty, or help the poverty-stricken inhabitants to enter the modern economy. The main reasons were that many such early state-driven financial interventions had weak incentive structures, were inefficient and the transaction cost of lending was high; they were highly bureaucratic, politicized, and often poorly chosen (Helms, 2006; Chamlee-Wright, 2005; Hoff and Stiglitz, 1990; Woolcock, 1998a; Bastelaer, 1999, 2000; Sobhan 1998; Adams *et al.*, 1984; Meier, 1984). According to Adams *et al.* (1984), the provision of subsidized credit for the poor led to the undermining of rural development, since neither the borrowers nor the bankers felt accountable to repay loans: both the local bankers and loan recipients deemed the money to be government handouts. The bureaucrats, and/or the comparatively local wealthy and powerful elite siphoned off aid money intended to help the poor via subsidies (World Bank, 1989; McGregor, 1988; Adams and Vogel, 1986). More to the point, the most economically disadvantaged and vulnerable inhabitants of developing countries were often denied access to financial organizations and were regarded as 'credit-ineligible' because they could not put up collateral accepted by formal banking organizations as is the case in industrial economies. Consequently, the 'economies of the bottom billion' were 'short of capital', thereby requiring 'private capital' (Collier, 2007: 87). On the other hand, the world's poorest people were considered to be 'billion bootstraps' (Smith and Thurman, 2007).[1] In reaction to this and in order to alter favourably the lives of the world's poorest people, Dr Muhammad Yunus, a Vanderbilt-educated professor of Economics at Chittagong University, and winner of the Nobel Peace Prize in 2006, launched the first systematic 'group-based' microcredit programme through Grameen Bank (GB) of Bangladesh in the mid-1970s.

Microcredit is conceived as the provision of small-scale financial loans to poor people for the purpose of undertaking small-scale economically productive enterprises. Bangladesh is the cradle of the microfinance movement.[2] The country is fast becoming one of the largest microfinance sectors in the world. The process of financial liberalization guided by the neoliberal agenda has transformed the microfinance landscape, which is reflected in the emergence of hundreds of non-governmental organizations (NGOs) throughout Bangladesh – a condition that has been eulogized by the World Bank as a 'catalyst of change' (cf. Karim, 2011). Two such NGOs, GB and the Bangladesh Rural Advancement Committee (BRAC), have successfully implemented a 'group-lending' banking system to provide money to the rural poor, predominantly women. These two NGOs achieved global recognition through their successful programmes (such as the number of clients, loan investments, and recovery rates on invested loans) and have assumed a hegemonic position in addressing both poverty alleviation and the social empowerment of women.[3] Both organizations claim that they do not require any form of collateral or conventional guarantees from the clients as security for loans. Individual loans are given to a small, self-selected and homogenous group of female borrowers (numbering between five and seven) who are collectively responsible for repayment of the loans. Women's access to credit can initiate a series of interlinked 'virtuous spirals' of economic empowerment, increased well-being for women and their families, and wider social and political empowerment through mobilizing and strengthening women's mobility and networks (Mayoux, 1999).

This book is a study of the way in which the provision of microcredit by two flagship microfinance institutions – GB and BRAC – influences the day-to-day lives of borrowers in rural Bangladesh. In particular, I investigate whether the group-based micro-loans that are channelled through women can actually facilitate social capital, reconstruct gender relations and provide a way out of poverty at the village level in Bangladesh.

Claims and research about microcredit

Microcredit has evolved into a global phenomenon, and currently is being implemented in many parts of the world including Latin America, Asia, Africa and even in developed countries such as the USA. The globalization of microfinance has generated a wave of enthusiasm in development discourses. Much of the impetus of microcredit policy is that it seems to negate all the errors of the previous top-down development paradigm and achieves what previous development approaches failed to achieve (Fernando, 2007; Chamlee-Wright, 2005). Bretton Woods institutions and United Nations (UN) agencies, in particular, adorned microfinance with many virtues in the fight against poverty and the pursuit of women's empowerment. In 1997, when the first microcredit summit[4] was launched in Washington, DC, USA, in support of the notion, it portrayed microcredit as the single most important weapon in overcoming poverty and as an approach that would be capable of reaching and empowering a large number of very poor women (Mayoux, 2000, 2002a; Fernando, 2007). Indeed, in the 1990s the World Bank and other donor agencies touted the microcredit programme as a central policy intervention for poverty alleviation and gender strategies (Mayoux, 1999, 2000, 2002a; Binswanger and Landell-Mills, 1995).

On 18 November 2004 the UN declared 2005 the 'International Year of Microcredit' in an effort to foster support for the provision of financial services to poor and vulnerable people who typically had been considered to be unbankable and ineligible for credit. The decision to promote this financial intervention was a part of strategic plan that would help to meet the UN Millennium Development Goals (MDGs). The MDGs list provocative development goals that not only take on the economic concept of poverty, but also promote more far-reaching measures of development that gauge development within a number of areas such as universal primary education for boys and girls; gender equality and women's empowerment; reducing child mortality; improving maternal health care; combating HIV/AIDS; ensuring environmental sustainability; and developing a global partnership for development (Montgomery and Weiss, 2011; Weber, 2004).[5] In 2006 the Nobel Peace Prize was awarded to Muhammad Yunus of GB for his 'efforts to create economic and social development below'[6], which again led to a broad media consensus regarding the virtues of microfinance in terms of poverty alleviation and women's social empowerment. According to the Microcredit Summit Campaign, by the end of 2010 more than 3,600 microcredit organizations had served 137.5 million clients worldwide, about 113 million of whom had been living on less than US $1 per day before their enrolment in microcredit programmes (Maes and Reed, 2012: 3).

This microcredit policy has earned an almost mythical reputation in development circles and has been widely considered to be a 'magic bullet' (Edwards and Hulme, 1996: 3), 'one of the hottest antipoverty strategies' (Gugliotta, 1993), 'global development architecture' (Weber, 2002, 2004), or 'a veritable panacea for poverty' (Rankin, 2001). While lauded in some quarters, microfinance has been criticized in others. There continue to be disparities between the hoped-for successes and the actual realities of micro-credit programmes. Carrying out detailed and rigorous impact studies is tricky, and as remarked in one review paper: 'thirty years into the micro-finance movement we have little solid evidence that it improves the lives of clients in a measurable way' (Roodman and Morduch, 2009: 3–4).

Most of the studies and claims about economic success and women's empowerment through the provision of microcredit in Bangladesh are based on statistical surveys, quantitative data and econometric analyses (e.g. Mahmud, 2003; Khandker, 1998, 2003; Pitt and Khandker, 1998; Hashemi *et al.*, 1996; Khandker and Chowdhury, 1995; Rahman and Khandker, 1994; Islam-Rahman, 1986; Hossain, 1988, 1984). These studies were conducted by the economists or the researchers who worked for the organizations involved. All the above-mentioned studies were donor-driven: i.e. they were sponsored by the World Bank, international organizations or the NGOs themselves. Some critics (e.g. Fernando, 2007; Karim, 2011) have argued that most of the current quantitative studies on microfinance have failed to explore its broader impact on social, economic and political processes beyond the local project areas.

Empirical work on GB carried out in the mid-1980s by the Bangladeshi economist, Mahabub Hossain, was the first piece of research into the economic impact of microcredit programmes. Hossain (1984) collected data from a sample survey of 613 bank officials, actual clientele of the programme and comparable non-members in other (control) localities. In addition, he used the bank's monthly statistics sheets and annual reports. He focused mainly on the success of GB in reaching the target group and the extent of the impact of the credit programme on income, and employment, and on the productivity of the borrowers. He showed that 59 per cent of the GB loan applicants were male and 41 per cent were female. At the time of loan application, 65 per cent of these women were unemployed. The remaining women were employed mainly in two occupations: domestic work and cottage industry work. About 36 per cent of all the applicants (male and female) reported that they did not have any productive employment at the time of loan application. Therefore, he argued that the GB credit programme had helped to create employment opportunities not only for the underemployed but also for those who previously had been fully unemployed. Moreover, Hossain's study revealed that the performance of GB microcredit in increasing per capita income and household income was excellent. Over a period of two years the per capita income of the borrower households increased by about 32 per cent, while per capita income in Bangladesh increased by only 2.6 per cent. In comparison with the income of control villages (those without credit programmes), the per capita income of the borrower households was also higher by about 31 per cent (Hossain, 1984: 27–28, 128). In 1988 Hossain followed up his earlier research by assessing the effect of GB on the economic prospects of the borrower households and he came to the same conclusion as before.

One oft-cited study was conducted by the World Bank economist Shahidur Khandker (1998) who examined the role of microcredit in relation to poverty alleviation through three major programmes: GB, BRAC, and Rural Development Project (RD-12). The analysis was based on data collected in a joint research conducted by BIDS (Bangladesh Institute of Development Studies) and the World Bank from a multipurpose household survey of 87 villages in Bangladesh during 1991/92. This study covered 'programme' villages for each of these three programmes and 'control' villages for which none these programmes or any other programmes were implemented. The main conclusion reached was that microfinance reduced poverty by increasing per capita consumption among programme participants and their families. Poverty reduction estimates based on consumption impacts of credit show that about 5 per cent of programme participants were able to lift their families out of poverty each year by participating in and borrowing from microfinance programmes (ibid.: 148). However, Morduch (1998) analysed the BIDS-World Bank survey data which had been used previously by Khandker but he applied a different research approach and found that microcredit did not have a significant impact on the increase of consumption levels and therefore on income increases and poverty alleviation. Similarly, David Hulme and Paul Mosley (1996), in a comprehensive study of 12 famous microcredit organizations in seven developing countries, including Bangladesh, arrived at the conclusion that microcredit had a negligible effect on the monthly income of poor members.

More recently, Haque and Yamao (2009) studied the impact of microcredit programmes on poverty alleviation in rural areas of Bangladesh. The study was based on primary-level data collected at random from 300 women who had borrowed microcredit from GB, ASA (Association for Social Advancement), and Thengamara Mohila Sabuj Sangha (TMSS) and other NGOs, who had been taking credit from these organizations for more than six years. The researchers found that the amount of credit granted was inadequate to carry out income-generating activities that could produce enough money to repay the weekly instalment after extracting the minimum sum requirements in order to survive. Their study concluded that microcredit is not an effective measure for poverty reduction among the very poor.

In the mid 1990s Ainon Nahar Mizan tested the relationship between women's economic activities and their conjugal decision-making power by using resource theory as the criteria (Blood and Wolfe, 1960) and resources in cultural context theory (Rodman, 1972). Mizan (1994) conducted her academic study of two selected GB projects in the Chittagong and Patuakhali districts in Bangladesh. The study concluded that GB participants enjoyed higher household decision-making power compared to non-borrowers, and that the relationship was statistically significant as assessed by bivariate and multivariate analyses. The finding is a reflection of the GB programme's considerable success in affecting women's status relative to men's in Bangladesh. Bank participation benefits women by providing them with valuable financial resources in addition to non-monetary assets (ibid.: 122–123).

A frequently cited study of women's empowerment through their involvement with microcredit in Bangladesh was conducted by the economist Syed Hashemi *et al.* (1996). The fieldwork for this study was undertaken in late 1992 and used a combination of ethnographic methods (120 households, about half of whom were participants in credit programmes) and a sample survey (about 1,300 married women under the age of 50 years who were borrowers and non-borrowers alike). The study employed eight indicators to measure the degree of women's empowerment in areas such as mobility in the public space; women's financial contribution to the household; ability to make both small and large purchases; involvement in major decision making (such as buying land, boats or rickshaws in order to increase take-home profit); freedom from family domination; and political and legal awareness. Their study argued that women's microcredit involvement in addition to their significant financial contribution to supporting the family serve as intermediate variables in studying the effect of credit on women's empowerment. The researcher also observed that even if women who had borrowed from GB handed over the entire loan to their husbands or other male relatives, they were more likely to be empowered than non-borrowers. Similarly, a number of studies (e.g. Islam-Rahman, 1986; Osmani, 1998; Pitt and Khandker, 1995; Amin and Pebley, 1994) confirmed the findings that female microcredit borrowers have greater decision-making power within the household compared to non-participants.

Although microcredit is a fairly well-trodden area of research, there have been relatively few qualitative studies (Karim, 2011; Rahman, 1999) that are based on long-term fieldwork and ethnography. Such studies on microcredit initiatives in Bangladesh have expressed deep scepticism about the donor-driven quantitative studies on the impact of microcredit on poverty alleviation, female autonomy, women's subordination or their exposure to domestic violence. The first major challenge to the concept of the empowerment potential of microcredit came from Goetz and Sen Gupta (1996). The authors considered the issue in their evaluation of the degree to which women actually control loans when they gain access to the credit programmes. The data for this study were obtained from GB, BRAC's Rural Development Programme (RDP), the CIDA-funded component of the Bangladeshi government's Rural Poor Programme (RD-12), and two women's NGOs, TMSS and Shaptagram Nari Swanivar Parishad (SNPS). Five categories were defined, each of which ranged from 'full control' of the entire production process of goods and services (including marketing), to 'no involvement' whereby women were not involved in any way in the use of their nominal loans. Goetz and Sen Gupta reported that 37 per cent of cases could be categorized as 'full' or 'significant control', compared to 63 per cent of cases that could be categorized as 'partial', 'very limited' or 'no involvement'. These findings gave the authors strong reservations about the empowerment potential of microcredit programmes for women in Bangladesh.

Similarly, Rahman's (1999) ethnographic study of the GB microcredit model found that its 'public transcript' of poverty alleviation and women's empowerment is at odds with a 'hidden transcript', which is patriarchal and involves the hegemonic exploitation of poor women by men and even by wealthier women. Rahman illustrates clearly that women are subjected to violence and aggression when they cannot repay their loans.

In recent years a growing number of studies have challenged the idealistic concepts of 'social capital', 'camaraderie' and 'participatory emancipation' involved in the notion of microcredit programmes as a noteworthy means towards sustainable development (Hietalahti and Nygren, 2011; Karim, 2011; Maclean, 2010; Bähre, 2007a; Elyachar, 2005; Molyneux, 2002; Rankin, 2002; Mayoux, 2001a). According to these studies, development practitioners and donor agencies have promoted microcredit programmes as 'magic bullets' for economic and social well-being which are based on crude presumptions about harmonic kinship and neighbourhood ties in the global south (Maclean, 2010; Rankin, 2002), about the gendered roles of women as money savers and business minders (Bateman, 2010; Molyneux, 2002), and about local communities as immaculate sources of social capital (Bateman, 2010; Bähre, 2007b; Hietalahti and Nygren, 2011; Maclean, 2010). These studies demonstrate that the social and gendered aspects of microcredit require deeper investigation. Furthermore, critical studies consider microfinance as the prime product of neoliberalism and capitalist technology which northern international agencies and neoliberal state bodies have actively promulgated over the past few years to alleviate poverty and empower women at the local level (Karim, 2011; Keating *et al.*, 2010; Townsend *et al.*, 2004; McDermott, 2001).

Microcredit, neoliberalism and the capitalist world system

Neoliberalism has become the dominant economic doctrine of our time (Peck and Tickell, 2002), hence Bourdieu and Wacquant portray neoliberalism as a 'new planetary vulgate' (2001: 2), Beck describes the same phenomenon as an ideological 'thought virus' (2000: 122). Anthropological scholars have viewed neoliberalism as a globally successful 'encompassing hegemonic project' involving 'the de-statization of governmental activity and the marketization of labour and budgetary austerity policies' (Hoffman *et al.*, 2006; 10–11). Through neoliberalism the state's role in people's lives is minimized and individuals are given the responsibility to take control of their own situations. Friedman offers this emblematic summary of neoliberalism: 'To the free man, the country is a collection of individuals which compose it … The scope of government must be limited … to preserve law and order, to enforce private contracts, to foster competitive markets' (1962: 2).

In *A Brief History of Neoliberalism* David Harvey points out that neoliberalism as a theory of political economy rests on the idea that human well-being can be best advanced by 'deregulation, privatization, and withdrawal of the state from many areas of social provision' (2005: 3). Thus, the social good can be maximized by exploiting the reach and frequency of market transactions, and it will seek to bring all human action into the market domain (ibid.). Harvey points out that although neoliberal states minimize their citizens' welfare policies, their governments have increased their interventions in other arenas in their efforts to construct social and political environments that actively encourage market rationality. In the same vein, Aihwa Ong (2006) indicates that neoliberalism is a technology of government which relies on calculable choices and techniques in the sphere of citizenship and governance.

The above interpretations of neoliberalism can be traced to Foucault's notions of 'governmentality' (1979, 1988) and 'disciplinary power' (1977). Through Foucault's early work (1977, 1978) we have come to see that he provided an account of a disciplinary society that functions through an incitement to regulation. Through his concern with the emergence of new power technologies during the eighteenth century, Foucault presented a picture of the domination of individuals through social institutions, discourses and practices. Individuals are also presented with a picture of subjectivities as they are shaped by disciplinary power. However, for Foucault power must not be understood purely in negative terms or as a repressive entity, but also in terms of its productive nature. In relation to the body, power does not merely repress its unruly forces; rather it incites, instils and produces effects in the body. In fact, as Foucault argues in *Discipline and Punish* (1977) power often has the effect of *enhancing* the capacities of those over whom it is exercised. The exercise of discipline can provide individuals with new skills and attributes, help them to control their own behaviour in trying conditions, and promote their ability to follow commands and to act in concert with others:

> But it should not be forgotten that there existed … a technique for consisting individuals as correlative elements of power and knowledge. The individual is no doubt the fictitious atom of an 'ideological' representation of society; but he is also a reality fabricated by this specific technology of power that I have called 'discipline'. We must cease once and for all to describe the effects of power in negative terms … In fact, power produces; it produces reality; it produces domains of objects and rituals of truth. The individual and the knowledge that may be gained of him belong to this production.
>
> (Ibid.: 194)

However, neoliberal governmentality in particular can be located in Foucault's notion of 'bio-power', a mode of governing that brought 'life and its mechanisms into the realm of explicit calculations and made knowledge-power an agent of transformation of human life' (ibid., 1978: 143). For

Foucault, power over life has centred on two poles of development. One of these poles considers 'the body as a machine: its disciplining, the optimization of its capabilities, the extortion of its forces' (ibid.: 139). The second pole focuses on the species' body as the basis of the biological life processes: propagation, birth and death, the level of health, longevity, etc. (ibid.).

Foucault considers governmentality as a mode of political rationality that emerges with the development of neoliberalism. A central theme of his work on governmentality is the way in which the modern state utilizes complex networks and techniques of power to control social actors and order social relations. According to Foucault (1991), governmentality refers not only to the regulation of the population but also to the regulation of the individual, of a household or organization, or even of a collectivity such as the poor, the sick or the unemployed. Rather than operating in a dominant manner in order to determine peoples' behaviour, governmentality, in Foucault's view, aims to affect their behaviour *indirectly* by influencing the manner in which people regulate their own behaviour. Thus, the aim of governmentality is to exert discipline upon the population with regard to their everyday conduct through systematic and pragmatic guidance in order to make them behave in a certain manner. The aim is not to engender human emancipation but rather to bring about modern domination, to create docile yet productive people, minds and bodies. In this respect, governmentality is associated with disciplinary power in so far as it annexes disciplinary techniques in order to attain its goal of regulating individuals (McNay, 1992; Dreyfus and Rabinow, 1982). In fact, by focusing on power and governmentality, Foucault revealed the association between the rise of the self-regulating and self-producing subject of liberalism and the enhancing infiltration of power and governance into both the social and individual body (Morgan, 2001). In his eloquent analysis of governmentality, Foucault wrote:

> I say that governmentality implies the relationship of self to self, which means exactly that, in the idea of governmentality, I am aiming at the totality of practices, by which one can constitute, define, organize, instrumentalize the strategies which individuals in their liberty can have in regard to each other. It is free individuals who try to control, to determine, to delimit the liberty of others and, in order to do that, they dispose of certain instruments to govern others.
>
> (1988: 19)

Foucault's concept of governmentality can be linked closely to the rules and procedures of microcredit organizations. Microcredit NGOs are institutions with their own organizational cultures, ideological commitments, goals, as well as power relations. Credit, which is offered to the poor to help them to become self-employed, is sanctioned through a range of social and economic laws, strict rules, norms and enforcement that govern the everyday behaviours of their borrowers, particularly rural women (see Table A.1 and Table A.2).

Together with the notion of microcredit as a key development strategy aimed at reducing poverty and empowering women, poor women, who represent 'the informal economy', have been incorporated into the market as 'projects' of market development (Cross and Street, 2009: 9; Elyachar, 2005), and thus produced as new entrepreneurial subjects and agents of governing (Elyachar, 2005; Karim, 2011).

In the microcredit business, according to Elyachar (2005), the notion of empowerment has become a component of a new mode of governance and power relations, in which the individual is the main agent of governance; i.e. 'the self is both subject and subjected' (ibid.: 193). Elyachar explains that microcredit, based on the notion of self-help, can be conceived as an empowering tool because the credit goes directly to the grass-roots level. As a result, microcredit organizations as 'representatives of the people' have been able directly to integrate the poor into the global market economy and transform those who used to remain in the informal economy into active subjects, 'the agents of their own empowerment' (ibid.: 192–194). However, the problem with this kind of integration is that the difficult realities faced by the poor during the course of their everyday lives are easily discounted, and the capability of the poor themselves to operate as economic actors is easily romanticized. What has followed, however, is that by appropriating the social networks for reproducing global markets without considering the realities faced by the poor at the grass-roots level, in many cases poor women have become 'dispossessed' of their own social capital (ibid.: 5–10, 192–195).

In her scholarly ethnographic study of GB and three leading microfinance organizations (ASA, BRAC, Proshika) in Bangladesh Karim (2011) discovered that microfinance loans have created new states of subordination and oppression for poor women both at the household and community level. According to Karim, although the loans are given to the women, the actual users remain their husbands or male relatives., In particular, Karim discusses how microcredit is characterized by a number of techniques that ensure the work of governing. In her study she explores the way in which Bangladeshi rural women's notions of honour and shame are instrumentally appropriated by microcredit organizations. She found that as techniques of governance, microcredit institutions operationalize traditional codes of honour and shame to manufacture 'a culturally specific governmentality'; or what Karim calls 'the economy of shame' (ibid.: xviii). For example, if a woman is unable to repay her loan on time, the microcredit organization has the power to shame that woman in public and cause her to lose face (ibid.: 84).

The global microfinance industry operates within a broad neoliberal agenda of diminished welfare states, drastically reduced social spending, and increased privatization and deregulation of public institutions. GB is considered a pioneer in promulgating ways for the neoliberal state to lessen the cost of welfare (cf. Karim, 2011). It seeks market-based solutions to a wide range of questions and uses the justification of individual liberty to deploy the strategies of self-help and responsibility rather than public responsibility. The bank also highlights high levels of recovery rate as evidence that poor women are creditworthy and are 'rational economic actors' in the challenges to their local social structure, whereby they use existing resources and invest loans themselves. In his essay '*Credit for Self-Employment: A Fundamental Human Right*,' Muhammad Yunus stated that:

> employment per se does not remove poverty. ... Employment may mean being condemned to a life in a squalid city slum or working for two meals a day for the rest of life. ... Wage employment is not a happy road to the reduction of poverty. Removal or reduction of poverty must be a continuous process of creation of assets, so that the asset-base of a poor person becomes stronger at each economic cycle, enabling him to earn more and more. Self-employment, supported by credit, has more potential for improving the asset base of the poor than wage employment has.
>
> (1989: 49)

The only unifying theme in this strategy is that it is the market that is alleviating poverty, not the state, and such transformations have caused people to behave in accordance with the 'market principles of discipline, efficiency and competitiveness' (Ong, 2006: 4). Harvey has argued that 'human well-being can best be advanced by liberating individual entrepreneurial freedoms and skills within an institutional framework characterized by strong private property rights, free markets, and free trade' (2005: 2). Microfinance harmonizes suitably with capitalist approaches endorsed by 'northern' lenders, and which are firmly entrenched in the ideals of self-sufficiency and free market capitalism (McDermott, 2001: 67 and 73). The president of the World Bank, James D. Wolfensohn, stated in 1996 that 'microcredit programmes have brought the vibrancy of market economy to the poorest villages and people of the world. This business approach to the alleviation of poverty has allowed millions of individuals to work their way out of poverty with dignity'. Yunus strongly advocates market economy as a means of eradicating poverty. According to him, 'the economic system must be competitive' and 'competition is the driving force for all innovation, technological change, and improved management' (2003: 206). He also claims that profit maximization is essential (ibid.: 205–207), a notion which again is ingrained with capitalist principles.

Today, microcredit programmes are not model non-profit financial services designed to alleviate poverty and empower women. They are currently caught up in a 'financial self-sustainability paradigm' (Mayoux, 2001b: 248; Yunus, 2003: 204). As a result, there has been a drastic shift in the focus of microfinance programmes from donor-driven schemes that provide subsidized credit to borrowers to commercially oriented operations that impose interest rates and emphasize profits that cover all costs and thus are financially sustainable (Montgomery and Weiss, 2011). Microfinance conveys a new promise: the 'bottom billion', the world's poorest, will serve as a 'frontier market' by opening up new horizons of capital accumulation (Roy, 2010). The 'commercialization of microfinance' has sparked an intensely heated discussion as to how far it matches the original microfinance programmes' mission. Some argue that as a result microcredit programmes may concentrate on their own financial sustainability instead of providing services to the poor (Montgomery and Weiss, 2005, 2011; Augsburg and Fouillet, 2010). One commentator has gone so far as to refer to the new mission 'a battle for the soul of microfinance' (Harford, 2008). In poor agrarian economies where most of the inhabitants rely heavily on agricultural work, small-scale production and small businesses, the prevailing neoliberal orthodoxy has presumed a distinctive feminization of poverty. This is because microcredit programmes specifically target rural women who have become major targets for would-be benefactors and agents of progress (Rankin, 2001).

This book is an attempt to grasp and to understand how microcredit relates to the social, cultural and economic processes affecting the lives of women and their households in rural Bangladesh. I shall not attempt to study the entire impact of microcredit programmes. Rather, my intention is to demonstrate how microcredit is related to the local lives of borrowers.[7] I have addressed the question of how NGOs use neoliberal policies and credit on the one hand, and also how local people access and appropriate credit on the other. I have endeavoured to contribute to an understanding of the ongoing focuses of microcredit initiatives within the context of Foucault's disciplinary power (1977) and governmentality (1978, 1979, 1988) against the background of neoliberalism. I stress the power relations, the processes and practices of governance, implications of enforced institutional discipline of microcredit organizations, and vulnerability of microcredit borrowers. Drawing on James Scott's notions of hidden resistance (1990) and the weapons of the weak (1985), I have focused on the way in which borrowers of microcredit criticize rules of programmes and procedures out of earshot and out of sight of the officials of the NGOs. Following the entitlement approach detailed by Sen (1981, 1987, 1999), I have also addressed the mechanism whereby poor people accept credit year after year and thus become further mired in debt.

This book examines three aspects: the social capital paradigm; the women's empowerment paradigm; and the poverty alleviation paradigm of the microcredit programmes. I have combined all three of them, unlike any prior study of microcredit in Bangladesh. I start by establishing whether women's participation in microcredit programmes solidifies and fosters social capital. I then focus on the way in which microcredit is related to gender relations within the familial web and within the community in which rural women are embedded. Finally, I address the question of whether microcredit programmes ensure a 'win-win' situation and achieve higher positive financial outcomes in the rural household economy. Fundamentally, the objective of this book revolves around the following questions:

- To what extent do microcredit programmes, purveyors of neoliberalism and capitalist world systems, interact with female borrowers to facilitate social capital, women's empowerment and poverty alleviation in rural Bangladesh?

- Does the collateral mechanism function or is it merely for procuring credit for the borrowers and a governmental technique for microcredit organizations to discipline the borrowers?
- Does credit offered to women represent a policy of women's empowerment or a plan for covert regulatory practice?
- What happens when multiple credit organizations offer loans simultaneously in the same locality?
- Do microcredit programmes ensure a 'win-win' situation of improved financial outcomes and enhanced well-being for the poor clients that those microcredit programmes promised to provide (Morduch, 1999, 2000)?
- How do microcredit borrowers criticize enforced institutional procedures out of the direct surveillance and gaze of NGO officials?
- Is a microcredit programme a launching point for capital accumulation, and can it therefore offer a route to enhanced access to resources and augmented welfare for poor borrowers?
- Are microcredit programmes simply an informal way of obtaining subsistence and a method of coping with temporary economic difficulties?

Understanding gender relations and women's empowerment

Some of the key factors (e.g. biological, sexual and sociocultural) are reflected in families, societies and communities. The social interactions between men and women in society result in socially constructed differential roles and identities for men, women, girls and boys. Gender relations in society are largely mirrored in gendered identities, perceptions and attitudes (Enarson and Chakrabarti, 2009). Gender relations come into effect in all areas of life: personal, social, economic and political; and are often unfavourable towards girls and women. Hanna Papanek writes: 'Gender differences, based on the social construction of biological sex distinctions, are one of the great 'fault lines' of societies ... those that mark the differences among categories of persons that govern the allocation of power, authority and resources' (1990: 163). Feminist scholars consider gender to be the social organization of sexual difference, or a system of unequal relationships between the sexes. As Moghadam (1990) points out, similarly to class, gender is not a homogenous category; it is inherently differentiated and elaborated by class, race/ethnicity, age, region and education. To paraphrase the sociologist Michael Mann (1986), gender is stratified and stratification is gendered.

Gender difference is more critical in Asian and African societies than in other parts of the world (Kandiyoti, 1988). Gender asymmetry is a universal fact and feminists share a commitment to the centrality of gender; they debate how to study it (Peterson, 2005: 499). Scott noted that the core idea of gender rests on an integral connection between two propositions: (1) gender is a constructive constituent of social relationships based on perceived differences between the sexes; and (2) gender is a primary way of signifying relationships of power (1988: 42).

Considering gender as a factor in relationships and hierarchical regimes of power is crucial because it helps to perceive women as active agents, rather than passive objects. As Mohanthy (1991) illustrated, it is necessary to look at Third World women as agents who make choices, evaluate their situations, and organize collectively. She provides sharp criticism of hegemonic Western scholarship in general and of the colonialism that is inherent within Western feminist scholarship in particular. She observes that development studies depict Third World women as a singular and monolithic subject, religious, family-oriented, legal minors, illiterate and domestic. Mohanthy argues that the discourse about the 'average Third World woman' exercises power by creating a hidden self-representation of the modern Western woman as the emancipated ideal (1991: 54–56). I concur with Mohanthy in that instead of assuming a singular and monolithic subject, Bangladeshi women's lives should be interpreted within the specific social and cultural context of Bangladesh.

Women's empowerment has become the mantra of development practitioners and scholars, although the meaning of the concept often remains vague and is widely debated (Afsar, 1998; Rowlands, 1997; Kabeer, 1994, 1999; Agarwal, 1994, 1997; Moghadam, 1990). In development literature the term 'women's empowerment' is usually used in reference to the level of female education; contraceptive use; employment; engagement in politics and governance; visibility, mobility and dress (UNICEF, 2007). This approach to women's empowerment is related to the conventional development indices, which represent women's empowerment in terms of changes towards more equal gender scores within these parameters.[8] This generalized approach can be extended to refer to almost any affirmative change for women. For example, increased income for women is considered by some researchers as 'economic empowerment,' even though women may be operating as individuals without any form of gender-based mobilization or help from their peers (White, 2010). The United Nations Development Fund for Women (UNIFEM) considers women's empowerment to be closely associated with social progress. It perceives empowerment as revolving around the issues of cognition and agency, namely critical consciousness of gender relations; a sense of self-worth and control over one's own life; the ability to exercise choice and bargaining power; and the ability to organize and influence social justice (DFID, 2000).

Rowlands (1997) took a broader analytical approach to the discussion of participation, power and empowerment on the basis of her interaction with women's groups in Honduras. She considered Foucault's notion of power as both relational and permeating everyday life, but added a feminist analysis of power that dealt with internalized oppressions and their role in maintaining gender inequality. She argued that 'empowerment is more than participation in decision-making; it must also include the processes that lead people to perceive themselves as able and entitled to make decisions' (ibid.: 14). It is personal, relational and collective. She noted that rather than a static end point, empowerment is a process that varies according to circumstance.

Chen and Mahmud (1995) defined different dimensions of empowerment on the basis of pathways of affirmative change. These included material, cognitive, perceptual and relational dimensions, the outcome of which is a woman's enhanced fall-back position and greater bargaining power. Material empowerment occurs through an expansion of the material resource base of women. Cognitive empowerment results from women's recognition of their own abilities and skills, as indicated by their greater self-esteem and self-confidence. Perceptional empowerment is mediated through changes in how others perceive women, as registered by their subjective increased social prestige and value. Relational empowerment takes place through changes in gender relations within the family and in broader society. It is indicated by a reduction in gender inequality in relationships. Chen and Mahmud (1995) and Rowlands (1997) did not view empowerment merely as a change for the better, but as a solid achievement of fundamental, structural transformation in the structure of gender relations. I have sought to place women's empowerment in this research as a structural process similar to the approaches taken by Rowlands (1997) and Chen and Mahmud (1995). In addition, I have emphasized the primacy of personal self-esteem and confidence for processes of empowerment and development of the ability to negotiate and influence gender relations within the family and in society as a whole.

Outline of the book

This book is divided into nine chapters. In the Introduction I extensively review the existing body of scholarship to set the theoretical framework and the research questions. I also briefly discuss the concepts of gender and women's empowerment. Chapter 1 covers the methodological aspects of the study. It delineates the problems encountered by the researcher in the field, discusses the ethical issues and the methods used.

Chapter 2 begins with an analysis of the interpretations of social capital and the allied solidarity, norms of reciprocity and trust, collective identity and actions based on the conceptualizations of Pierre Bourdieu, James Coleman and Robert Putnam. It debates whether participation in microcredit-providing organizations solidifies, perpetuates and even fosters relationships (i.e. social capital) between women within groups or between groups in the research study areas. Microcredit programmes are based on social collateral mechanisms, whereby one client stands as another's guarantor. An individual poor woman cannot simply ask for a loan from a microcredit organization. As a condition for receiving credit she has to be a member of a group and visit the centre in order to pay weekly instalments. My interest lies in exploring whether microcredit membership and its collateral mechanisms facilitate social networks, norms of reciprocity, collective identity and action among the borrowers, as well as political participation by women in rural areas. The chapter looks into the question of whether the group principle works as an instrumental strategy used by microcredit organizations to discipline borrowers and to recover credit instalments within the set time. It analyses the way in which the social collateral mechanism, poverty, competition for limited resources and insecurity erode the web of social connectedness and the fabric of social trust.

Chapter 3 expands the analysis to deal with the issue of how microcredit borrowers choose to build social capital by using credit to pay for dowries when a family member marries. What is the logic behind giving household items at marriage ceremonies in the research areas? Both in the rules and decisions of GB and BRAC it is stated that borrowers are strictly prohibited from taking any dowry at their sons' weddings; nor shall they give any dowry at their daughters' weddings. I examine how microcredit borrowers view the NGOs' rules in relation to widespread dowry practices in their respective areas. Before embarking on that discussion, I briefly study the marriage practices in my research areas.

Chapter 4 provides an overview of how women's participation in microcredit programmes is related to their intra-household decision-making power and conflict negotiation capacities within the realm of the conjugal household. More specifically, throughout the chapter I debate the following questions: how does microcredit involvement relate to gender roles, and women's participation in intra-household decision-making processes? Does microcredit increase women's confidence, self-esteem, and recognition by others within the household? How do women evaluate these changes? How is microcredit linked to reproductive behaviour, fertility practices and women's exposure to violence?

Chapter 5 takes a bird's-eye view of microcredit, gender relations and practices. I explore the way in which microcredit programmes targeted at women are associated with the dynamics of gender relations in which they are embedded. More specifically, this chapter seeks to establish the extent to which rural women microcredit borrowers are 'rational economic actors' in the challenges vis-à-vis their local social structure, whereby they use existing resources and invest loans themselves. I endeavour to trace the reasons that trigger most women to turn over the credit to the men of the household instead of making investments themselves. I ask why microcredit NGOs offer credit through women and seek an answer to the question: is it a well-meaning initiative or a mechanism devised to exert *power* over women's bodies and thoughts (Foucault, 1977)?

Chapter 6 seeks to demystify what happens when several credit organizations simultaneously offer loans in the same locality. The microfinance sector in Bangladesh witnessed rapid growth under the framework of neoliberal policies in the late 1990s. As a result, commercialization and competition have increased among microcredit organizations, and this has led to companies establishing new branches in the same area where a competitor already exists and is serving their clients. Relatively little information about this issue currently exists in the debates on microcredit. This chapter explores the way in which microcredit organizations compete with each other for the same clients by appropriating neoliberal policies, and also by targeting richer clients for profit to strengthen their own sustainability. The issues of drift and diffusion of microcredit programmes within the local settings are also covered.

Chapter 7 focuses on whether microcredit programmes ensure a 'fair deal' situation in which both the organizations and the client parties can profit. In the spirit of Michel Foucault's theoretical concepts of *disciplinary technology* and *governmentality* this part of this book illustrates processes and practices of governance of microcredit organizations. Credit, which is disbursed to promote self-employment and increase household incomes, is sanctioned through a set of social and economic laws, strict rules and procedures, enforcement (which is referred to as disciplinary technologies/governmentality) that govern and discipline microcredit borrowers to achieve chosen goals. I also describe the way in which microcredit borrowers widely criticize the rules and procedures of microcredit programmes when they are outside the direct surveillance and gaze of the NGO officials. The interrelation between structure and agency is explored by showing how some clients manipulate the rules of the NGOs to their own advantage and how some of them have emerged as informal money-lenders who divert their loans to other people at a high interest rate. This analysis owes much to Scott's concept of hidden resistance and weapons of the weak.

In Chapter 8 the concepts of insecurity and vulnerability, and the entitlement approach developed by Sen (1981, 1987, 1999) are described. Following Sen's ideas about *direct entitlement failure* and *trade entitlement failure*, I explore the reasons for which poor people take credit year after year despite becoming permanently indebted. By the same token, this present study data also provide some insights on who benefits from credit and why.

In conclusion, Chapter 9 brings together the ethnographic interpretations of the earlier chapters and returns to a more theoretical level, to the conceptual questions presented in Chapter 1.

Notes

1 On this subject also see de Soto (2003).
2 The terms microcredit, microfinance and micro-loan are used interchangeably in the literature but do not reflect any change in the underlying premise. However, 'microfinance' is a more recent concept than 'microcredit.' It was developed in the early 1990s to include both the borrowing and micro-saving aspects of financial interventions for the poor (Bastelaer, 2000). Nowadays, it is the word of choice, mainly because it avoids the connotations of debt that microcredit seems to imply (Jansen, 1999). I use the terms microcredit, microfinance, micro-loan and microenterprise interchangeably throughout this book.

3 At July 2012 GB had 8.379 million borrowers, 96% of whom were women. With 2,567 branches, GB provided services to 81,382 villages, covering 97% of the total villages in Bangladesh (GB Monthly Report, July 12, 2012, no. 390. Available at: www.grameen-info.org/index.php?option=com_content&;task). The Bangladesh Rural Advancement Committee is one of the largest NGOs in the world. About 6.77 million borrowers are involved in the programme run by BRAC (BRAC Annual Report, December 2011. Available at: www.brac.net/content/stay-inform ed-brac-glance).

4 www.microcreditsummit.org/resource/58/the-microcredit-summit-declaration-plan.h tml.

5 See also www.unmilleniumproject.org.

6 www.nobelprize.org/nobel_prizes/peace/laureates/2006/.

7 The reason is that impact analysis is strongly related to the notion of causation or causal effect analysis, which nearly always makes a study quantitative. There are many factors that influence human lives which we are not always able to control or measure, so I avoid impact analysis study.

8 Various methodologies have been developed to measure empowerment including the Gender-Related Development Index (GDI) contained within the United Nations Development Programme's (UNDP) Human Development Report, the Gender Empowerment Measure (GEM); the Organisation for Economic Co-operation and Development's (OECD) Social Institutions Indicator. The World Economic Forum has introduced the Gender Gap Index, and the World Bank advocates economic empowerment through Smart Economics by making markets work for women.

1 Methodological choice

This chapter presents the methodological considerations of the study. It begins by describing the problems encountered by the researcher in obtaining the relevant and necessary permissions from the microcredit organizations in the project areas in Bangladesh. I describe in detail the process through which I selected the research locations, made contact with the field level microcredit officials and entered into the field study areas. The chapter describes the methods and techniques employed – including surveys, didactic themed and in-depth interviews, case studies and personal observations – and discusses the ethical issues and gendered choices. I also provide an overview of the locations where the fieldwork was carried out.

Encountering the field study areas

Grameen Bank's almost mythical reputation and acceptance within and beyond Bangladesh has always fascinated me. I was enthralled by the story of how Muhammad Yunus had spread a small idea all over the world and launched a new wave of development paradigms. That the international organizations and development practitioners of the north often talked about a 'southern idea' of development and took the initiative to implement it in many parts of the world amazed me. As a citizen of Bangladesh, I also observed the revolution of the microcredit industry in the country. Owing to my position as a PhD researcher at Helsinki University, Finland, and a public university teacher in Bangladesh I was readily given permission by GB to conduct fieldwork and collect information from GB microcredit borrowers in Sylhet, Bangladesh. However, I was to discover that the reality was very different from my initial perceptions of microcredit in Bangladesh.

I visited a branch of GB in Sylhet upazila (sub-district), Bangladesh in early June 2010 and met a bank official to whom I explained the purpose of my visit. The official listened and then stated that he was unable to give me permission to carry out my research, but suggested that I go to the regional administration office and submit an application to explain the purpose of my research. That same day, I visited the regional office, met with one of the office assistants and again explained my position. A letter from the postgraduate coordinator of the Department of Sociology at the University of Helsinki was also shown. The official told me to submit my application, which would then be passed to the regional manager who might give permission when he was available. I asked him whether it is possible to meet with the regional manager that day and he nodded his head and advised me to wait. However, despite waiting for some time, I was unable to meet the manager that day as he was occupied elsewhere. The assistant suggested that I could return to the office the following morning to meet the manager. This I did, and was given the opportunity to meet the manager. The manager read my application and I tried to explain the purpose of my research to him. During my conversation with the manager, an audit officer from the bank's head office in Dhaka was also present. The officials were interested to know more about my political ideology, so I sought to explain to them that my research was purely academic and that I had no particular political affiliations. The officials explained that because GB is a Nobel Peace Prize winner the bank must give careful consideration before giving permission for academic research to be carried out. They repeatedly expressed their powerlessness regarding any decision to grant me permission to conduct my research. 'According to the rules of the organization we have no authority to give you permission. If anybody wants to conduct research among GB borrowers, GB handles it from its head office. The head office decides the time and place of research, and the place of residence of the researcher', said the audit officer.

As a researcher in sociology and development studies, I am familiar with the centralization of power and the bureaucratic administrative structure of Bangladesh, but I was confounded when I found out that an NGO such as GB adheres to the same strictures. Nevertheless, the area manager could see that I had no political agenda against GB and its unique mission. He disregarded the audit officer's argument and initially gave me permission to start my work, but told me that he would discuss the permit further with the bank's head office. The area manger suggested that I meet the branch officer of Fullbazar (pseudonym) and selected the centre. Accordingly, I visited the branch office, explained to the branch manager and a number of loan collectors that I wanted to participate in the weekly credit instalment meetings since the initial aim of my research was to find out whether female borrowers' participation in the group meetings facilitates social capital among the borrowers within and beyond the group. Therefore, I felt that it was necessary for me to participate in the group meetings so that I could observe the activities of the borrowers and how they spent their time during the payment period. However, I learnt that as the borrowers carry out a variety of jobs they do not spend much time at the group meeting places. The borrowers or their relatives visit the group meeting places, pay their weekly instalment and depart immediately. Thus, I began to realize how lax the rules of the GB credit programme are. Neither the group meeting nor the presence of all the borrowers of a centre at the same time is a requirement for getting a loan, which I will elaborate on later.

The following week, I met the branch manager of Pujabazar (pseudonym) and travelled to the countryside to select the present study's research villages. With the consent of the branch manager, I selected the Shantigaon (pseudonym) GB centre in Sylhet district as one of my research villages. The officer assured me that he could at least arrange an official meeting for me; introduce me to his 40 borrowers of the centre and give me any help if needed it. I selected this particular village because it is located some 16 kilometres from a suburban area.

The branch manager kept his promise and on the day that weekly instalments were made he arranged a meeting in Shantigaon. The area manager, branch manager and the loan collectors were present at the meeting. Normally, the GB clients of Shantigaon centre would begin to arrive at the centre to pay their weekly instalments at 9.30 a.m. but due to heavy rain I was late and the GB officials persuaded the borrowers to wait for me. I reached the meeting place at around 10.00 a.m. The area manager introduced me to the borrowers and all the members who followed the officials' instructions and introduced themselves to me one by one. Next, the officer told the borrowers to describe the improvement that the loans had made to their socio-economic situation. I observed a new kind of 'patron-client relationship'[1] between the officials (patron) and the borrowers (client), who appeared submissive and obedient before the officials. The officials were authoritarian towards their clients; they seemed to know the borrowers' economic situations better than the borrowers did themselves.

The officers introduced a number of borrowers telling them to describe how well they had done as a result of participating in the programme. The borrowers obediently demonstrated their allegiance to their patrons, perhaps to increase their access to more credit services. When the GB officials requested Aritri (the leader of the centre) to talk she instantly stood up and enthused about the number of microcredit NGOs now operating in Shantigaon village, including GB, ASA, BRAC, FIVDB (Friends in Village Development Bangladesh). All except GB are newcomers. She stated that the villagers do not take credit from the other programmes as they are are not good nor helpful for them. She told me that the bank has been operating a microcredit programme in the village for about 18 years and that she has been taking microloans from the bank since it began its activities in a nearby village. She informed me that at present 95 per cent of the occupants of Shantigaon take out loans. I asked her who does not take part in the credit programme, and she replied that as almost everybody in the area takes out loans, it is very difficult to say who chooses not to.

I learned from her that some clients have let their memberships lapse for a certain period of time due to their inability to pay their instalments, but most of them try to maintain their savings accounts so that they can meet future loans. She said that a few households who have no business, male provider or a steady source of income do not take credit for the fear of not being able to pay it back.

Like the group leader, Raduni (45 years old) has been taking credit from GB for the past 18 years. She claimed that now everybody, rich and poor alike (*dhani-gorib*), take out loans, because many organizations offer credit in Shantigaon. She also claimed that many other banks (microcredit NGOs) now work in Shantigaon but they never approach them. They like GB because it stays with them 'through thick and thin' (*shuk-dhukhe ache*). While listening to the two women I observed that some of the other borrowers who were sitting at the back smiled at one another, but I failed to understand the significance of this at the time. Later, I was to learn that despite Aritri's and Raduni's claims that GB borrowers do not take credit from other organizations, some do indeed take loans from BRAC in the same way that they do from GB. As the meeting came to a close, the officials indicated that I should ask the borrowers about the improvements to their socio-economic circumstances, but I told them I would talk to them tomorrow.

The next day, I visited the village alone and spent all day with the villagers talking and gossiping and explaining to them that I intended to write a book about their village. I found a tea-cum-grocery shop owned by Mehedi, whose brother works as an official at my university. This man is also a BRAC microcredit borrower who promised to help me at any time and told me that if I visited his shop over the course of some days he could introduce me to many of the microcredit borrowers' husbands and I would be able to chat to them. My visits to the shop helped me to socialize with the locals. The microcredit borrowers often had tea in this shop, or came to top up their mobile phones, or just to chat. As I had come to the village through the auspices of GB, the locals initially thought that I was an NGO agent. I repeatedly had to clarify my purpose for visiting the village and to state my position as a university teacher at the public university in Sylhet. During the initial stage of my research I spent much time chatting and drinking tea with the villagers. It fascinated me that these very poor rural people soon forgot all about their bodily ills and economic difficulties when they started to gossip. They expressed their opinions about religion, local as well as national politics, NGOs, the environment, and so on. Through my conversations with the rural people in this shop I became part of the local society. The shopkeeper, Mehedi, is a knowledgeable person with closely knit networks in the Shantigaon area. He knew who was involved in the microcredit programme, which microcredit NGOs operate in this area and who does what with microcredit. Thus, I spent the whole week developing closer ties with the microcredit borrowers' households and local people in Shantigaon.

During this time I became acquainted with an older female microcredit borrower, Alapi (a Hindu housewife) who had a good relationship with most of the female microcredit borrowers. She had once worked as a group leader for GB in Shantigaon. I talked to Alapi and her husband many times and discovered her to be a knowledgeable woman. Alapi left school after the fifth grade but despite this she was articulate and capable. She told me that she could help me to visit the homes of all of the microcredit borrowers. She became my assistant and subsequently helped me to complete my data collection from the microcredit borrowers of Shantigaon.

However, I should mention here that after spending two weeks in Shantigaon I observed that the GB branch manager was always behind me observing where I went and what I talked about. The borrowers felt uneasy in his presence and were reluctant to talk frankly with me. Similarly to Scott's (1990) study of everyday forms of protest and boycott of subordinate groups in a Malaysian village, I observed that the microcredit borrowers talked one way in front of the official but differently when he was not present. This posed a considerable constraint on my data collection. So I changed the technique of collecting data. I told the branch manager that he need not spend his valuable time with me because I knew the villagers and could collect the data myself. Initially, he turned down my proposal but eventually I managed to persuade him. Owing to this experience, I did not go to the other GB microcredit village, Zelegaon (pseudonym), via GB or in the company of one of the bank's officials. Instead, I went to the village and became acquainted with the microcredit borrowers and local people with the help of a local man, Azad, who works as an assistant at a university where I was as a faculty member. As Azad's family had been involved previously in the microcredit programme, he had good networks with other borrowers. Azad and one of his female neighbours, who had been involved in a microcredit programme for the past 18 years, worked as my assistants. They introduced me to all the microcredit borrowers and we visited the borrowers' homes together.

It was comparatively easier to obtain permission and to collect data from the BRAC microcredit borrowers than from GB. In mid-June 2010 I visited the regional office of BRAC in Sylhet to request a permit to carry out my field research on two BRAC microcredit centres in Sylhet district, Bangladesh. I met one of the officials to whom I explained the purpose of my visit. The official without any circumlocution informed me that BRAC operated a micro-lending programme in every part of Sylhet district. Therefore, I could select any centre according to my convenience. The officer did not try to influence my selection but suggested that I select areas near the roads because during the rainy season it would be very difficult to work in villages located in the interior. I understood his point but explained that I wished to carry out my research both in an interior centre and in a centre near to the suburban area. The officer gave me a phone number suggesting that I talk to the branch manager of Nodigaon (pseudonym) village to select research sites. In my presence the officer also called the branch manager to inform him that a university teacher wanted to meet him about doing research with the borrowers at his centres. I called the manager and said that I would come to his office soon. Later that day, in spite of heavy rain, I visited the office at Nodigaon and met the branch manager there. After discussing my research proposal with him, in the evening I travelled to the village with the official and selected Nodigaon village as one of my research areas. I chose this village because it was situated within two kilometres of my place of residence and had good road connections. I would be able to visit this village easily and the manager promised me that he could introduce to the microcredit borrowers of the Nodigaon centre.

Later that morning, I visited the loan administration centre again with the branch manager to participate in the repayment instalment meeting. The officer introduced me to the loan collection official who was cordial. She tried to introduce me to the borrowers or their representatives who came to pay their weekly instalments. However, like the GB centre in Shantigaon, I found it difficult to organize all the members in the weekly instalment place at one time. The field officer told me that during the morning the women were busy doing housework because their husbands were leaving for work outside of the home, therefore they or their representatives came to pay their instalments and departed soon afterwards. She introduced me to a borrower and asked her to help me. Later, I found another woman to join me on door-to-door visits during my fieldwork in Nodigaon village.

During the first week of my fieldwork at Nodigaon, I was introduced by phone to the BRAC branch manager of Pujabazar (pseudonym), which is situated about nine kilometres from the Sylhet-Sunamganj highway. After several postponements, I was able to meet the branch manager of Pujabazar to select another research site. Since the official had been informed of my arrival, he accompanied me to a BRAC centre in Shivpur (pseudonym). The village was about two kilometres from the BRAC branch office at Pujabazar but it took about one and half hours to reach it because the road was muddy and partly flooded. I understood that it was not possible for me to collect data from this interior village centre but I spent all day with the officer in order to record his views and the microcredit operations in the area. As a result of spending time with the micro-lending official I could only admire the official's motivation, skill and patience and appreciate the scale of the intensive networks that NGO personnel must build and maintain in rural areas. For example, I saw him speak persuasively to a grocery shopkeeper, saying 'I have observed that you run your shop nicely but why don't you invest more capital and keep more goods in the shop? How long will you run your business in this way? You are young and this is the time to do something with your life. I have already advised you to collect your mother's signature so that I can arrange a loan for you. If I can do something for you I will be very happy.'

When the official talked to the group leader at Shivpur he called her two sons and gave them TK 40 to buy two pairs of trousers. The official had tried repeatedly to convince the group leader's husband, a rickshaw puller, to take out an additional loan in order to restore the roof of their house. When we left the group leader's house, the official asked me, 'Do you see how we work at the village level?' I recalled one outspoken NGO consultant who explained to the anthropologist, Julia Elyachar, in Cairo in 1995:

Money is empowerment. This is empowerment money. You need to be big, need to think big. Borrowers here can be imprisoned if they don't pay, so why be worried?

In America we get ten offers for credit cards in the mail every day. You pay incredible real interest rates for that credit, something like 40 percent. But the offer is there, so you get the card, stuff your wallet full of credit cards. You feel good. It should be the same thing here, why not help them get into debt? Do I really care what they use the money for, as long as they pay the loan back?

(2002: 510)

Research methods and the main sources of data

The empirical data for this study were collected between June 2010 and December 2010 from 151 married female microcredit borrowers in two of GB's microcredit project areas and two of BRAC's project areas in the district of Sylhet, Bangladesh. The project areas were purposely selected from three separate villages: Zelegaon, Nodigaon and Shantigaon. From each project area I collected information only from those female borrowers who had been involved in microcredit programmes for one or more years. The broad aim of this study is to grasp and contribute to an understanding of how microcredit is linked to social, cultural and economic processes of women's lives and their households in the local communities.

Zelegaon village lies about five kilometres inland from the Sylhet-Sunamganj highway. The road access between Zelegaon village and the city is good and could easily be accessed from my residence by rickshaw in 25 to 30 minutes. People can visit this village from the urban areas by three-wheelers and rickshaws but local people often use three-wheelers as they are a cheaper form of transport. I selected the Zelegaon village as one of my research areas because GB had been operating its credit programme in this village for the past 18 years. GB had been operating credit programmes via two centres in this village: the east *para* (neighbourhood) and south *para*. I collected data only from the east *para* because the south *para* centre had started its operation with 25 members just a few months prior to the data collection period. There were 90 households taking out loans from the east *para* GB centre. Of the 90 GB borrowers' households, I collected data from 76 households because five households declined to give me information, five borrowers were unmarried and the remaining four households had got involved in the credit programme only a few months prior to the data collection period.

Nodigaon village is adjacent to the Sylhet-Sunamganj highway and is easily accessible. The river Surma flows just behind the village. The village is adjacent to the suburban area and it took only 10 to 15 minutes to travel there from my residence by rickshaw. BRAC had been operating its credit programme in this village for four years prior to this study. There were 44 households in receipt of the BRAC microcredit programme but I collected information from only 37 households because two borrowers were unmarried and the other five households had been taking credit less than one year prior to the study.

Shantigaon is an interior village located approximately 16 kilometres inland from the suburban area of Boropur bazaar (pseudonym) although the road communication networks between this village and the suburban area is good. People can easily visit this village from the urban area by three-wheeler. I selected this village as one my of research sites because both BRAC and GB have been operating microcredit programmes there. BRAC had been operating in Shantigaon for four years prior to the study data collection period, whereas GB had been present there for 18 years. There were 40 households who took credit from the GB centre of Shantigaon and 18 households from the BRAC centre. I collected information from 38 households because there were 10 households who simultaneously took loans from both BRAC and GB. The remainder had been taking loans for less than one year. I considered this village to be an important research site because both Muslims and Hindus live there. As a result, I saw a supplementary opportunity to examine whether microcredit participation cultivates communal harmony and strengthens networks among Muslims and Hindus in this village.

My most important research material is qualitative and my analytical approach is interpretative, although I also collected census data. As mentioned earlier, I started my fieldwork by using observation and holding informal discussions with the selected borrowers and members of their families in order to familiarize myself with the villagers and the social issues in their communities. These discussions and observations helped me to compile a semi-structured questionnaire for collecting some quantitative/survey data. The survey examined the following aspects of the respondents' households: sex and age of all family members; marital status; education and occupation; land ownership; how long the respondent had been married; number of births and number of surviving children; family planning; monthly income and expenditure; duration of microcredit membership; and current loans and associated investments.

In addition to the ethnographic observations and surveys, ethnographic (in-depth) interviews and case studies were also conducted. After I had become more familiar with each microcredit borrower family I began to collect more qualitative data. First, case stories were collected from 35 female borrowers (25 from Zelegaon, five from Nodigaon and five from Shantigaon villages) who had been actively involved in microcredit programmes since their inception in the respective villages. These data facilitated a study of the population and helped me to build a mutual rapport with other microcredit borrower families, and this in turn aided the ethnographic (in-depth) themed interview process. In the themed interviews, specific questions were asked. For example, the first theme was about social capital for which information was sought on how women microcredit borrowers form their credit group; how credit is allocated; whether the members regularly attend the weekly instalment meeting; if the members are familiar with other group members; how well the microcredit group members trust each other; how solidarity is shaped; and whether microcredit involvement increases women's active participation in local politics. Another theme was gender relations, which included information about who asked for credit; who controls credit; reasons that hinder women from investing in credit themselves; reasons to give credit through women; women's intra-household decision-making capacities; fertility behaviour; domestic violence; and dowry practices. A third theme was household economy for which information was sought on income; expenditure; problems with paying credit instalments; problems with credit programmes; and economic gain through credit. Each in-depth themed interview took two hours or more. Initially, the interviews were recorded but when I noticed that this made the respondents feel uneasy notes were subsequently written in Bengali.

I held in-depth conversations with GB and BRAC micro-lending officials in my research areas to understand their opinions about microcredit programmes and how they saw the microcredit business at the present time when a number of different credit programmes were being offered in the same area. I had informal conversations with these officials at their branch offices, ate with them many times and travelled with them to see how they operated their programmes. Almost every week I tried to be present when weekly instalments were being collected in Nodigaon and Shantigaon. In short, the bulk of the material of this study was collected through didactic themed and in-depth interviews, case studies and personal observation.

My decision to study microcredit programmes in Bangladesh is rooted in my conviction that a qualitative study approach has much to offer to research into this global development paradigm. Qualitative research provides information in a particular but meaningful context (Tedlock, 2000) and this method is suitable for policy contexts as well. For case studies one of the common ways to carry out qualitative inquiry is described by Stake (1994, 2000) who writes: 'Case studies can be a disciplined force in public policy setting and reflection on human experience' (1994: 245). I do not equate my scholarship with the existing quantitative studies based on large data, econometric and statistical analyses. The findings of this research cannot be extended to wider populations or be generalized with the same degree of certainty that the existing quantitative studies on microcredit can. However, my ethnographic approach will provide a complete and detailed description of the appropriation of credit as part of the local economic, social and cultural settings and customs of the studied villages. I aim to find out what is really going on in the local settings.

Focusing on three villages in the same upazila, all within 18 kilometres from each other, has helped me to produce a nuanced understanding of the local meanings, picture, and to some extent the 'generalizability'[2] of the microcredit programmes. I am aware my research often crosses the local boundaries. My study focuses on women but in relation to men, and most of my respondents are women. When I collected information from female microcredit borrowers I often talked to their husbands and older sons. I also talked to local elderly people to find out what they thought about microcredit programmes in their community. Throughout this research, I relate my information and observations to the existing studies on women's microcredit involvement, social capital, gender relations and poverty alleviation in Bangladesh and elsewhere. I provide respondents' quotations which are representative of the relevant ideas and cultural principles. Whenever I encountered different points of view on the same theme, I cite quotations illustrating those multiple ideas.

I conducted this fieldwork in Bengali which is my native tongue. I personally interviewed the respondents with my assistants. With a few exceptions, in their homestead areas the female respondents exchanged their views frankly with me. They often covered their heads with their *sarir achol* (the lower part of a *sari*) when talking to me.

Ethical issues

The main ethical issues raised by ethnographic research deals with privacy. I took this question into consideration by informing each community about the object of my research so that the people involved were fully informed and thus equipped to decide whether their voices in the study should be presented under their real names or whether their identities should be concealed. Most female microcredit borrowers interviewed for this study did not wish to use their real names, particularly when they criticized NGO activities. This was because the relationships between the NGOs' officials and the respondents are unequal; rather, they were characterized by a vertical relationship structure. Therefore, throughout this study I have used pseudonyms. I try to avoid elaborating on the respondents' personal backgrounds or pointing out which statements are from the same respondents.

From a gendered perspective working as a male researcher on women's involvement in microcredit systems in a patriarchal rural community might seem odd. While it is often argued that in a setting in which women are segregated and secluded, only female researchers can hope to glean a 'true' perspective of women (Papanek, 1964: 161–162), I did not consider it to be a huge problem. As a Bangladeshi, I understand the cultural of codes of conduct, and I am familiar with local dialects, and verbal and non-verbal modes of communication. James Gregory also contended that the traditionally accepted view of the 'inaccessibility of the women's world' to male researchers is 'largely a myth' (1984: 316). During my fieldwork in Nodigaon, Shantigaon and Zelegaon I hired female microcredit borrowers from each village as my assistants because I had observed that women could easily discuss certain issues with other women, which I as a man could not. In particular, I found that my respondents were too ashamed or embarrassed to talk to me about contraception and domestic violence. It could be argued that a female researcher might have obtained different answers to questions. I often arranged tea and snacks with the help of my local assistants for the household members and they also arranged food (such as home-made cakes) for me, which helped to develop trust between the microcredit borrowers' families and myself, thus enabling embedded participant observation. During field-work and chatting with the villagers, I was frequently asked questions about my research, such as whether and what kind of benefits it would bring to them. Would my research facilitate any financial help from the government for them or foster development projects in their areas? Could my recommen-dation reduce the interest rates set by microcredit NGOs? Once it became known that I am a faculty member of a public university, I often received requests to arrange petty official jobs for the villagers' sons at my university. I felt sorry when I repeatedly had to explain that I was unable to help. When one family found out that I was studying in Finland they asked many times whether I could send their sons to Finland. Some poor microcredit borrowers requested financial help to cover the cost of hospital treatment or marriage expenses for their daughters, but I could not help them.

An overview of the localities

As mentioned above, the fieldwork for this study was conducted and com-pleted among the microcredit borrowers of Zelegaon, Nodigaon and Shanti-gaon villages. Due to constraints of time and manpower it was not feasible for me to conduct a detailed survey of all the villagers. I only collected data such as the number of households, occupations, literacy levels and religious composition of Zelegaon and Nodigaon and partially that of Shantigaon. In this section, I present a brief account of the socio-economic organization of these villages.

Zelegaon is a comparatively big village. At the time of conducting the survey there were 251 households in this village and all its inhabitants are Muslim. There is an Islamic Madrasha and a government primary school in this village. A number of micro-lending NGOs such as GB, ASA, BRAC, Grameen Shakti and FIVDB operate credit programmes in this village. Con-sequently, most villagers have become involved in the microcredit pro-grammes. Most houses are tin-roofed with mud floors. Only a few houses have brick walls. Most of the households have a shared concrete ring latrine and a shallow tube well. Generally, between three and five households use a common latrine and a shallow tube well. Most of the heads of household and married women have not received an institutional education. However, most women have learned to write their names in order to take micro-loans. Nowadays, most girls get a primary education but do not attend secondary school because there is no such school in the village or nearby villages.

Nodigaon is a smaller village. There are 95 households and all the inhabi-tants are Muslim. A number of microcredit organizations including GB, ASA, BRAC and FIVDB operate credit programmes in this village, and most of the households have become involved in the credit programmes. Similarly to Zelegaon, most of the older men and women in Nodigaon have not attended school. At the time that the study was carried out, the trend had changed, and boys and girls were going to school.

Access to land or land ownership[3] is the main indication of wealth and social hierarchy of a household in rural Bangladesh. Nowadays, education, income and emigration also contribute to social position. An overwhelming majority of households in Zelegaon and Nodigaon have no cultivable land. Despite the fact that all the households have their own homestead lands, their ownership of land is negligible and varies from 3–15 decimals[4] per household. As a result, most households in these two villages belong to the same category in terms of land ownership. However, emigration by some family members is contributing to a change in class structure.

Although Islam as a religion does not recognize nor permit a caste system, traditional Muslim society is generally divided into three hierarchical groups: *Ashraf* (highest status, noble category), *Atrap/Ajlaf* (lower status, literally ordinary people), and *Azal* (degraded status people). The *Ashraf* class is divided into four sub-groups: *Syed, Shekh, Mughal* and *Pathan*. The *Atrap* and *Azal* groups include various occupational or peasant groups in addition to those who have converted from indigenous tribes or from other religions (Arefeen, 1982; Uusikylä, 2000; Jansen, 1987). The Zelegaon and the Nodigaon villagers belong to the same occupational *gushti* (lineage), *maimol* (fishery). Among the *maimol* of Zelegaon and Nodigaon, there is one sub-group that is *bangal*. I got the idea that the *maimol* are skilled at catching and selling fish whereas the *bangal* do not catch fish but they do sell it. However, the lineage of *maimol* and *bangal* is the same that is, *chotomanush* (lower status) lineage. Nowadays, many households switch their occupations and work as day labourers, construction workers, vegetable sellers and grocery shopkeepers, but the dominant occupation remains fishing. The villagers are conscious about the low status of their *gushti* title. They often described themselves as poor people but the young generations do not like to introduce themselves as *maimol*. When I collected data from the elderly women, the young boys often intervened by stating: 'Don't say *maimol*, say our *gushti* title is fishery.' Some elderly women did not introduce themselves as *maimol*, but introduced themselves through their natal families' titles such as *Syed, Khan* and *Chaudhuri,* which are regarded as higher status (*bhala* lineage) (see also Gardner, 1995). For example, when Hashi, a microcredit borrower from Nodigaon village, introduced herself as a *maimol*, her widowed mother-in-law Mamtaz said to her, 'at present you are no longer *maimol,* you are now the wife of *Bhyian* family' (higher category). Likewise, Minu a microcredit borrower from Zelegaon village gave her family title as *Syed* while all the other inhabitants of her village were *maimol*. According to her, a marital relationship between the *Syeds* and the *maimol* is not possible (*Syed – maimol-e biya hoy na*) because the *maimol* belong to the lower status (*choto*). With few exceptions, the inhabitants of Zelegaon and Nodigaon predominantly marry into other *maimol* families from other villages. For the most part, endogamy is practised and prevails among the villagers (see Chapter 3).

Shantigaon is a big village and there are 315 households. In the rainy season it was difficult to travel from east *para* to south *para* of the village. I collected data from the microcredit borrowers living in the jungle *para* of Shantigaon village. There are 135 households in the jungle para, of which 29 households are Hindu and the rest are Muslim. Of the households, 65 household heads were day labourers. The villagers carry out various kinds of work such as agricultural day labour, the production of bamboo materials, stone crushing, small shopkeeping, masonry and carpentry. There are two primary schools in this village and a nearby high school. Apart from one household, all the inhabitants have their own homestead land. About 40 per cent of the households in the jungle *para* possess some agricultural land, but often this is not cultivated as it is marshland (*haor*).

There are two Hindu castes in this village: the *Nath* and the *Sharma*. The *Sharma* belong to the upper caste or *Brahmin*, whereas the *Nath* belong to the Kayastha. Among Muslims there is no specific *gushti* title. With the exception of two households, none of the villagers to whom I spoke had a *gushti* title – they described themselves as ordinary Muslims. The first household told me that they are *Chaudhuris* and the second that they are *Syeds*, but the other inhabitants and elderly people of the village informed me that these are artificial classifications. According to them, despite the fact that the villagers belong to different *bari* (homestead, normally comprising several households) and *ghors* (houses), unlike Hindus Muslims in reality have no original *gushti* or family title. People often use their achieved status title. For example, the home of the head master (head master-er *bari*), the home of the advocate (*ukil shaheber bari*) and sometimes by indicating the names, for example, the home of Rahim (*Rahimer bari*). Despite this seemingly hierarchical structure respondents said that the villagers have no hierarchies in terms of *gushti* titles. When I asked Rahim, a microcredit borrower and the secretary of the local mosque if he would allow his daughter to marry into any of the families in this village, he answered that despite there being no *gushti* titles among the villagers, not everyone can socialize (*samaj*) with everyone else. Each villager knows very well with whom they can forge relationships.

Notes

1 A patron-client relationship is defined as 'a special case of dyadic (two persons) ties involving a largely instrumental friendship in which an individual of higher socio-economic status (patron) uses his own influence and resources to provide protection or benefits, or both for a person of lower status (client) who, for his part, recipro-cates by offering general support and assistance, including personal services, to the patron' (Scott, 1972: 92). The patron-client relationship is commonplace in rural politics and social organizations in Bangladesh (Jansen, 1987; Jahangir, 1979; Gardner, 1995). Generally, the social position of the patron is based on land hold-ings and on his political affiliations. This tradition is based on economic

dependence. This type of relationship predominates in rural areas. The landless and the poor try to associate themselves with rich peasants (Jansen, 1987: 178; Jahangir, 1979: 3).

2 According to Miles and Huberman, 'Having multiple sites increases the scope of the study... By comparing sites or cases one can establish the range of generality of a finding or explanation, and, at the same time, pin down the conditions under which that finding will occur. So there is potential for both greater explanatory power and greater generalizability than a single case study can deliver' (1984: 151). Note: the authors use the terms 'site' and 'case' interchangeably.

3 Land is considered the most important means of production. Social hierarchy in rural Bangladesh is generally understood in terms of people's access to land. Most commentators on Bangladesh invariably assess rural class on the basis of land ownership beyond all else (Jahangir, 1979, 1982; van Schendel, 1981; Jansen, 1987; Gardner, 1995).

4 100 decimals = 1 acre.

2   Microcredit and social capital
Dynamics of conflict and cooperation

In the 1990s social capital and group-based microcredit programmes were introduced as major strategies of development interventions. Both strategies identified the need to mobilize social factors in the alleviation of poverty and social stability. The group-based microcredit programmes are considered to be effective policy instruments for creating and strengthening the social capital of the community. This is because in order to reach as many clients as possible microcredit programmes provide credit using social mechanisms such as self-selected group formation, social collateral mechanisms or joint-liability and regular presence at a weekly instalment group meeting. Muhammad Yunus also declared that the system of microcredit values 'gives high priority on building social capital' (cf. Woodworth, 2008). Notwithstanding social capital forms as an important dimension of the microcredit process, very little attention has been given to the association of social capital with microcredit credit programmes in Bangladesh. This chapter contributes to the continuing debate about how or if group-based microcredit facilitates the formation of social capital at the local level in Bangladesh. Specifically, I endeavour to answer the following lines of enquiry: does microcredit membership and its collateral mechanism mobilize women's social networks, promote collective identity and cultivate trust among the borrowers and produce successful outcomes in the rural areas? Does participation in a credit programme increase women's active participation in grass-roots politics? Does the group mechanism function or is it merely a means for procuring credit for the borrowers and a governmental strategy for microcredit organizations to fit the demands of the market?

Social capital and microcredit programme: drawing the link

Social capital is recognized as the missing link in development theory; a remedy for the social decay caused by neoliberal policies aimed at getting the price right (cf. Maclean, 2010). In recent years, social capital as a development strategy in the south has gained huge attention, and therefore we are witnessing a burgeoning interest in, inter alia, social capital formation and discussions about applications of the concept across sectors and disciplines. However, the concept of social capital is neither an entirely new nor a monolithic concept. Rather, it has a long history in the arena of social science – particularly in sociology and political science. A number of scholars (Portes, 1998; Flora, 1998; Woolcock, 1998b; Portes and Sensenbrenner, 1993; Swedberg, 1987) have showed how the current theoretical foundations of the concept of social capital were derived from the work of Alexis de Tocqueville, Durkheim, Marx, Weber, Tonnies, Simmel, and Talcott Parsons. Woolcock (1998a) identified Lyda Judson Hanifan (1916) and Jane Jacobs (1961) as the first proponents of the contemporary concept of social capital. Jacobs remarked on the value of social capital in 1961 in his discussion of the vitality of cities.[1] Hanifan's idea[2] of social capital encompasses the current themes and understanding of social capital, but the French sociologist Pierre Bourdieu and the American sociologist James Coleman established the systematic analysis and conceptual framework of social capital (DeFellippis, 2001; Portes and Landolt, 2000; Portes, 1998; Flora, 1998; Portes and Sensenbrenner, 1993).

The concept of social capital first appeared in Bourdieu's work *La Reproduction*, published in 1970.[3] Bourdieu presented a systematic discussion of the concept in his writings under the title 'The Forms of Capital', defining the concept of social capital as 'the aggregate of the actual or potential resources which are linked to possession of a durable network of more or less institutionalized relationships of mutual acquaintance or recognition – or in other words, to membership in a group – which provides each of its members with the backing of the collectivity-owned capital, a *'credential'* which entitles them to credit in the various senses of the world' (1986: 248).

According to Bourdieu, social capital incorporates obligation, the advantages of connections or social position, and trust. Connections and obligations are not given, but are the product of investment strategies 'consciously or unconsciously aimed at establishing or reproducing social relationships that are directly usable in the short or long term' (1986: 249). Bourdieu also deals with the interaction between capital, social capital and cultural capital and argues that they are all interconnected and can be converted into economic capital, and that people purposefully invest in relationships that could bring them future benefit (ibid.: 243).[4] According to him, the amount of social capital that people or a group of people really hold depends on the network they can efficiently mobilize, and on the composition of different forms of capital – economic, cultural or symbolic – that they are able to attain through their links. Bourdieu's clearest definition of social capital is considered to be a theoretically useful and sophisticated attempt to deal with the issue. However, it was Coleman who provided a comprehensive analysis of social capital in mainstream American sociology and brought social capital into widespread use in the social sciences (DeFellippis, 2001; Portes, 1998; Serageldin and Grootaert 2000: 45). Coleman presented a sophisticated analysis of the role of social capital in the creation of human capital in his book entitled *Foundations of Social Theory*, which is the culmination of a series of publications. He considered social capital as a 'particular kind of resource available to an actor' (1988: S98). Individuals can obtain these resources by reaping the benefits of the social structure within which they exist. Coleman defined social capital in terms of its function as a variety of entities that all comprise some aspect of a social structure that in turn helps certain actions of individuals who are within the structure. He viewed social capital as productive and argued that unlike other forms of capital (e.g. human capital, physical capital) social capital exists in the structure of relations between persons (1990: 302).

For Coleman, social capital exists in the structure of relations among individuals and is thus largely intangible. Its potency can be realized through its capacity to facilitate individual action towards a purposeful end. By giving this definition of social capital Coleman then delineated the differences between physical, human and social capital. In his view social capital as a resource enhances cooperation although physical capital is a tool that facilitates production. Social capital is different from human capital, which is embodied in individuals who possess knowledge and skills. As a result, they can perform a particular kind of action. Social capital is not embedded in the actors themselves; rather, it exists in the structure of relations among actors (1990: 304).[5]

Coleman argued that social capital can be obtained by groups and also by individuals. Through purposeful action corporations, social movements and communities can possess social capital just like individuals (1988: S98). Social capital can be created, but by the same token it can also be destroyed (1990: 310–321). Coleman mentioned three forms of social capital: (1) a structure of obligations, expectations and trustworthiness whereby people always carry out activities and tasks for other people with no immediate return or assurances derived from social capital and its roots in mutual trust; (2) information channels (an important form of social capital) that provide a basis for action; (3) social norms and effective sanctions that inhibit negative social actions (e.g. crime) and reinforce socially acceptable behaviour (Coleman, 1988: S101–S104). It is obvious that Coleman identified social capital as a feature of social structure that facilitates action.

In fact, social scientists' explanations of social capital have focused on relationships between individuals or between an individual and a group. Such analyses focus on individual development that flows from social capital, or the way in which actors accrue benefit through their involvement in networks or broader social structures (Bourdieu, 1986; Coleman, 1988, 1990). Now, however, the attention of scholars has shifted to the role of social capital in community development (Portes, 1998; Portes and Landolt, 2000; Woolcock, 1998b; Evans, 1996; Ostrom, 1994). The principal source of the idea for community development practitioners and researchers is Robert Putnam (1993a, 1993b, 1995a, 1996, 1998, 2000). Through Robert Putnam's scholarly work the concept of social capital has gained widespread acceptance and since the early 1990s has become an extremely influential concept in development discourse. Putnam referred to social capital as 'the norms and networks of civil society that lubricate cooperative action among both citizens and their institutions' (1998: v). He continued, 'The core idea of social capital theory is that social networks have value ... social capital refers to connections among individuals – social networks and the norms of reciprocity and trustworthiness that arise from them' (2000: 19). Consequently, social capital is closely related to what some have treated and described as 'civic virtue' (ibid.: 19). According to Putnam, 'A society of many virtuous but isolated individuals is not necessarily rich in social capital' (ibid.). Therefore, voluntary associations are the 'features of social organization, such as networks, norms, and social trust, that enable participants to act together more efficiently pursue shared objectives' (1996: 34). People's involvement in a community or association is an indispensable feature of social capital. Putnam purported that social capital is a resource that individuals or groups of people can either possess or fail to possess. He argued that one of the important mechanisms for creating trust, norms, social engagement and cooperative behaviour is participation in networks of voluntary associations (1993, 1995a, 1995b, 2000).

Since Robert Putnam, a plethora of literature has been developed on social capital resulting in a myriad of conceptualizations but most of them along the ideas of Bourdieu, Coleman and Putnam, which view social capital as relying upon networks, norms, trust and associational memberships (Offe and Fuchs, 2002; Narayan and Cassidy, 2001; Angelusz and Tardos, 2001; Scheufele and Shah, 2000; Lin, 1999; Hofferth *et al.*, 1999; Krishna and Shrader, 1999; Teachman and Paesch, 1997; Ostrom, 1994).

Group-based microcredit programmes are regarded as a preferred way of mobilizing social capital. Scholars argue that microcredit-providing organizations facilitate social capital in the form of solidarity group formation, group lending or group guarantee (Dowla, 2006; Anthony, 2005; Bastelaer, 1999). Regular weekly instalment meetings are perceived as an appropriate place for discussion, and for building networks and finding new opportunities. Ostrom has noted that routine meetings, frequent interaction, and collective credit goals can aid communication, understanding about fellow members and trust as a precondition for collective action (1994: 532). Likewise, based on the findings of her study on GB members, Larance (1998) suggested that women microcredit borrowers can establish new networks and strengthen existing social ties that reach beyond their living quarters and familial networks by attending weekly centre meetings.

Following Putnam, most academic scholars draw a straightforward relationship between organizational memberships and the development of social capital in a positive sense, social capital is not immune from negative externalities. Understanding social capital as a public good pays no attention to the downside of the concept such as exclusion of outsiders, excessive claims on group members, restrictions on individual freedom and success, and downward levelling norms (Portes, 1998: 16).[6] Social capital within the framework of microcredit programmes can be seen as a modern mode of governmentality, which is related to the creation of a set of rules and procedures that help to regulate microcredit borrowers' conduct to achieve specific goals (Foucault, 1979, 1988). According to Jacob Yaron (1991), solidarity groups of microcredit programmes function primarily to provide lenders with a mechanism for 'slashing administrative costs … motivating repayment [and] introducing financial discipline through peer pressure'. Critiques of microfinance interventions have demonstrated that the outcomes of using social capital in microfinance are positive at the institutional level, but claims about women's social capital, collective identity and participatory emancipation are not clear-cut (Moodie, 2008; Maclean, 2010; Mayoux, 2002b; Elyachar, 2005; Bateman 2010, Molyneux 2002; Rankin, 2001, 2002; Bhatt, 1995). Social capital in the microcredit programmes functions as a vehicle for neoliberal economic policy that emphasizes local capacity building and focuses on the poor as agents of their own survival (Rankin, 2002).

Faranak Miraftab of the Department of Urban and Regional Planning at the University of Illinois, USA, was also critical of neoliberal development projects, including policies that focused on participatory development and decentralized development programmes. Miraftab (2004: 240) pointed out that many neoliberal programmes result in the opening of markets and a reformation of public sector services that the poor rely on, which has a negative consequence on the poor. She argued that neoliberal projects effectually keep out marginalized groups under the guise of symbolically incorporating them. Miraftab wrote: 'the neo-liberal emphasis on community participation, communities' social capital, civil society, and decentralization are all closely related ways in which this new governance model tries to "manage" or offer a "social fix" to the inherent tensions of the capital accumulation within capitalist, racialized, and patriarchal societies' (ibid.: 53).

In what follows, I would like to address the way in which membership in microcredit organizations relates to the notion of social capital at the local level. By social capital I mean collective identity, actions and networks and how they facilitate access to resources, trust and political engagement.

Group formation, mobilizing women and the myth of collective identity

The people of rural Bangladesh live in small *bari* [7], *para* and villages. They are not isolated from their social groups, kinship and social relations, and they maintain their social hierarchies through daily interaction. I began my research by exploring the way in which female microcredit borrowers form their self-selected groups.

Both GB and BRAC have adapted the tenets of the group-lending mechanism. According to microcredit rhetoric, the members of a group function as the collateral for credit. In other words, repayment is based on group liability among the members of the microcredit group. If one member fails to repay their instalment, other members contribute on behalf of that woman, so that the group members can go forward together. The rule is that if one member is lagging behind economically and another is forging ahead, the prospering member's credit may be deferred until the other achieves the same standard.

From the social capital perspective, the issue of group formation is very important in the sense that by joining a group, borrowers are supposedly able to gain access to group resources and convert them into other types of capital (cf. Bourdieu, 1986). Group formation is related to disciplines, the facilitation of social networks, the development of a particular type of social norm of regularly attending weekly instalment meetings, and democratically electing a group leader. More specifically, microcredit group membership can become a means for female borrowers to maintain regular interaction with other borrowers and the NGO officials. Such interaction may nurture a sense of mutual understanding, help to increase the chance of collective identity and action, allow borrowers to establish networks and strengthen them (both horizontally and vertically) and build trust within and beyond their own homesteads or kinship groups. Thus one can argue that on the one hand microcredit organizations solidify women's existing social capital, and on the other hand they generate new social capital at the village level.

GB first started its activities in the village of Zelegaon about 18 years prior to the data collection period for this study. When the first branch of GB opened in this area, GB employees persuaded some families by saying that since they were poor they could take out loans from GB for small businesses or other activities and repay their loans via weekly instalments. However, the condition was that first they had to find at least ten members and form a group. Suchona (45 years of age) has been serving as a GB group leader and the centre chief (*kendra prodhan*) of Zelegaon since the inception of the centre. She informed me that when the bank first came to her area some people, including her husband, were motivated to take loans by the GB official; consequently, they took the initiative to develop the centre. 'My husband got a specific amount of cash for his fishery business, so we decided to join the microcredit programme', said Suchona. She claimed that since all her neighbours were poor and had financial difficulties they also came forward to access the credit programme. In fact, when the centre was established in Suchona's house, she had also motivated some of her neighbours to take credit otherwise the centre might not be established here. I asked Suchona how she encouraged people to take part. She replied:

> I know my neighbours; either they belong to the same gushti [lineage] or they are related through kinship. They are not strangers, so this was not a problem. The group consisted of our neighbourhood [para-*protibeshy*] people. First we formed a group of 18 members but after a couple of months of the formation of the group we took on four new members and excluded four old members from the group because they could not pay the instalments. They always caused trouble.
> Q: Did you select members carefully?
> Yes, when we formed the group we chose only those with whom we had

good relationships [moner mil ache] and who would be capable of paying instalments. Yet some members faced problems with repaying credit instalments because their businesses were not doing well.

As in the case of Suchona, the group and centre leaders of Shantigaon and Nodigaon interviewed in this study confirmed that when the micro-lending programmes started their activities in their areas the NGO staff encouraged some local people to take out loans and in turn these people encouraged their neighbours to follow suit. When they formed borrowing groups they emphasized the members' honesty and financial ability to pay instalments, and the pattern of kinship networks and relationships. The respondents pointed out that they considered these characteristics to be important because if a person was unable to repay their credit instalments who would take responsibility for them? As a result, the self-selection practice underlying the group formation mechanism quickly resulted in the exclusion of the poorest people who were not financially well-off or who had no steady source of income, and did not belong to the same *gushti* or *bari*. Therefore, in the early years of microcredit each microcredit borrower group also represented a kinship group or a lineage group and not a solidarity group, as also observed by Ito (1999).[8]

It is no longer always necessary to motivate people to become members of the credit programmes because people now take credit on their own initiative. Of 151 married women microcredit borrowers 20 per cent had been helped to join microcredit programmes by various microcredit officials and some senior members of the NGOs . Nowadays, I observe that the NGOs officials or field assistants generally motivate two groups of people to become members or to maintain the existing membership: the financially well-off families who have a steady cash flow or income and the members who have a good record for paying their instalments on time. The kinship networks and neighbourhood relationships are the key resources, which to a large extent influence local people to participate in the microcredit programmes. The majority of my respondents unanimously stated that poverty and sometimes immediate financial constraints prompted them to become members of microcredit programmes. Generally, the men send their wives, mothers or mothers-in-law, sisters or close female relatives to access credit. Previously, the clergy (i.e. *hujur, mawlana, mullah* or the mosque's imam) avoided credit programmes but now they too send their female family members to take credit. As some female clients said, 'Nowadays the religious leaders copy what the general public does in society. They used to be against the NGOs' loans, but now they are not'. This was a significant change in the local religious stricture about providing credit at a profit because earlier the religious groups had attacked the NGOs' activities in many places of Bangladesh including Sylhet. Previously, they ostracized women who worked with the NGOs, and forbade women to be seen in public without wearing the *burqa* (full veil). They even forced 50 women to divorce because their marriages were considered 'un-Islamic' (Hashmi, 2000).[9] The religious leaders strongly believed that

Islam strictly prohibits taking or giving loans with interest. However, when I sought answers to questions about the apparent change in attitude towards microcredit from an *imam* of a local mosque he avoided giving an answer. Instead, the secretary of the mosque explained that this religious stricture could not be followed perfectly owing to the economic conditions and the constraints that they imposed on the population.

The formation of a new group or self-selected solidarity group is no longer a requirement for taking credit from micro-lending organizations. Currently, in order to be eligible for the scheme, an applicant has to have high individual collateral and the capacity to repay loans, and is only asked to collect two signatures from two female members and the centre chief to accept them as members in the group. Dropping, excluding or including new members is a continuous process within the microcredit programmes; it does not cause any anxiety among new or existing members since the sense of solidarity or degree of cohesion is low among the borrowers. The group leaders play a decisive role in membership arrangements. They know the details about the inclusion and exclusion of members but the majority of the borrowers are not interested in who takes credit or not. The centre chiefs have links with many borrowers at the individual level as well. For instance, the group leader of Zelegaon village confirmed that the centre comprised 90 members and that she was acquainted with most of them as she had been working as the centre leader since its inception. When I asked her if all members knew each other, and she replied:

> I don't think all the members know each other because some are not interested in knowing who takes credit or who leaves the programme. For me it is very important. I have to keep them in mind, because I have to ensure that they make their repayments each week. Every week the borrowers or their representatives [e.g. sons, daughters and husbands] come to my house to pay their instalments. They do not visit me without a reason and nor do I visit them. I have some close neighbours with whom I socialize.

Group meetings or weekly credit instalment meetings are perceived to be the main method of constructing particular social norms and social capital among the microcredit borrowers. Scholars (Dowla, 2006; Bastelaer, 2000; Jain, 1996; Ostrom, 1994; Schuler and Hashemi, 1994) have argued that social capital or a particular cultural habit is facilitated when microfinance organizations such as GB and others like it require all of their members to repeat certain of the bank's rules and regulations as a matter of course every week, such as reciting the list of decisions that accompanies group membership. As noted by Schuler and Hashemi:

> Grameen Bank's weekly meetings, the chanting, saluting, and other rituals are important in creating an identity for women outside of their

families ... The programme gives women socially legitimate reasons to move about and associate with one another in public spaces ... Ironically, Grameen Bank's more regimented approach appears to be more effective than BRAC's in strengthening women's autonomy.

(1994: 73)

My observations and data do not support the findings of Schuler and Hashemi. Every week I went to the GB payment/administration centre to observe the weekly instalment meetings but observed that the loan collector sat on the verandah of the group leader's house and the borrowers or their representatives duly paid their instalments and left the premises. I got a strong impression from the borrowers that previously, when microcredit programmes started up in the research areas, GB in particular insisted on group meetings or borrowers' presence at weekly instalment payment places but this requirement now has completely lapsed. Currently, the organization does not attribute any importance to group meetings. I observed that many women sent their husbands or close relatives to make their payments. Some women never visited the centre. Instead, they authorized their husbands or sons to carry out tasks such as paying instalments, meeting with bank officials, etc. The financially well-off families and some old people never sent their wives to the centres to pay their weekly instalments. Often their husbands visited the centres and paid the instalments and in some cases the microcredit officers themselves collected the credit instalments from the borrower's place of business. I asked the female respondents why they did not visit the centre to make their credit payments. Some chose not to respond to the question. However, based on the interviews, the most common reasons were lack of interest, everyday engrossment in household chores, and to some extent husbands' unwillingness or religious transgression. I argue that microcredit programmes in my research areas do not facilitate group-meeting norms. The micro-lending business has to a certain extent become individualized owing to the laxity of rules and decisions. For example, Minara (a 45-year-old GB microcredit borrower) explained that members actually send their credit instalments when it suits them, depending on their work schedules. According to her, the loan officer generally collects weekly instalments in her centre between 9 a.m. and 11 a.m. Consequently, most borrowers do not visit the centre at the same time. Moreover, she thinks that since some women prefer not to come at the centre they are not aware who takes credit and who has left the programme. Minara does not visit the instalment collecting centre (*kisti toler kendra*) every week. I enquired why this was so, and she replied:

What is the necessity to go there? For me, the main purpose of going there is to get the loan, to pay my instalment [*kisti*] and put money in to my savings account, nothing more. I do know that if I sought help from other group members I would not get it. If you have nothing nobody will help you.

However, I was able to find some women who do regularly visit the centres to pay their credit instalments. However, they demonstrate that they feel good about the opportunity to talk to other women and, to some extent, they can enquire about other people's news. They share ideas and form acquaintances with women outside of their kinship groups or hamlets. At least one day a week they can wear their neat and clean dresses and small items of jewellery. Nowadays, they also change their mode of dress and some women copy one another and wear lipstick. As the husband of one microcredit borrower said, 'For giving instalments when some women walk the road-side wearing their good *saris* and chatting with each other it looks beautiful. Even some years ago we did not observe this scenario in this village.' Another female respondent added, 'Not only that, in the payment centre we can talk to each other, which helps to develop face-to-face relations'. In other words, to some extent microcredit group memberships have helped to change the self-image of these women. However, whenever I asked the female microcredit borrowers whether such relationships would result in any mutual productive benefits or help to form some form of collective identity I was amazed at the pessimistic outlook they had about collectiveness. Most of the narratives express the feeling that credit relationships cannot produce any mutual or shared benefit, nor some form of collective identity or norms of reciprocity. Nasibun (38 years old) sums up the women's views:

> The members do not help one another. The NGO boss does not say anything about this. Nobody wants to help others unless it benefits them. If any member helps you to pay an instalment, they always expect you to help them in return. If you fail to offer similar help, then the relationship will be destroyed. If someone has money, they don't want to give loans themselves; rather, they are directly advised to take a loan from the NGO.

When I asked my respondents whether they consider the members of their group to be equal, a number of women said that as human beings they are equal but according to the mentality and to some extent their socio-economic circumstances they are not equal. Not everyone can do *samaj* (i.e. socialize) with everyone else. They often asked me, 'are the five fingers on one hand equal?' or 'are the fingers on our hands equal?'[10] Many borrowers described the prevailing features of unity thus: 'The poor people always show less unity and solidarity towards their neighbours, and the poor cannot tolerate another poor person's good circumstances or happiness'; 'If a poor family can improve their financial circumstances, within a few days they forget their poor kin'; 'Everybody is busy with themselves or their families, so they do not come forward to help if they see that someone has a problem'; 'When a poor family gets rich in the rural areas, other families become envious [*hingsha*] of this family and try to harm them'.[11] Nasibun often visited the microcredit centre and explained her position as follows:

Every week I visit the group leader's house to pay my instalment. Being a woman of this village [gramer *meye*] I know many members and their houses. I do not know everybody's names but their faces are familiar to me. There is no unity among the members. If a family becomes rich, other families become envious of this family. Everybody is busy with their own family. This is the practice [niyam] of our society.

Jesmin (39 years old), a microcredit borrower in Nodigaon, admitted that she knew most of the group members because she got involved in microcredit when the BRAC started its operations in her area. She actively worked to develop this centre and has tried to maintain good relations with other members but she feels isolated. I asked her the reason for this, and she explained to me: 'Here all belong to the same *gushti*, that is, *maimol*. Some of them have good relations with each other but I am alone, I am *abadi* [outsider]. So in this village even many of the group members do not like me – they are envious [hingsha *kore*] of me.' Jesmin said that her family came from Jessore. They bought land in the village of Nodigaon and also built a house many years ago but villagers often said to her family, 'They bought our land and built house although they are outsiders'. Jesmin's husband informed me that he is a member of the village *panchayat* (traditional village council) but the neighbours do not like them. Sometimes they try to quarrel with his family. However, since a girl from the village started addressing Jesmin as a fictive mother (dharma maa) and her son as a brother, neighbours no longer try to harm them. Jesmin's fictive daughter's husband was a small fish trader who often enquired after them. Jesmin also helped her fictive daughter; she took credit from a microcredit NGO on her behalf. However, I observed that Jesmin has a reasonably good relationship with some members of the group as well as with the group leader, but when I asked her about this relationship she explained, 'I have tried to get to know some members who live near my house despite the fact that they still do not like me. Now I always try to maintain a good relationship with the group leader *apa* [sister], because if I have any problems in paying my instalment the group leader will not cause any difficulties.'

Collateral mechanism and the market principle

I asked my respondents why the NGOs disbursed credit through a collateral mechanism whereby an applicant has to collect the signatures of two female borrowers and the group leader as guarantors. The analysis of data ascertains whether microcredit-providing NGOs accurately work according to the logic of the market principle and place. Most of the respondents acknowledged that micro-lending organizations collect the signatures of two female borrowers and the group leader to enable the applicant to run the NGOs' business smoothly in the local community. According to them, the NGO officials are not the inhabitants of the village, so they do not know all the villagers.

Therefore, they cannot sanction a loan on behalf of people who are unknown to them. So that they can recover instalments when they are due without facing any hassle they disburse credit through guarantors and the group leader. The respondents often argued that the NGOs seek to 'fill their own bellies through the help of others' (i.e. the clients). According to some of my respondents, when a member defaults the NGO official use a group of women against the woman to recover the unpaid instalment which causes conflicts, creates disturbances and destroys prevailing social relationships.[12] They do not consider their guarantors or groups as mutual helping groups: instead, they view them as pressure groups:

> [The collateral mechanism] is like frying fish in its own oil. If someone wants to take credit the NGO's official compels her to collect two other women's signatures and the signature of the group leader. As a result, three people, including the woman's own family members, are involved in that woman's loan. Now, if a woman fails to pay her instalments at least five people go at the same time to make that woman pay the instalment. That can cause arguments and conflict and requires arbitration among the members. The NGO officer does not have to cope with any problems.
>
> (Afia, 36 years old)

The above statement suggests that microcredit programmes engage the group mechanism only in the most instrumental manner as a governmental strategy to reduce administrative costs, to ensure through the maintainance of financial discipline that repayments are made, and to improve the financial health rather than the welfare of the borrowers or the strengthening of ties among the members.[13] Most respondents claim that the guarantors are often their close relatives or neighbours. If a woman works as the guarantor of another woman, she hopes that the borrower will reciprocate the contractual relationship when the guarantor in turn becomes a borrower. As a result, mutually beneficial reciprocal relations are formed whereby guarantors work for each other. I found no clear example of joint-liability arrangements whereby group members took responsibility for other members' repayment problems in the study areas.[14] 'If people take out loans it is their duty to pay them off, not that of the guarantors or the group members', said Fouzia, a BRAC microcredit borrower. In addition, the micro-lending officials do not advise members to help one another. Some borrowers who have long-term microcredit involvement use their micro-savings in the case of default.

With regard to peer group pressure and recovering instalments, all the group leaders confirm that they have to play a decisive role in ensuring that borrowers pay their weekly instalments. The group leaders have friends and enemies. Some may indulge in back-biting but some also praise the group leaders. If a member is delayed they have to talk to her family and motivate them. However, I got the impression that today these kinds of problems occur less frequently:

Sometimes I have problems with some members. These families do not understand that the bank follows its own rules, not my rules. But the problem is now less than it was earlier.

(Alapi, 43 years old)

In contrast to the comment above, one group leader said:

Sometimes I am faced with considerable problems which can breed conflict with others. If any borrower fails to pay her instalments I have to talk to her, motivate her to repay the credit, which is a waste of time for me. I have decided to cut my name from the programme, in order to be relieved of this burden.

(Jarina, 40 years old)

I do not have many observations on how group pressure functions; I only observed one such case at Nodigaon. I saw Rahela (55 years old) arrive at the group meeting place and wail that she had failed to arrange for the repayment of her instalment for the last two consecutive weeks. When I enquired about the matter, I knew that she took credit in order to finance her son's second-hand three-wheeler. Through driving the three-wheeler, her son pays the instalment of the loan, but 15 days ago the police had arrested her son and impounded the three-wheeler. Police claimed that he had stolen this three-wheeler. Rahela suspected that probably the person who had sold this three-wheeler had stolen it and then sold it on to them. The documents belonging to the three-wheeler most likely were forgeries. Now she did not know what to do nor how she would pay the instalments. Her family had no additional income or property to pay the instalments. She went to the police station but they did not give her any time or assistance. However, the loan collecting staff said: 'I am not interested in your son nor in the police case. I must have the instalment.' Rahela wept and begged the other members to pay her instalments but they declined and said that they could not. The group leader and some of the members said to her, 'Do not cause us problems: you took out the loan, you must pay it back as well as any fines. It is not our duty [*kaj*] to show you where you will collect the money. You and your son are trying to cause us problems. Go and find the money.' Thus, in this case, altruism, which according to Putnam (2000: 117) is a significant indicator of social capital normally fosters co-operation. It nurtures norms of reciprocity as well as encouraging economic productivity, and could not be taken for granted.

I assumed that Fuglesang and Chandler's description of GB's activities typified the norm throughout Bangladesh: 'Throughout the GB the prevailing attitude is that the group must progress as a whole. ... [Field staff] use every occasion to reinforce the message: You must go forward together and help each other' (1993: 100). In contrast to the above experiences, I discovered that microcredit organizations in the research areas of this study operate in the line with the idea of supporting the entrepreneurship of the poor, where clients are considered to be active agents in their own development (cf. Elyachar, 2005). Clients are responsible for the investment of credit, income generation or the elimination of poverty. An individual borrower is responsible for the success or failure of her credit investments. The NGO officials do not give any advice about the use of credit. 'To be honest, it is not our duty as to how the borrowers invest the money and pay the instalments', said one of the branch managers. By and large the main task of a member is to solve her own financial problems by herself. What struck me in this respect was that the overwhelming majority of the borrowers viewed the microcredit organization first and foremost as a money-lending business (*shud-babshaw*), and they considered their debts to be a private matter. All the respondents from these villages unanimously stated that their organizations had not called any meetings (*karmoshala*) at the centres for several years. The NGO field staff have three main duties: providing credit; bringing in new members; and recovering instalments by the due date.

The concept is very clear and one that each borrower easily comprehends: each individual is responsible for paying off credit and it is impossible to avoid making credit payments. Nowadays, the NGO field assistants maintain extensive networks and door-to-door contacts for collecting instalments. As a result, I have observed the development of a new kind of patron-client relationship between loan officers and borrowers in my research areas. Furthermore, some of my respondents have told me that it is pointless to follow up their credit investments because it creates an antagonistic environment if one enquires whether she invests her money herself or practises money-lending which incurs repayments at high rates of interest. Other researchers reached the same conclusion: when group members monitor one another's consumption and repayment patterns in accordance with programme incentive structures, they can generate a hostile and antagonistic environment rather than the one that unites them (Ackerly, 1997; Fernando, 1997). I also understand that some behind-the-scenes negotiation takes place between group leaders and members about the use of credit. Not all borrowers are honest about the use of credit; some work as money-lenders. Although fieldworkers are supposed to visit clients individually and monitor the investment of credit, in fact they are reluctant to find out for what purposes the borrowers actually use their credit.

Solidarity is expected to provide a productive or a valued resource flow. Hence, this is what sociologists have characterized as social capital (Coleman, 1990: 300–302). In the same vein, Putnam (1993a, 1995a) has also argued that associational membership teaches cooperative behaviour and attitudes for mutual benefits. However, it is not obvious in what situations members of a group get involved in reciprocal relationships. The overwhelming majority of my respondents do not have the economic ability for reciprocity. Owing to their appalling financial circumstances they cannot lend money to each other. For example, although neighbours and relatives might lend each other a pot of rice or some kitchen equipment thus helping each other to a certain extent, their financial situation does not permit them to help others more altruistically. Nowadays, the people who have financial ability do not lend money, but instead suggest taking loans from microcredit organizations. Instead of borrowing from fellow villagers, many people get involved in the microcredit programmes. The impoverished microcredit borrowers try to maintain good relations with their richer kin in order to get help (*shahajja*). They often expect assistance from their relatives, close friends and kin not rather than from others, but this does not mean that the relatives do not resort to arguments and conflict (*jhogra*) in the event that someone defaults on their repayments.

Squabbling as a part of life

Arguments, disunity, envy, expectations that are not met, competitiveness and individualistic self-interest have always been an inherent part of normal family life for poor people,[15] but they are currently on the increase. I find the economic downturn as the major cause. Here I present briefly two cases to illustrate how arguments, disunity, jealousy and competition take place within the extended family in the local communities. I do not argue that before microcredit involvement rural people or the families were free of conflicts. I show that despite the fact that these families reside in the same homestead areas and take credit from the same organization, they lack solidarity and unity.

Case 1: Jarina and Parul

The first case study sheds light on the causes of arguments in the household. Jarina and Parul are elderly microcredit borrowers who have been taking credit from BRAC for several years. They are both housewives and sisters-in-law and reside in the same compound in two separate houses that have corrugated iron roofs, brick walls and mud floors. Both women took credit in order to construct their houses. The distance between the front doors of these two houses is no more than 25 feet but they are separated by bamboo fencing. Their husbands are rickshaw pullers and both families have several children. That is where the similarities end.

Jarina has been serving as a group leader for the BRAC microcredit programme in Nodigaon village for the last four years. During my fieldwork in Nodigaon I usually visited Jarina's house every week and stayed there between 9 a.m. to 11 a.m. to observe instalment collecting activities. Her family is poor so there is no furniture in her house and she could not complete furnishing the house. The household has two *chokis* (basic wooden beds), a small work table, two chairs and some cooking utensils. In early July 2010 I talked to Jarina about her credit involvement and improvements. Jarina did not complete her story because some male and female borrowers came to pay their instalments. The men paid quickly because they had to hurry to work. However, on one occasion the loan collector told me that she had to go next door to Parul's house to collect credit. I asked the official why Parul did not come to Jarina's house, which was immediately adjacent house. The officer replied that Jarina and Parul's families do not talk to each other, and Parul does not visit, so the official always collects Parul's instalments from her house. I had talked to Parul previously but I was not told about the ongoing conflict between Parul and Jarina. The loan collector suggested that I could find out more from Jarina or she would take me with her and I could talk to Parul again. I took the opportunity to do so because I felt that I could talk with Jarina later as she is the group leader. When I visited Parul's house, she arranged two *moras* (stools) for us but the loan collector left the house immediately.

My field assistant and I chatted to Parul for about an hour and I asked Parul what the problem was with Jarina and why she did not visit her house. Parul told me that her family's financial circumstances are very bad in comparison to that of Jarina's family, so they do not like her household. According to Parul, her husband Latif once asked his brother (Jarina's husband) for help, but instead of helping him his brother hit him hard with a wooden stick and used abusive language. Latif did not get any justice (*bichar*) from the local *panchayat* because his brother accused him stating that 'despite the fact he is junior to me he behaved badly to me'. The neighbours also insisted that an elder brother can beat his younger brother. Parul told me that his brother-in-law took over their property. Upon marriage Parul acquired her brother-in-law's extended family. They lived and ate together. At that time, Parul's husband handed over his earnings to his brother but Parul did not say a word about this. Parul's brother-in-law made all the household items when they were living together as extended family. According to Parul, when she became the mother of two sons her brother-in-law began to quarrel with her and her husband, and accused them of eating more than their income covered. Parul's brother-in-law eventually forcibly ejected her family from the house.

Parul regards her brother-in-law as perfidious (*beimaan*) because when he ejected them Parul's family only got two poor-quality wooden beds and a few cooking utensils. According to Parul, her brother-in-law deprived them of everything. Some of the neighbours also requested him not to do this, but he ignored their pleas. Parul claimed that she cried a lot and left the extended family. As her family had nothing at that time, they went to her parents' house and resided there for some months. Later her father and her brother gave her some money, so her family returned to their homestead land (*vita-bari*) where they built a bamboo thatched house. 'How selfish my brother-in-law is!' said Parul. 'Now he does not even allow us to fetch water from the tube well. So I fetch water from further away. Many of our neighbours treat my brother-in-law as *Ajajil* [Satan]; he is such a cruel character. The elder brother kicked his younger brother in the belly, but what can other people do?'

According to Parul, after about one year of separation her brother-in-law became severely ill. At that time her husband did not contain his sympathy; he borrowed money from others and took his brother to the doctor. Parul's husband bore all the cost of medicine and food. This state of affairs lasted only for a few months. Some time later, Parul's husband suffered from acute fever and thus could not pull his rickshaw for nearly a week. As a result, the family faced a serious economic crisis. They had no money to pay their credit instalment, or buy food and medicine. Parul had no other option but to ask for some money as a loan but her brother-in-law, and instead was abusive to Parul. Parul left her brother-in-law's door, and borrowed money from another relative to pay her loan and to complete her husband's treatment. At the time of writing, Parul's family had not maintained any form of relationship with her brother-in-law's family for the last three years. I asked Parul, 'how did you get credit? Did your sister-in-law cause problems as a group leader?' She replied, 'I collect credit from the officer and try to pay the instalments by the due date, so what is the problem with her? The credit is not her money. The microcredit official knows very well that we do not get on with one another.'

Later, I talked to Jarina (Parul's sister-in-law) again but neither she nor her husband wanted to talk about this family conflict. Jarina heard my conversation with Parul. According to Jarina, she has to follow her husband's orders so she does not talk to Parul and her husband. Jarina regarded her brother-in-law's family as bad and selfish. She claimed that her family did a lot for her brother-in-law's family but this help was never acknowledged. Her husband also pulls a rickshaw just as her brother-in-law does. Both families are poor. As a group leader of the credit programme she helped Parul by giving her signature in support of Parul's application.

This case study illustrates how despite the fact that both the households are in the same compound and both take credit from the same organization, they do not interact with one another and microcredit membership does not contribute to unity between them. Let us turn to the second case study. The following story explores how cooperation, jealousy and competition can occur under the same roof.

Case 2: Alapi and her brother-in-law's family

Alapi is a Hindu woman who lives in Shantigaon village. She is one of the oldest microcredit borrowers and she had been taking microcredit for the past 18 years from GB and from ASA and BRAC for the past four years. Alapi's husband Robi is 50 years old and a *van* (cart) driver who now only works occasionally due to poor health. Her eldest daughter got married five years ago and has two children, but now resides with her natal family owing to her husband's violent behaviour. Alapi's household has no homestead or cultivable land. Now they reside in a room in the house of Alapi's brother-in-law (her husband's younger brother). 'Life was good about 25 years ago, when I came to this family as a bride. Day by day life became more difficult, and struggling with poverty became a part of everyday life,' Alapi recalled.

Within the caste system, Alapi's husband belongs to the weaver community but he did not follow this profession. Since his youth her husband has sold *chira* (flattened rice) -*muri* (puffed rice) in different villages but his income did not cover food, minimal clothing and other living and family expenditures. He ran his business by taking loans from local money-lenders with interest. As a result, he was always incurring losses. Her husband gradually sold his homestead land to settle different types of loans. In 1983 he fell seriously ill and as a result the family became paralyzed financially. He could not work, so he had to borrow money to maintain the household. In addition, he had some loans from local money-lenders carrying a 100 per cent interest rate. The money-lenders applied tremendous pressure to get the money through village arbitration (*bichar-shalish*). Therefore, Alapi's husband decided to sell his homestead land and thatched house to his younger brother, Raton. Raton is known to be one of the successful microcredit borrowers in Shantigaon centre (see Chapter 8 in this volume). Since then the family has been home-less. There is nowhere for them to take shelter. The family have sometimes resided in an abandoned house. However, Alapi's mother-in-law could not accept the appalling situation which her eldest son's family found itself in. She cried and begged her younger son Raton to give them a room in his house to live in. Thus, for the past few years the presence of Alapi's family has been a burden upon her brother-in-law's household.

Alapi first took GB credit for the sum of TK 2,000 to finance her husband's *chira-muri* business. Alapi prepared the chira-muri and her husband sold it in different villages. Since this work was laborious and he could not run the business in the rainy season, he left this business and started a tea stall on the pavement of Bandor bazaar in Sylhet by using a GB loan. This business was successful, and Alapi's family hoped to overcome their poverty, but after two years the tea stall was evicted by the government. Alapi's husband was again unemployed. As a result, the family found it difficult to pay the instalments to GB in time; thus Alapi took a new loan from ASA. Some years ago she also took credit from BRAC in order to buy a *van* for her husband. 'I do not like taking loans simultaneously from different microcredit organizations because it is very hard to pay the instalments and it is also against the rules to take credit but poverty and debts compel me to do this year after year', said Alapi of the vicious spiral of her family's increasing debts.

After losing the homestead land, the family never took credit from local money-lenders. Alapi considers them to be pirates. She hates them enor-mously. She says that the NGOs' credit system is good because it saves her family from the greedy hands of local money-lenders. Poverty forced her third son and fourth daughter to stop school at grades four and three respectively. The third son was sent out as an apprentice in the hope that he might help to lessen the family's financial burden, but the boy does not like his work. I observed that the family suffers great poverty. Alapi's husband is always sick or idle. He spends most of his time asleep. Her daughter suffers from vitiligo. Alapi's eldest son maintains the family. He drives a rented three-wheeler. During the past year, he has made almost all the payments required for GB credit and BRAC instalments. How long can the son work to reduce poverty and vulnerability of the family? What is the future of this family?

Alapi's family lives in her brother-in-law's house but Alapi and her husband Robi say that their brother Raton is not a good man. According to them, Raton is financially well-off but he is not willing to help them. The couple consider Raton to be a selfish person with an acquisitive mentality. They told me that nobody trusts Raton. He thinks only about himself and seeks to become ever richer. They believe that they made a mistake in selling their homestead land to Raton. Now they do not like living in Raton's house. They applied for a loan to buy a three-wheeler for their son and to buy homestead land so that they can build a house for themselves. Robi claimed, 'As a brother if Raton helps us a little what is the problem? We will not bother him to pay back loans. We understand everything. If our son buys a three-wheeler and drives in this road, our brother thinks that his income might decline. He only wants our son to drive a rented three-wheeler.'

However, I also talked to Raton and his wife. Raton told me that despite the fact that his brother's family has been taking out credit over the years, they still have not been able to improve their financial situation. They are very poor because his elder brother Robi is unintelligent and lacks entrepreneurial skills. His sons are the same. 'So where will this family get money from? What can I do for them?' Raton asked. 'I provide a room for them. It is not my duty to give them shelter. My brother's family does not do anything for me. Nowadays nobody gets this type of opportunity, but my brother's family does not understand it,' Raton continues:

> My brother's family envies me. Now they are trying to take credit to buy a three-wheeler, but is it easy work? In this road now there are more three-wheelers than passengers. I am also doing this work, so I know the difficulties of this business, but who will make them understand? They have nothing yet they try to compete with me.

These two cases show how poverty and competition over limited resources can erode the fabric of social life and reduce solidarity among the poor in the local communities of Bangladesh. Indeed, family fights, tensions and competition over scant resources[16] seemed to be commonplace in most families. Within the household domain these fights and tensions are structured as brother vs brother, mother-in-law vs daughter-in-law, sister-in-law vs sister-in-law, husband vs wife. People get entangled in conflicting familial and kinship relationships too. Based on my findings I suggest that poverty, lack of employment and competition over limited resources among the poor micro-credit borrowers are omnipresent (see Chapter 8 in this volume). I argue that these problems will be exacerbated in the future and they are bound to generate a climate of envy and hostility that in practice atomizes social relations rather than bringing people together.

To conclude, the social cohesion, joint-liability or a sense of mutual inter-dependence, shared objectives or the attitudes towards the importance of the group as expressions of collective identity is barely detectable among the borrowers. By and large the collateral mechanism or group membership works as an entry route to access credit programmes for the borrowers, but for NGOs it is an instrument for promoting their governmentality over the borrowers and a furtherance of capitalist gains through collecting instalments at due times. An applicant's ability (individual collateral) to repay her loan is the main criterion for access to a credit programme. The microcredit offi-cials simply enforce repayments, whereas the credit groups that originally were intended to boost social capital and solidarity among women are either impotent or actually help to enforce the payment of the defaulted repayment. The social capital school, especially Putnam (1993a, 2000), argues that membership of associations (e.g. microcredit organizations) facilitates face-to-face interaction between people, creates a common set of norms and an environment for the development of collective identity. I argue that in a poverty-stricken environment, the supposed connection between organizational mem-berships or collateral mechanism and building collective identities or provid-ing a platform among the microcredit borrowers is much less clear-cut than is commonly assumed by scholars. More specifically, this study suggests that microcredit programmes have not strengthened solidarity or favoured the creation of solidarity in the poor localities. Rather, the group-lending system and joint-liabilities appear to have intensified various anxieties and squabbling among the borrowers, in particular when they are struggling with scarce resources.

The fabric of social trust

Social capital scholarship (Fukuyama, 1995; Putnam, 1993a; Coleman, 1990) has a broad consensus about trust as the central ingredient of social capital. Putnam, for example, considered trust to be a central element of social capi-tal: 'One of those features of social organization' that along with norms and networks 'can improve the efficiency of society by facilitating coordinated action' (1993a: 167). Trust determines the performance of a society's institu-tions. People who are trusting are more optimistic, altruistic, more likely to donate to charity, work to solve community problems, vote, and be willing to serve on a jury (1995a: 22). Social trust accommodates social capital facil-itating the creation of cooperation within a society. It builds a spirit of com-munity and strengthens social ties to others within a system. Francis Fukuyama is one of the principle scholars who defined trust as 'the expectation that arises within a community of regular, honest and cooperative behaviour, based on commonly shared norms' (1995: 26).

Social trust is generated by individuals when they regularly interact with each other in the same environment or social structure. Membership of associations facilitates face-to-face interaction, a common set of norms, and creates an environment for the development of trust. This fundamentally presumes the validity of a micro theory of social capital that hypothesizes a causal link between association membership (e.g. microcredit) and trust. When referring to the goals of the microcredit programme, Muhammad Yunus argued that the mission ought to help the poor to help themselves to conquer poverty, that it should target poor women in particular, and that it must not be based on collateral but on trust (cf. Woodworth, 2008). Taking this into account, I asked the following questions: does participation in microcredit organizations foster trust among the borrowers in the research areas of this study? Do microcredit borrowers trust each other? When I raised this question, Begum (aged 55 years), a microcredit borrower from Nodigaon village, told me that she cannot trust anyone, even her very closest friends or relatives. When I asked her why she was so cynical, she related a sorrowful story about her daughter.

Begum married twice because her first husband died when she was just 15 years old. She got married for a second time to a man who already had a wife. The man hid this information from Begum's natal family. Begum found out after she had spent a few months at her new husband's house. However, at that time she had no alternative but to stay. Later, the husband arranged two separate houses, one for his first wife and one for Begum. In spite of this, Begum's co-wife (*satin*) did not tolerate Begum. She often quarrelled with her. According to Begum, two years ago her daughter Hashi (then 22 years of age, and was born to her second husband) sat an examination. One day, as Hashi was studying at home, Begum returned to her natal house for a few hours. During this time Hashi's step-mother and brothers secretly entered the house and threw acid over Hashi. As a result, part of the right side of her face, head and hands were burnt. When Begum heard the news, she immediately took her daughter to hospital where the girl received treatment for about two months. The doctors operated on her face and head seven times. Begum claimed that her elder son from her first marriage bore all the cost of Hashi's treatment, not her father. Not only that, the husband was furious when Begum filed a case against her husband's first wife and sons. The police arrested them but they were only jailed for one year. As a result, according to Begum, her husband refused to let her live in his house and she and her sons now reside in her natal house. Begum asks, 'can you give an example where a father supports this type of heinous attack on his own daughter?' She states that although she knew people can enter into conflict with one another, she could not believe that anyone could perpetrate such a heinous act. Her daughter now goes to college with her face veiled. She often cries when she sees her burnt face in the mirror. She is ashamed to show her burnt face and head.

The above-mentioned brutal event is a one-off example which is not related to the microcredit programme, but it would appear that trust is not a one-way relationship. Rather, it must be mutual. Trust must be seen in the societal context within which it prevails. We can only trust people we know reasonably well (cf. Hardin, 1999). Trust is a central component in building a cohesive and integrated community; it is the *glue* that binds people together. Its presence undoubtedly has a positive impact on social life, while its absence may cause a breakdown of social institutions and relationships (Franklin, 2004). Nevertheless, whenever I asked to what extent microcredit borrowers trust one another, surprisingly the majority of the respondents often claimed that 'It is very difficult to trust or believe others in society'; 'It is not easy to find a trustworthy or reliable person'; 'We have now entered in an era [*juge*] where even the brothers do not trust each other'.The older respondents in particular often claimed that trust, as well as morals, in their neighbours have drastically declined. They frequently characterize today's society as being bad. These views are probably related to their everyday experiences. For example, I asked Karimunnessa (aged 60 years) whether she believes all her group members, and she replied:

> There are various types of people in society: is it possible to believe them all? We live in bad times now – you cannot trust anybody.
> Q: Do members of your group help you as a guarantor so you can take credit?
> They are my close relatives and my neighbours. They are personally known well to me. I also work in support of them. They work as only guarantors but I am obliged to pay off my credit. If I have problems paying instalments, do you believe they will help me? No, rather they will hold me tightly. … We are living in a society so we have to trust some people who live nearby and are known well.

Another borrower, Jesmin, added that 'I trust my group leader and the officer of the bank (BRAC) because all my savings are in the microcredit bank. If I do not trust them I cannot do anything.' However, she argues that one has to be alert by keeping one's eyes and ears open in such a society. The microcredit borrowers in my research areas agreed that trust is very important; yet trust towards other borrowers is exceptionally low. I think this is not unexpected in a country with dysfunctional politics, strong clientele relationships, political patronage, widespread rent seeking, weak accountability and virtual state monopoly over new sources of development capital (Wood, 1994; Sobhan, 1998). However, the vast majority of the borrowers in my research areas do not believe that people are trustworthy in society in matters related to money or valuable materials (see also Hulterström, 1995). They believe that if anybody drops/loses money or something valuable there is little chance that they will get it back again if it is not handed in to close family members. In other words, people maintain a negative attitude or do not trust outsiders who are not close family members and neighbours.

The group leader of Zelegaon told me that despite the fact that she works as a group leader of the centre, she does not trust the other members of her centre. She asked me, 'Is it possible to trust the others in this society?' Suchona recounted an event by way of illustration. One day the microcredit officer was collecting money instalments and three other borrowers were sitting there. One of their borrowers was in a hurry so she asked Suchona to take her money. Suchona took TK 1,160 from the borrower and put it on the table in front of the official and the other three members. Sometime later she noticed that the money was no longer there; the official asked everybody and searched them but could not find the money. Later, she paid the money through great personal suffering: 'You cannot believe how I felt having to pay this money – my blood boiled. This is the world in which we live and interact! If you have this kind of experience, will you trust others? No, I think not,' Suchona said.

Another dominant idea revealed in this ethnographic account is that people are motivated by self-interest. They try to extract profit or interest from any-thing, even from other family members. One of my respondents said that her husband was falsely accused of a crime and was fined TK 100,000. As her husband was in prison she asked her mother-in-law to take out a loan from the microcredit bank in order to help her to release her husband, who was after all her son, from jail but her mother-in-law would not help. When I suggested to my respondent that as an older member perhaps her mother-in-law knew the rules of the credit programme and this was why she did not agree to take a loan for this purpose, the respondent rationalized her position thus:

> No, my mother-in-law said that she could not take credit. However, you will be astonished to hear that she took out TK 100,000 as a micro-loan and lent it to one of her relatives at a high rate of interest but she did not help her son because she would not have received the interest from her son. My mother-in-law is an old woman but she is so greedy and lies to us. She did not trust her son, so how I can trust my mother-in-law and respect her. My mother-in-law only knows how to look after herself but does not know how to help her own son. This is just one example. You will find many similar examples in our society.

Trust towards people of another religion is even more complicated. The microcredit centres of BRAC and GB at Shantigaon village are situated in a Hindu *bari*. Therefore, the Muslim microcredit borrowers also travel there in order to pay their credit instalments. As a result, the interactions between Muslims and Hindus have increased in comparison with the days before microcredit involvement. Respondents of my study unanimously stated that the communal harmony among the villagers is exceptionally high. Research-ers (e.g. Hulterström, 1995; Stenman *et al.,* 2004) studied trust and religion, and could not find any significant evidence that religious allegiance affects the level of trust in rural Bangladesh. However, in the present study most Muslim women asserted that Muslims were more trustworthy than Hindus. By the same token, Hindu women held the opinion that Muslims were not as trustworthy as they were. Only a few respondents claimed that they trusted both without prejudice and reservation.

When I visited the house of a group leader in the company of an NGO staff member she received me and made tea. While I was there some Hindu and Muslim borrowers came to pay their instalments. I observed that Hindu borrowers entered the house itself, but the Muslims remained outside on the verandah. I asked the loan collector, 'Could you call them in here to collect their instalments?' The official replied, 'No, I will go outside and collect instalments from them.' I understood that it might be a matter of purity pollution or religious belief of the Hindu religion. I felt uneasy because as a Muslim I had entered the house. However, in reality the difference in behaviour was not simply explained by ritual purity and practices. Instead, I found that the matter is strongly associated with the question of trust and security. When I apologized that I had made a mistake in entering her house, the group leader and another women said, 'No, you are not a problem.' It seems to me that the concept of ritual purity is symbolic, so when I asked the Hindu women, 'Why don't you allow Muslim women to enter your house?' All the respondents unanimously stated, 'If we allowed them to enter our houses we would have to offer them a seat, then we would have to provide them with food and then maybe somewhere to sleep.'

Taking the above factors into consideration, it is possible to suggest that Hindus do not trust Muslims and feel insecure as a minority group in the village. The Hindu women argue that if they invite Muslims into their houses the Muslim boys will form relationships with their daughters and violate their *izzat* (honour), and who will take responsibility for that? The Muslim men and women also confirmed that Hindus avoid entering their houses not just because of religion but also because of distrust and insecurity. I got the impression that the Muslims of Shantigaon always try to avoid getting involved in any conflicts with Hindus because conflicts will be interpreted as minority repression. This is illustrated by the fact that Muslims in Shantigaon village secretly refer to Hindus by the derogative word *malaun* and similarly Hindus refer to Muslims as *bangal*.

In sum, trust among microcredit borrowers is exceptionally low despite the fact that the borrowers have been taking out credit from the same organization and most borrowers are interconnected with one another through the collateral mechanism. Poverty, a lack of resources, and to a certain extent insecurity erode the fabric of trust in a society. In particular, people do not trust one another on matters related to money or valuables and politics.

Civic networks and political engagement

Women's political participation is one of the most important ways of gauging women's networks, consciousness, decision-making capacity and ability to influence matters that affect their lives in the community and in society as a whole. Women's political empowerment and effective representation in decision-making institutions are crucial factors for implementing changes in the power dynamics between the sexes in society. Historical records document the mass participation of Bengali women in a broad range of political movements such as the nationalist movement waged against British colonial rule, the Tebhaga movement in 1940s and the independence movement from Pakistan in 1971. Some studies (Bailey, 1990; Mizan, 1994) noted women's minor or non-participation in political activities in the Indian sub-continent. Historically, women's voting rights in Bangladesh were established long ago. Constitutionally, women can join any political party in the country and stand as candidates in national elections. The constitution of Bangladesh provides for the 'dual representation' of women in the parliament and in the local government. The constitution ensures women's participation in all spheres of national life but in reality women's political participation in rural areas is low.

Bangladesh has been ruled by two women since 1991. Nevertheless, their high positions in politics do not reflect women's position in politics in general in Bangladesh. The scarcity of women in the political party structures and in parliament is indicative of the low level of their involvement in the country's political arena and legislative processes. Nowadays, women vote in local and national elections in the country. For example, 70 per cent of women in Bangladesh voted in the 1996 parliamentary elections (CPD, 2000). Most NGOs, women's organizations and civil society organizations work to promote women's effective participation in politics. In 1997 Bangladesh introduced an affirmative action quota system for women's participation in politics at the local level, i.e. 25 per cent of seats were reserved for women by direct election. The implication of reserved seats in Bangladesh has been considered as a historic step, not only to increase the number of women in formal politics but also to bring about a qualitative change in their role perception (Chowdhury, 2002).

I have investigated whether microcredit-providing NGOs have implemented and nurtured democratic practices at their respective credit centres and whether they promote leadership among women. According to GB microcredit rules, the centre chief must change each year. However, unlike arguments put forward by Larance (1998), I found that the same women have served as centre chiefs or group leaders in the villages in my study areas for many years. For example, Suchona had served as a centre chief for the GB microcredit programme in Zelegaon village for 18 years prior to the study. Sorola had worked for the GB centre in Shantigaon for eight years, while Jarina and Alapi had served the BRAC microcredit programme for the last four years. In other words, a change of leadership does not occur annually as stipulated. I found that leaders are not selected democratically. The micro-lending officials select as group leaders women who have the potential to give time to the NGOs and commute to the centre in order to collect weekly instalments and to govern efficiently. When I asked what criteria would make a woman particularly eligible to be a group leader, Suchona said:

> I told you that my family has a commitment to develop this centre in this village and you know since its inception the bank has performed all its functions via my house. I provide this facility without any interest. I think because of my contribution the officer selected me as group leader. ... There are also many members who like me. I work to the advantage of the borrowers as well as the bank.

By the same token, it is also true that many women do not wish to be group leaders because the work is complicated, time-consuming and sometimes stressful and antagonistic. Consequently, sometimes women themselves refuse the position of their own volition and sometimes the husbands asked their wives not to become group leaders. The respondents also pointed out that the officials prefer those women as group leaders who can efficiently work on behalf of the NGOs and whose family members have good relationship with other households. Therefore, microcredit NGOs utilize marginalized women's social capital (social networks) and governing capacity to run their businesses efficiently at the local level, as also explored by Besley *et al.* (1993: 794) in their study of Rotating Savings and Credit Associations in India. Moreover, I understand that a group leader must be clever, vocal and have the capacity to pay back their own instalments by the due date. If a group leader fails to pay her own instalments in addition to collecting the instalments of her peers efficiently, the NGO officials will not retain her as a group leader. For example, Alapi worked as the group leader of the GB centre in Shantigaon village but when she faced severe difficulties in paying back her instalments the officer terminated her position.

Organizational membership can effectively increase people's awareness, greater democratic vitality, and political activity (cf. Putnam, 1993a). In his seminal work on social capital, *Making Democracy Work*, Putnam, inter alia, focused on the positive social virtues of voluntary associations and showed how voluntary associations promote greater democratic vitality in northern Italy compared to southern Italy. To understand the political awareness of microcredit borrowers in my research areas, I asked the respondents whether they knew the names of their respective local union chairman. All my respondents claimed that they knew the names of their local representatives. Surprisingly, this awareness is apparent in their voting habits. I found that the overwhelming majority of female microcredit borrowers whom I studied had been instructed by others, particularly the men, how to vote. When I asked my respondents about their own voting patterns, many borrowers maintained that they have voted in all the national and local elections. One of the changes they have observed is that now more women have voted than previously because the political leaders are active during the election time. They even bear the cost of women's transport to visit the centres. Micro-lending NGOs do not teach their borrowers about politics and political involvement.

The respondents repeatedly regarded politics as 'rich people's games' (*boro lokder khela*). They often considered politics to be men's work or women say they do not know about politics. Even so, this does not mean that women are not involved in political affairs. I observed that party politics and networks have extended to the grass-roots level in Bangladesh. Whenever I talked about politics many women discussed the party affiliations of various families in the neighbourhood. Political factionalism is increasingly becoming part of village life in rural Bangladesh. I asked Zamila's husband (aged 40 years) why rural women are not knowledgeable about politics. He replied:

> Actually, women in this village have less interaction with people outside of the village. They have limited mobility outside the domain of homestead areas. Most of the time they stay in the household areas or in the *bari* so they do not know about politics, good or bad candidates in local elections or who would be beneficial for them. Some women now vote in local elections but they are influenced by their husbands or their sons. The bank does not say anything about elections or politics. Women go there for taking out a loan or paying instalments, nothing more … What do women know about politics?

Still, there were some women who voted according to their own preferences:

> When my husband was alive he decided who I should vote for. Now sometimes my sons advise me but most times either I decide for myself or I make my own decisions by talking to my brother-in-law's wife.
>
> (Suchona)

> My husband is a simple-minded man [haba-goba], he does not under-stand anything. I have voted according to my own choice. I know some women in my area who decide themselves who to vote for.
>
> (Nasibun)

Among the 151 female microcredit borrowers interviewed in the three research areas of this study, their voting patterns were such that only 15 (about 10 per cent) women voted according to their own preference. Two per cent of women were instructed by their sons but most respondents (88 per cent) reported that they had voted according to their husbands' instructions.

Trust in political leaders or their pledges was exceptionally low among the respondents (see also Hulterström, 1995). They believed that because of their poverty their demands were ignored by the political leaders. Most of my respondents informed me that the political leaders in the rural areas have no moral principles and they do not help local people with their problems. The political leaders are too busy reaping benefits and filling their own pockets. The respondents often pointed out that before an election the political leaders visit their houses but do not return afterwards. The leaders promise many things during an election campaign but afterwards they forget their pledges. This shows that female microcredit borrowers are aware of matters relating to communal welfare. For example, Samirun (aged 28 years) explained:

> Suppose that in our area there is no high school, this means that when our children have finished at primary school they cannot attend high school. The nearest high school is about seven kilometres away from the village so poor parents cannot send their children. It is also risky to send a girl too far away from the village. The political leaders have not carried out any developmental work in our area. The poor people always remain poor; their problems always remain the same so why does it matter if we vote?

Women's political involvement in the ballot in rural Bangladesh does not mean active political participation at the local level. Women's direct involvement in politics is minimal because involvement is incompatible with women's everyday activities, sociocultural norms, and religious attitudes embodied in the social structure of rural Bangladesh. Women are not supposed to interfere with political affairs between men because to do so gets them up against *lojjasharam* (shame and modesty) and *pardah* practices (see Chapter 5 in this volume) of society. Additionally, poverty is the key factor that works against the political participation of women. Gender is a significant factor in poverty in Bangladesh. Poverty is over-represented among women. Women's inferior economic status keeps them financially dependent on men. They are rarely considered to be independent political actors. As Kabeer points out, 'Gender asymmetries in relation to resources and opportunities made women far more dependent on men than men were on women' (2001: 80). This dependence is also an important factor that limits a woman's freedom to participate in politics. I found two microcredit borrowers (out of 151) who stood in the local union council elections.

Aroti and Fouzia: two politically active women

Political participation or active involvement by women impinges upon social capital including class, caste, kinship networks and the idea of relatedness. For example, Aroti (40 years old) is a GB member of the Shantigaon microcredit programme and has been serving as a local union council member for the last eight years. She has been married for 20 years and is the mother of three sons. She used to live in a different village in the area. Aroti's husband Ranjon obtained a Diversity Immigrant Visa for the USA in 1998 and made all the preparations to go there but was not able to go in the end. His brother-in-law intentionally misguided him and seized all his lands. Thus, Aroti and her family now have to reside in her natal house as Aroti's parents and brothers live in Australia. I asked Aroti what made her decide to stand in the local union council elections. Aroti replied that previously she did not know anything about politics because she was a housewife. However, in the last union council election some of her neighbours and local people persuaded her to stand in a membership election. At first she refused, but they insisted. Eventually, the local people convinced her on the basis that as Aroti had had some academic education (to tenth grade) and was an articulate woman from a good family, she might do well in the election. As they were so insistent Aroti talked to her brothers and cousins and then stood in the election. Her uncle's sons bore all her election expenses.

I enquired about the other factors that helped her to win the election. According to Aroti, the high status of her family played an important role. She claimed that when people asked her to stand they said that they needed a candidate from a good family. As mentioned above, there are two castes among the Hindus in Aroti's village: the *Nath* and the *Brahmin*. The *Brahmins* are the priests of the Nath caste. Aroti belongs to the *Nath* caste and they form the majority among the Hindus. One of her cousins is a tax inspector and his wife is a doctor. The other brothers are also educated; they often visit the village and help the local people.

It is evident that Aroti considered a number of factors that were embodied in structural relationships including her hierarchical family status, socio-economic position, and perceived fitness in society for winning the election. The religious differences of Shantigaon do not cause any problems for Aroti's involvement in politics. As the microcredit centre of Shantigaon village is in a Hindu house, Muslim microcredit borrowers also have to travel there in order to repay their credit. Microcredit involvement also paved the way for Aroti to maintain a relationship with other borrowers. Aroti regularly visits the microcredit centre for weekly instalments payments, so she can meet some of the members, which helps her to develop face-to-face relations and civic engagement. As Putnam observes, 'Networks of civic engagement, like the neighborhood associations, choral societies, cooperatives, sports, clubs, mass-based parties, and like ... represent intense horizontal interaction. Networks of civic engagement are an essential form of social capital: the denser such networks in a community, the more likely its citizens will be able to cooperate for mutual benefit' (1993a: 173). Putnam argues that social connections developed through regular gatherings mobilize social capital because they 'facilitate gossip and other valuable ways of cultivating reputation: an essential foundation for trust within a complex society' (ibid.: 37).

As a local union council member Aroti has organized vulnerable group feeding (VGF) cards for the poor and allowances for widow and destitute women. As Aroti has been working as a local council representative for several years and has developed her political skills and confidence, I asked her if she was going to stand in the next election. Aroti replied that she did not know at present. Her uncle and cousin's brother will decide whether she will stand or not. It depends upon them. I could have asked her uncle who came into the house during our interview, but chose not to. Although Aroti said that her uncle and brother will decide whether she will stand as a candidate in the next election, I observed that Aroti was active in local politics and had built up strong networks in her area. People in the surrounding area generally valued her activities. Many men and women knew her mobile phone number. She also gave her phone number to me and told me that if I needed any help she would give me as much assistance as she possibly could. She was simple but articulate. I talked many times to her husband but he was not active politically and did not want to discuss Aroti's activities.

To investigate further I asked Aroti why rural women did not get involved in local politics. She replied that it is difficult for them because most of the women living in her area are poverty stricken, illiterate and have no political acumen. Women are busy in the home; they cannot move or work like men in the rural areas. They cannot participate in local arbitration. Their husbands or the elder members of the family do not support women's involvement in politics. Aroti pointed out that politics at the local area is actually the work of rich people (*boro lokder kaj*); the politics of the poor is how to ensure the provision of two meals each day.

Scholars have noted the widespread presence of patron-client relations and factionalism in rural Bangladesh (Jansen, 1987; Jahangir, 1979; Bertocci, 1970). The poor people of the villages I studied are now less dependent on local money-lenders and rich people owing to the microcredit programmes. Consequently, the typical patron-client relationship has become weaker. The poor people considered the local elders, the elite and the *panchayat* of their respective villages to be 'no good' (*bhala-manush na*) and unhelpful. They could not rely on local arbitration and panchayat as the local leaders often take bribes and make biased judgments. As a result, the interaction between the poor and the local elite has decreased. As one of the microcredit borrowers explained, 'In the rural area, now there is no judgment. If anything happens, people have to walk many times behind the local elder people. These people often take bribes. They talk and work in favour of those who give the bribes.'

Local politics is also related to family disputes. Disputes occur between different households which may extend to different *para* and *gushti*. For example, Fouzia (a 41-year-old BRAC microcredit member from Nodigaon village) who stood in the local union council election but did not win, sees local politics in the following way: 'It is always difficult to say who will win in the local election. Local people consider many things when they vote.' Fouzia claims that last time she did not win the local membership election because some of her neighbours created a conspiracy against her and defeated her. According to her, her family has had a family conflict about land since the time of her father. During the time of election these people took revenge because of this conflict. They filed a false case against her husband and got him arrested. As a result, she became weak and lost in that election. However, she hopes that next time they will not succeed, because she has tried to maintain good relationships with everybody.

I observed that Fouzia knows everybody in her village. She often makes contact with women and enquires about their news. She thinks that they will vote for her. She pointed out that despite the fact that women are guided by their husbands, not all of them actually follow their husbands' suggestions. Fouzia claims that she advises many households about taking out loans and she also acts as guarantors for some clients. I asked her whether it creates bad relations, and she replied: 'Yes, sometimes it happens. But it concerns the group leader, not me. I have tried to avoid this type of problem.'

Like Aroti, Fouzia thinks that generally women who reside in their natal village are at an advantage when they enter local politics. I observed that Fouzia is well known in her village. Membership of the microcredit organization helps her to expand her existing networks. She generally tries to visit the credit centre every week in order to meet other members who visit there. As a result, she can enquire about other people's news and can build closer relationships. I also observed that Fouzia often walked from one *para* to another and gossiped with other women. Moreover, she maintained extensive networks via her mobile phone. I never saw her without her mobile phone in her hand. When I asked her whether her husband interferes in her political involvement, she replied, 'It is none of his business' (see Chapter 4 in this volume).

In this section, I have argued that microcredit programmes are related to some of the changes that have taken place in politics and patron-client relationships. The microcredit programmes have attenuated the traditional patron-client relationships. The poor people are now less dependent on local money-lenders and rich people owing to the micro-lending programmes. Nowadays, many people do not rely on the local arbitration system; instead they prefer to seek support from legal institutions. However, the findings of this study indicate that microcredit organizations in the area that I studied failed to promote women's political capabilities or civic engagement since these organizations mainly concentrate on the services of credit distribution and instalment collection, and have deviated or shifted away from community mobilization (see Chapters 6 and 7 in this volume).

This study has found that women's participation in politics is impeded by their lack of education, experience and skills in the rural area. Traditionally, women are preoccupied by their domestic activities, which keep them isolated and obstruct the advancement of their interests and involvement in politics. Traditional gender roles, cultural norms, religious beliefs and codes of conduct for women also restrict women's networks and involvement in politics (see Chapter 5 in this volume). Apart from these factors, political party patronage plays a decisive role in women's participation and candidacy in elections at the local level. Local elections do not have to be partisan according to the constitution of Bangladesh, but in reality party affiliation does matter.

Families who can maintain trusting relationships with local political leaders can ensure their nominations and support from the political parties during elections. By these means, local politics is integrated into the larger political systems. The cases of Aroti and Fouzia also demonstrate particular political party identities in village politics.

My study illustrates that only a few women can use microcredit memberships to widen their networks for political gain. Women from high-status families in terms of class, caste, lineage or kinship networks have done well in local politics and this is not unusual. The kin-based patronage networks are the bedrock of politics in many countries of the world but they are usually exploited for the benefit of male relatives. When women exploit the same networks, there is a tendency to explain it somewhat condescendingly in terms of male kinship. Some critics (e.g. Nanivadekar, 2003) have argued that the impact of the quota system has been negligible. They argue that rather than leading to political empowerment, it creates 'proxies' or 'token' women i.e. women without true power. These women in reality advance the patriarchal interest of the family as their participation in politics is in itself patriarchal participation. However, as I have illustrated Aroti and Fouzia did not act as 'token' women. Their activities indicate that older women can become directly involved in political affairs, albeit more informally than men. A wife or a daughter may initially serve as a proxy for a man. Nonetheless, one can hope that eventually she will be able to use her family to access true political power and then use that same power to question and subvert the hierarchical patriarchal structures of the family and of the wider community.

Notes

1 According to Jacob, self-government requires that there 'must be a community of people who have forged neighbourhood networks. These networks are a city's irreplaceable social capital. Whenever the capital is lost, from whatever cause, the income from it disappears, never to return until and unless new capital is slowly and chancily accumulated' (1961: 138).

2 'Social capital ... refer[s] to ... those tangible substances [that] count for most in the daily lives of people: namely goodwill, fellowship, sympathy, and social intercourse among the individuals and families who make up a social unit ... If [an individual comes] into contact with his neighbour, and they with other neighbours, there will be an accumulation of social capital, which may immediately satisfy his social needs and which may bear a social potentiality sufficient to the substantial improvement of living conditions in the whole community' (Hanifan, 1916: 30).

3 The English translation of this book was published with the title *Reproduction in Education, Society and Culture* in 1977.

4 According to Bourdieu, Depending on the field in which it functions, capital can present itself in three fundamental guises: 'as *economic capital,* which is immediately and directly convertible into money and may be institutionalized in the form of property rights: as *cultural capital,* which is convertible, on certain conditions, into economic capital and may be institutionalized in the form of educational qualifications; and as *social capital*, made up of social obligations ('connections'),

which is convertible, in certain conditions, into economic capital and may be institutionalized in the form of a title or nobility' (1986: 243).

5 According to Coleman, 'Just as physical capital is created by making changes in materials so as to form tools that facilitate production, human capital is created by changing persons, so as to give them skills and capabilities that make them able to act in new ways. Social capital, in turn, is created when the relations among persons change in ways that facilitate action. Physical capital change is wholly tangible, being embodied in observable material form; human capital is less tangible, being embodied in the skills and knowledge acquired by an individual; social capital is even less tangible, for it is embodied in the relations among persons. Physical capital and human capital facilitate productive activity, and social capital does so as well' (1990: 304).

6 On this topic the reader is also referred to Gambetta (1988, 1993) and Hardin (1995).

7 A *bari* is a collection of households which has divided and sub-divided, and they are almost always patrilineally linked (Todd, 1996; Gardner, 1992). Several *bari* cluster together into a *para*, or neighbourhood (Todd, 1996).

8 Sanae Ito (1999) revealed in a study on GB that the bank's staff and the borrowers generally shared the assumption that it is more natural for members of the kinship group rather than the solidarity group to be held responsible for a borrower defaulting on a payment.

9 See also Karim (2004).

10 On this subject see also Kotalova (1993); Uusikylä (2000).

11 Streefland *et al.* (1986) in a study of microcredit borrowers and non-borrowers in Bangladesh wrote that their respondents often said that in the rural areas a poor man only thinks about himself and will try to become rich even at the expense of his brothers.

12 Montgomery (1996) and Ito (2003) also mentioned that 'staff pressure' sometimes leads to violent action by fellow members against defaulters.

13 In her study of microfinance and social capital in Nepal Rankin (2002) also reached the same conclusion.

14 Matin reported a general breakdown of joint liability in one of GB's oldest branches. He wrote that 'to the extent that the effectiveness of peer pressure decreases as the proportion of irregular borrowers increase, the bank will focus effort in containing irregularities by encouraging individual liability (even partial) and thereby rewarding the relatively regular borrowers. This implies that the potency of enforcing joint liability in triggering peer pressure is highest when it may be least required (i.e. when most borrowers are regular repayers) and fails when required the most' (1998: 75). In a study of BRAC's microcredit members Montgomery (1996) observed that borrowers' groups did not resort to joint-liability arrangements to maintain repayment discipline.

15 On this subject see also Arens and Beurden (1977); Jansen (1987); Streefland *et al.* (1986).

16 On this subject see also Jansen (1987); Streefland *et al.* (1986); Gardner (2012).

3 Credit, dowry practices and social capital

> No marriage takes place in our area without the giving of household items [*khat-maal*]. We arranged our daughter's marriage by giving some gold ornaments and household items. Despite the fact that the groom's family did not demand these things, we had to give them to follow the practice of our society [*somajer niyam*]. We covered the expense by taking out a GB loan and getting some help from our relatives. Still, I bear the burden of repaying instalments on the GB loan.
>
> (Maya, a 50-year-old widow and the mother of six daughters and two sons)

I was to hear the above statement many times during my fieldwork. It illustrates how dowry payment in the form of household goods financed by the bride's family has been widely practised in the rural area. Both GB and BRAC state clearly in their rules and regulations that borrowers are strictly prohibited from accepting any form of dowry on the occasion of the marriage of a son, nor should they give any dowry when their daughters marry (see Table A.2). This chapter looks at the way in which microcredit borrowers choose to build social capital by using credit for dowry gifts on the occasion of marriage. More specifically, I explore the following questions: what is the logic behind giving household items in the event of marriage in the research areas? How do microcredit borrowers perceive microcredit-providing NGOs' rules in relation to widespread dowry practices in their respective areas? Do dowry gifts strengthen social capital at the local level? Before embarking on this discussion I briefly describe the marriage practices in my research areas.

Marriage practices

In South Asian societies reproduction is only permissible within marriage. There is no socially recognized status for women outside marriage, so it is widely believed that women have to be given in marriage and should not be kept in their parents' house for too long. A woman can only become a complete person when she becomes a mother. Therefore, it is an important duty of the father to find husbands for his daughters. The presence of marriageable women is considered inauspicious for men of the house, and the fear of incest is strong (Fruzzetti, 1990: 31). In Bangladesh marriage is not an option for a girl, rather it is universally understood that a woman must be given in marriage at least once (Blanchet, 1986). Bangladeshi society has a long tradition of girls' being married at an early age (Aziz and Maloney, 1985; Maloney *et al.*, 1981), because 'keeping a postmenarchal daughter or sister at home for too long dishonours her guardians, lessens her own value and draws unfavourable attention to the whole family' (Kotalova, 1993: 190).

There is a broad consensus among parents that a girl should get married as soon as possible after the girl has reached puberty (*sabalika*) and preferably before she is 18 years of age. All the daughters' mothers strongly believe that marriage is an integral part of a woman's life. I found evidence that the number of child marriages is declining, but to be an 18-year-old unmarried girl is considered inappropriate within the sociocultural norms. There is a widespread belief among mothers that nowadays there are more girls than boys in society. Consequently, families feel pressured to marry off their daughters. Research has shown that some parents maintain that it is their religious duty (*foraj kaj*) to marry off their daughters before the onset of puberty (e.g. Ashrafun and Uddin, 2010; Todd, 1996). Failure to get one's daughter married is a source of shame and dishonour for the family. Meherun (52 years old) illustrates the issue:

> I feel ashamed. I cannot show my face to the other neighbours. I cannot arrange my daughter's marriage. She is now 21 years old. She now always stays at home. I made the mistake that by taking micro-loans and selling land I was able to send my son abroad … I thought that when my son sends money I will arrange my daughter's marriage by giving *khat-maal* as marriage gifts but now no proposals come as my daughter is getting too old. Only Allah knows my sufferings about my daughter's marriage. Why does Allah give me this grief?

Marriage practices in the study areas are uniform, in the sense that most marriages are arranged and usually the fathers and the elder people of the house take the initiative to look for suitable grooms for their daughters. Sometimes the mothers also try by using their contacts to find suitable husbands for their daughters. During marriage negotiations a girl's opinion about the choice of groom or the time of marriage is not always heard. Generally, when the groom's party comes to see a girl, the girl is asked to talk to the visitors or serve them food. Sometimes the groom also joins the visitors to see the 'candidate wife'.

The respondents who I talked to arranged their daughters' marriages according to the best of their abilities. Of great importance are a suitable groom (*daman or bor*) and a good family (*bhala ghor-bhalamanush*). The desirable characteristics of a suitable groom are a good character, a nice appearance, a compliant nature (*bhodra*), and good health. The ideal groom is also skilled and has not been married previously. In addition, the respondents also stipulated that the groom should have some financial means, and this has recently emerged as a dominant factor in marriage arrangements. Financial means are considered a predictor for upward mobility. The groom should have the financial ability to provide a better standard of living (*bhronposhon*) including better food, clothing and shelter for his wife than that which she was used to in her parent's household. The same stipulations were also reported by Geirbo and Imam (2006) in a study made in Nilphamari District in Bangladesh. With regard to a good family, a smaller family size is highly desirable. Most of my respondents confirmed that their families often try to avoid marrying their daughters to husbands who come from to large families, such as those with several young unmarried girls, since a boy coming from such a family often incurs an extra economic burden associated with arranged marriages. Moreover, familial conflicts also often occur in this kind of family. A girl's guardians often prefer a boy who is at least three to five years older than their daughter.

A common principle in Bangladeshi culture is that the bride should be less educated than the bridegroom. Uusikylä confirms this tendency in her study: 'But if a girl is educated, she is valuable when she will have her own children, she can teach them … a son can help his father in his business and accounting. If the husband and wife are educated and literate, the husband should be more educated than his wife. She should be a bit inferior' (2000: 58). Most microcredit borrowers' daughters in the villages of Zelegaon and Nodigaon have educated to primary level (fifth grade), so they believe that their sons-in-law should at least know how to read and write. In Shantigaon, some girls have received a secondary level education, so they prefer their daughters' grooms to have had at least the same level of education. However, there is no hard and fast rule in this regard. They argue that they often emphasize a boy's financial means instead of a higher level of education.

Family background or lineage (*bongsha*) is not a decisive factor in arranging marriages in the study villages. I have already described the Muslim and Hindu social stratification systems in the villages of Zelegaon, Nodigaon and Shantigaon. The Hindus of Shantigaon village generally arranged marriages within the same caste according to their abilities. In Shantigaon there are two castes: *Brahmin* and *Nath*. A *Nath* boy generally marries a girl from the Nath caste. However, he can marry a *Brahmin* girl, but not a girl who belongs to a lower caste than *Nath*. The Muslim respondents in Shantigaon informed me that there is no ascribed noble status or elite family (*Khandan* or *Ashraf*) in Shatigaon village. They are ordinary Muslims and are divided into their occupational hierarchies (achieved status). Therefore, when they arrange marriages they seek families who belong to the same occupational category. Most respondents from Zelegaon and Nodigaon villages are Muslim and they work in the fishing business (*maimol*). They arrange marriages with families from similar backgrounds, though not as rigidly as the Hindus do. Vreede de Stuers (1968) analysed North Indian Muslim women and reported that within the high-status *Ashraf*, a rule of equality in the status of those giving and receiving wives is followed, after the Islamic principle of Kafa's (equality in marriage). This means that in principle at least, there is rigid endogamy: *Ashraf* families will only marry into other *Ashraf* families (ibid., quoted in Gardner, 1995). The people of Zelegaon or Nodigaon belong to the *Azral* category (lowest status) and not to the *Ashraf* or *Atrap* category. Yet to a certain extent equal-status endogamy marriage (a *maimol* family with another *maimol* family) has existed in the two villages.

In South Asia Women's fluidity is important to the construct of kinship and it is more extreme than that of men. Through marriage women are absorbed into another kinship group (Säävälä, 2006). The patrilineal and patrilocal residence is the norm in the present study villages. Some of the older respondents informed me that in their father's or grandfather's generations, the majority of their family's marriages were arranged with relatives or kinsmen or within the same village or in nearby villages. Nowadays, marriages are rarely arranged within the same village or with maternal and paternal cousins. Most marriages are arranged outside the girls' natal villages, so the girls normally move from their parents' house (*bari*) and village (*gram*) to that of their in-laws, and thereby generally their labour, guardianship and loyalty shift to their husband's family.

In the context of West Bengal, Fruzzetti and Ostor (1976) mention that sisters in Bengal are members of their father's *gushti* but only their brothers can pass on their blood and family name to their children. According to Fruzzetti, 'When a virgin becomes a wife … to her in-laws and to her husband … she is cancelled [cut off] from her father's collection of ancestors in the line [bangsa bali]. She is now of her husband's *gotra* and is added to his *bangsa bali*' (1990: 99). The term *gushti* can be taken to mean 'symbolic domain' (Schneider, 1984) in Bangladeshi society where genealogical and blood relations are not only concepts that define relatedness, rather they denote a person's country, village, region, origin or homestead (Uusikylä, 2000; Gardner, 1995). A woman's *desh* (village of origin) is not fluid; it is her father's village, not her husband's house (Gardner, 1995). Unlike Hindus (Davis, 1983: 66), a Muslim woman holds a dual membership of *gushtis* through marriage. Todd (1996: 4) argues that although married women lose their natal families they retain strong links with their natal families. Their own families are both a refuge and an economic resource. Santi Rozario (1992) has considered it as the 'residual membership' that makes women's position anomalous. She argues that a married woman is made to feel an outsider as long as her mother-in-law is alive. By the same token, Jitka Kotalova (1993) has called this state 'belonging to others.' She claims that marriage divides a women's sense of belonging between her natal home and husband's home. She retains a dual membership of both. She does not quite belong to either her natal family nor to her husband's family. Both Rozario and Kotalova emphasize the structural significance of the patrilineal and patrilocal aspects of the kinship resulting from the total transfer of the women from parental to the affinal kin and they overlook the complexity of the kinship relations of a woman and deep bondages between brothers and sisters.[1]

Cases of *ghor jamai* (when a husband lives in his wife's household) are uncommon in my research areas. This type of marriage is viewed in South Asian cultures as foolish and unmanly; hence, such arrangements are not desirable although there are exceptions in some communities (Gardner, 1995; Kotalova, 1993; Cantlie, 1984: 110; Bertocci, 1970). Nowadays, love marriages or self-arranged marriages also take place although most parents to whom I talked do not support this development. They argued that love marriages should be discouraged because this type of marriage clashes with family status and violates social norms. Most daughters' parents feel that the girls are susceptible to violence in such marriages because the grooms' families often treat them as 'bad girls' and do not to accept these marriages. Kanu Bibi, a microcredit borrower from Zelegaon village, provided an example:

> My son secretly married a girl for love [*prem-bhalobhasa kore*] but the daughter's parents did not accept this marriage. Our family title is *maimol* [fishery] but the girl's family is *khan* [grocer] and they have a small grocery business, so they did not accept this marriage. My son now lives with his wife in a rented room in a colony [slum] and works in a workshop. He no longer enquires about my news.

Most of my respondents said that when they were young they were always obliged to do what their parents had decided, but today's society is different. Boys and girls no longer listen to their parents. It is necessary to watch over young boys and girls carefully, in case they make the mistake of falling in love and marrying before they are able to support a family. Some respondents dislike mobile phones because they make it easier for their children to begin and carry on affairs. Even so, some respondents explained that sometimes parents who have many daughters do encourage their daughters to have affairs and marry in order to avoid having to give dowries.

Despite there being no drastic changes in marriage practices, some changes have taken place in my research areas. First, nowadays most marriages are arranged outside the local areas due to the expansion of communication and mobile phone networks. Second, economic class is considered to be a dominant criterion for arranging marriages in the local communities. Third, a small number of self-arranged marriages or love marriages also take place. Next, I will examine the logic behind dowries, whether the practice of giving dowries has increased as a result of microcredit programmes, and whether dowries strengthen social bonds and kinship networks in the local areas.

Dowry or marriage transactions

Dowries or marriage transactions as comprehended by South Asian societies, conflate with the different kinds of gifts and cash that are given by a girl's parents to a bridegroom and his family when a marriage takes place (Uberoi, 1997: 232). In West Bengal the Hindus view dowries as gifts. The most auspicious form of marriage in Hindu culture, *kanya dan*, literally means the gift of a virgin, or the exchange of a virgin (Fruzzetti, 1990). According to Fruzzetti (ibid.), in Hindu marriage rituals two types of gift are made: the gift of a virgin, and the payment of the dowry. 'The first is a sacred gift, the highest possible, and can be neither argued about nor contested, whereas the second gift is a *dabi*, a demand rightfully made by the groom in return for accepting the bride. A girl's father has both gifts in mind when he starts looking for a groom. Both dowry and bride represent wealth' (ibid.: 30).

The giving of dowries (*pon, dabi, joutuk*) is a near-universal practice for virtually all groups of people in Bangladeshi society. Money, jewellery and household items are often demanded as dowries on the occasion of marriage in favour of the groom's party. Some families even demand luxury goods such as televisions, furniture, motor-bikes, or even jobs abroad. It has been widely documented that payments are increasing among Muslims and Hindus in Bangladesh (Todd, 1996; Gardner, 1995; Rozario, 1992, 2001; White, 1992), although the practice of giving dowries whereby the bride's family gives gifts to the groom's family has been outlawed by the government of Bangladesh. The government, individual women, women's organizations and NGOs try to reach out to people with the message that dowries are a social disease, and the struggle against this problem continues. Among Muslims dower or bride wealth (*mohar*) is religiously and rigorously sanctioned. The bride wealth is payable at marriage by the husband to his wife out of honour and respect and as proof that he honestly wishes to marry her with a sense of responsibility and obligation (Monsoor, 2003). Bride wealth also acts as security for the bride in case of divorce or marital breakdown, although in Bangladesh this is generally paid only in the case of divorce (Ahmed and Naher, 1987).

There is no unique theory as to why or how the bride wealth transactions shifted into dowry payment in South Asian society. Most explanations have considered the 'marriage squeeze' theory, which upholds the notion of there being a surplus of unmarried women relative to men (Mari Bhat and Halli, 1999; Amin and Cain, 1997). Other explanations include women's inferior status in productive roles, the devaluing of women, and their dependence on men (Rozario, 1992, 1998; Sharma, 1980), in addition to the policies promulgated under British colonial rule and the masculinization of the economy (Oldenburg, 2003) in South Asian society. Boserup (1970: 37–50) argues that dowry is paid when a woman does no productive work. It is given to her parents-in-laws to support her financially. However, when a woman does productive work, a bride-price is given to the natal household to compensate for the loss of her labour: this is customary in parts of Africa where women have a central role in public production. However, scholars have noted how higher dowries are linked to perceptions of women's decreasing economic value. As a consequence, Sharma (1980) has argued that higher dowries are a signal of the increasing dependence of women on men. Kishwar (1986) also considers women's inferior economic roles and dependency to be accountable for maintaining the dowry practice in society. She states that the giving of gifts by a brides' family to the groom constantly underpins the bride's inferiority to her husband. According to Kishwar, a dowry is not given to secure a daughter's happiness, as is often claimed, but to increase her dependency (ibid.: 9). Scholars have also noted that dowry is associated with high status and is part of the process of 'Sanskritization' (Srinivas, 1966). In a study carried out in Sylhet, Bangladesh Gardner (1995: 178) observed that to a large extent the dowry custom is related to competition between in-laws; the use of marriage to achieve upward mobility; the need for women and the material goods they bring with them on marriage; and to its importance as a sign of the reputation and social position of their natal households.

The practice of giving dowries in Bangladeshi society varies in relation to class, caste or the social stratification system of the society. Consequently, it is difficult to develop a uniform explanation for the practice. Whatever the reason for making dowry payments, much of what has been written on the subject has focused on the dark side or the detrimental aspects of the practice such as divorce, victimization, and the subordination of women, and domestic violence by husbands and in-laws. The focus on the depressing aspects of dowry practices impedes a deeper understanding and logic behind the practice. The studies on microcredit programmes are divided into two approaches. In advance of Geirbo and Imam's (2006) study of the motivation behind the giving and taking of dowries, many studies have investigated whether microcredit borrowers give and take dowries when arranging marriages (Khandker *et al.*, 1994; Rahman, 1986a) or have attempted to prove that microcredit borrowers take out credit to pay for dowries rather than investing in business (Ahmad, 2007; Rahman, 1999, 2001). As documented in Todd's (1996) study on GB in the Tangail district, and Geirbo and Imam's (2006) study of BRAC in Domar upazila in the Nilphamari District, Bangladesh, all my respondents unanimously stated that it is customary to give household items in the event of marriage. Of my respondents, 24 borrowers whose daughters were married, confirmed that they had previously used microcredit to bear the cost of the marriage transactions.

Next, I will analyse how spending money on dowry gifts for a wedding as a part of a gift-giving practice is fundamentally related to local social norms, cultural and social identities, emotional patterns and the system of social relationships.

Dowry as social capital

Giving dowries in the form of gifts (such as household items and furniture, ornaments or cash) in the event of marriage is extensively practiced throughout rural communities in Bangladesh. Most of my respondents acknowledged that parents generally give household items to their daughters and sons-in-law 'out of pleasure/familial love' (*khushi hoye dei, khushi mone dei*), and for their 'daughters' happiness'. However, it has become a social obligation, a norm and a demand of society. Following the practices of financially well-off families, it has rapidly spread among all types of people across class boundaries, religions and castes. The families of both the bride and the groom expect household items to be given on marriage, and hence the cost of marrying off a girl has increased gradually.

My respondents are aware of the rules and decisions of GB and the BRAC which prohibit the granting of loans for dowries but they do not think that it conflicts with the mission of microcredit programmes. One of my respondents, Rahima (55 years old and the mother of five sons and one daughter) has maintained GB membership since the inception of the centre in Zelegaon village in the early 1990s. I asked her how she viewed microcredit-providing NGOs' rules and and the widespread dowry practices in this area. In response, Rahima claimed that she knows all 16 decisions of the Grameen Bank (See Table A.2) which state that borrowers should not take or give dowries at their sons' and daughters' weddings. However, she thinks these are mentioned incidentally:

> It is a statement in the rule book [*boier kotha*] which has no value to me or the local people in our area. Before GB, the government also said that people should not to give or take any dowry, but no one listened to this. People do not follow the government rules. Can you tell me who is more powerful, GB or the Bangladesh government? Do GB officials follow this decision in their own lives? No, they also give and take many things at their sons and daughters' marriages. In a *Sylheti* marriage, parents give dowry items at a daughter's marriage and they accept dowry goods on their son's marriage.

Rahima demonstrated that the locals follow the social norms and practices (*samajer niyam*) just the other people do or practice in the same society. According to her, even parents who have no money or who live from hand to mouth also try to give something at their daughters' wedding ceremonies. Rahima thought that the educated and rich people make up the rules but they too give generously on their marriage of their sons and daughters. She could not see why poor people should not give and take gifts on the occasion of the marriage of their sons and daughters. She argued that rich and poor alike love their daughters. She observed that some people accept gifts even if they are getting fair-complexioned girls as their sons' wives. Similarly, some parents are always ready to give gifts, even though their daughters are beautiful. According to her, the parents of dark-complexioned girls are always aware that they have to give something at their daughters' weddings. To Rahima's way of thinking, parents always try to arrange marriages even for girls with grave physical defects by giving something, although nowadays marriages of dumb, blind or lame girls are rare.

Rahima confirmed that she received household items including a bedstead, clothes rack (*alna*), chair, prayer table, and some kitchen utensils as a dowry from the bride's family on her oldest son's marriage. For her part, she gave a few items to the bride. Now her son and his wife reside in a separate room in the same compound and can use all these things. Rahima argues that if her daughter-in-law had not brought these goods with her they would have faced economic pressure to buy them. When her second son married, Rahima also received some household items and gave some gifts in return. Unlike her first son's marriage, this time she only directly demanded (*dabi kora*) TK 5,000 from the bride's parents to repay a loan, which her son took himself. I enquired, 'You demanded TK 5,000 but if the bride's family had not given any furniture what would you have done?' She replied to me that generally such a thing does not happen in her society. Parents always try to give as much as possible with their daughter, but if they do not give furniture their daughter might be asked for it. Rahima has decided that she will also take household goods from the brides' families when her remaining two sons marry. She is aware that her daughter will also marry one day too. As she gave gifts on the marriage of her sons, I asked her whether she is prepared to make a gift at the wedding ceremony of her daughter. She replied:

> My daughter is not handicapped or blind, so I will not be dishonoured by her marriage. I love my daughter. If she can lead a happy life at her husband's house it will be a great pleasure for me. I have decided to give some household items – as many as I can afford - on the occasion of my daughter's marriage if I can find a good boy and house for my daughter.

In order to pay for gifts, Rahmia took out a TK 100,000 (1 US $ = 75 Taka in 2010) loan from the GB microcredit programme in 2009 by explaining that the purpose of the loan was to buy a three-wheeler for her son. In reality she lent the money to her nephew (her brother's son) on condition that he pay her TK 15,000 in profit. She has saved that money to cover the cost of her daughter's marriage.

The case of Rehana (40 years old) is different. She gave some household items and gold ornaments on her two daughters' marriages, so she has determined that she will demand the same on the occasion of her two sons' marriages as well. She explains her decision thus:

> We arranged our daughters' marriages by giving one *vory* of gold [1 ounce = 2.65 *vory*] and household goods. We gave these things to follow others and it is the accepted practice of our society. As I had followed the practice of the society when my daughters married, why should I not accept a gift when my son marries?

According to Rehana, even parents who have some reason to be ashamed or who lack money do not send their daughters to their husbands' homes empty-handed. Arranging a marriage without any gifts does not look good in the eyes of in-laws and neighbours. If her daughters-in-law bring something with them, she (Rehana) can proudly show these things to other people, which will improve her social standing and that of her daughters-in-law among the neighbours.

From the above cases we see how dowry (particularly the giving of house-hold goods) functions as a form of gift-giving norm or social obligation in rural communities. On the one hand, parents take gifts on their sons' mar-riages but on the other hand, they give gifts on their daughters' marriages. Although dowries play a pivotal role in weddings, most of the respondents do not perceive these gifts as dowries per se; instead, they see it as giving household items:

> People in our area do not regard marriage gifts as dowry; instead, we say *khat-maal dewa* [we are giving household items]. Most of the time it is not necessary to demand a dowry for a wedding. The bride's family gives it willingly and the groom's family receives it enthusiastically. It is a well-known tradition.
>
> (Suchona)

During marriage negotiations, two types of marriage transaction take place: giving household items and dowries. There is a subtle difference between giving household goods and paying a dowry. Brides' families by and large willingly give household goods as a local practice but dowry is not given willingly, it is usually demanded by the groom's family. The groom's family usually overtly states if they have dowry demands, such as cash, a sofa suite, TV or gold ornaments. However, usually they do not talk openly about giving household goods. When a marriage has been settled, the bride's family has to give household goods as gifts at their daughter's marriage according to the local norms. Generally the matchmaker (*ukil*), family friends or close relatives act as mediators between the two parties in the dowry negotiations. Most poten-tial sons-in-law do not directly participate in such negotiations, but usually let the more senior family members carry them out. Negotiations are influ-enced by factors ranging from the family's financial position to the bride's complexion. If a girl has a light complexion then her family is likely to encounter fewer problems in arranging her marriage than if she has a dark complexion.

The bride's family in the studied villages usually gives the following items as *khat-maal* with the bride for her new home: a bed, cupboard, clothes rack, prayer table, mattress for the bed, pillow, bed sheet, mosquito net and household utensils. They also provide the groom's wedding outfit such as a shirt, trousers, *pajama-panjabi, lungi*, T-shirt, shoes, and sometimes a watch. The groom's family generally also provides wedding clothes including a sari, petticoat and blouse, shoes, make-up for the bride, and sometimes gold ornaments such as gold nose pins and earrings.

Some parents do not prefer to take or give household items as marriage gifts; rather they prefer cash to invest in business. Senora (50 years old) informed me that she had decided to arrange her daughter's marriage to her sister's son, if she agrees. For this marriage Senora will take out a micro-loan again. She decided that she will not give any household goods for this marriage; instead, she will give some cash, so that the groom can invest it in his fishing business. Likewise, she prefers to take cash instead of household goods when her sons marry, so that they can use the money to improve their fishing businesses and ensure a livelihood. Senora maintains that it is unnecessary to take household goods as marriage gifts, because if anybody needs money they cannot sell such goods to raise it.

Giving khat-maal or household goods is not simply an economic arrangement nor does it reflect Boserup's (1970: 37–50) observation about compensation to the groom's family as they receive a woman who does no productive work. Rather, most of the respondents who took part in this study perceived it as a social norm. It as an integral part of a wedding which is deeply rooted in the gift-giving norms, values, moral obligation, emotional patterns, and the system of relationships in society. It is related to the reconstruction of a girl's new sociocultural identity in her marital home. The financially well-off families send household goods to the groom's family by truck or by bus, whereas the poor people send them by handcart (*van*), which can be viewed as a material display of local face value, social status and class in Sylhet. Tenhunen wrote about a village in West Bengal in India, 'Yet money is not the only agent in the process. Giving gifts are essentially about constructing social and cultural identities: the interconnected domains of gender, kinship, caste and class' (2009: 136). I found that giving household goods as wedding gifts had acquired an emblematic position in the rural communities of Sylhet. Following Bourdieu (2002), it can be termed as 'symbolic capital', which enhances honour, prestige (*sanman-marjada*) and recognition of bride's family or 'brightening the face' (*mukh uzzal kore*) of a new bride (*notun bou*) when she goes to her marital home, and it also strengthens relationships. The husband's family members cannot criticize or undervalue the bride when the appropriate gifts have been given.

Sometimes gift-giving also proves the nobility of mind (*boro hridoy*) of the bride's family. It increases welfare, injects courage or the bargaining capacity of a girl in her marital home. After marriage, when a new bride goes to her marital home the neighbours and relatives curiously enquire what she has brought from her natal family. Has the new wife come empty-handed (*khali haat*)? If they hear that their new bride has brought household goods with her they are happy and will not whisper that the new bride has come from a chicken-hearted (*chotomon*) or a very poor and unsocial family, and could not bring anything from her parents house. As Tenhunen (2009: 133) also argued about a village of West Bengal in India, wedding gifts contribute to a 'positive self-image' of their daughters when they enter their in-laws house.

Giving gifts on the occasion of marriage contributes to forging connections between the bride's and groom's families. Gifts are often given to strengthen the marriage and increase the status of the bride in the affinal home. Aysha, a 40-year-old microcredit borrower from Zelegaon, provided an example of how this practice has intensified the connections between both marriage parties' families. As a result of taking microcredit Aysha has been able to make *nakshi-khata* quilts for many years and thus she covered all the expenses of her older daughter's marriage. At the marriage she gave a necklace and a pair of earrings to her daughter and a finger ring to her son-in-law. In addition, she gave all the usual household goods. According to Aysha, her daughter is now leading a happy life with honour (*marjada*) in her in-laws' house. The mother-in-law of Aysha's daughter is also very pleased and she helps her daughter. When Aysha gets many orders for *nakshi-khata* she gets help from her older daughter to avoid work pressure, and the daughter's mother-in-law does not cause any problems.

In different way, Banu, a 55-year-old widowed microcredit borrower from Zelegaon village explains how microcredit helped her to arrange her dark-complexioned daughter's marriage. Banu has been taking credit for some years. She uses the credit to invest in making bamboo-cane goods and to pay for her everyday costs. Banu has always tried to put aside some money from her earnings for her daughter's marriage. According to her:

> My daughter is dark like me, so I was aware of that without khat-maal and dowry I would not be able to arrange my daughter's marriage. Some years ago when my daughter was 18 years old I gave her away in marriage to a truck driver. I used my savings and some micro-loans for this marriage because I gave household goods and some ornaments to my daughter. The groom's family demanded some cash, so I also gave some cash to my son-in-law. Without cash and household goods I think it would not have been possible to arrange my daughter's marriage so nicely.

The above statement suggests how both economic and symbolic capital functions together (Bourdieu, 2002). Giving a dowry to one's daughter manifests a girl's status in her parental home, daughter-parents relationships and is a way of demonstrating love and affection towards her (Saavala, 2010; Tenhunen, 2009; Geirbo and Imam, 2006; Trawick, 1990). Trawick (1990: 108–109) notes that the hardship parents must undergo in order to scrape together a dowry for their daughter and marry her off well in a Tamil village in India is often interpreted as an act of loving sacrifice perpetrated for the daughter's sake. Both feelings of love and feelings of pride are manifested through gift-giving. Most women in this study stated that mothers always yearn for the happiness of their daughters. They always want to see their daughters in a happier position with more than they had before. They often argued that the girls belong to their mothers (*meyera mayer jaat*). Only mothers can understand their daughters' happiness and pain. The mothers know how their daughters can lead a happy life in their husbands' houses. Therefore, mothers give them as much as they possibly can. As one mother stated:

> I have already arranged half a *vory* of gold, I will take a loan again so that I can give some household goods on the marriage of my daughter, if I get a good boy and a good family … If a mother does not give something to her daughter, where else will she get anything or who else will give her anything? If I do not give something when my daughter's marries and if she faces problems or feels shame as a result, it will be very painful for me.
>
> (Sanjida, 50 years old)

Another woman added:

> In our society the boy child always gets a greater share of a parent's property than a girl. Our society also has a tendency to deprive the girl child, so I think it is good to give something on a daughter's marriage by hook or by crook.
>
> (Saleha, 55 years old)

Still, some respondents believe that completing a marriage through giving gifts to the groom's family is socially pleasing. If a family can arrange their daughter's marriage through giving gifts to the groom's family, they think that their daughter has gone out into the world with good luck (*boro kopal*). As Maya explained:

> In many marriages I saw the grooms' families give only a few items to the brides' families. But when my older daughter got married the groom's family did not look to us or demand anything. They told us that it is not necessary for us to give anything to our daughter; they would 'embellish our daughter-in-law with goods'. The groom and his family is so good, they gave everything such as wedding clothes [saris], shoes, cosmetics, a pair of gold earrings and a nose pin for the adornment of our daughter.

Microcredit programmes have brought changes to the dowry or gift-giving practices of local communities. Before the establishment of the microcredit programme people mortgaged their valuable properties such as land for dowry gifts but now they no longer do that. As stated above, during marriage negotiations, girls' opinions about their choice of the bridegroom is generally not sought, but they are not completely passive when the topic of marriage gifts is discussed. Many of my respondents tell me that nowadays the girls also often do not wish to go to their husbands' houses empty-handed. I discovered that some teenage girls in the villages, sometimes with the help of their parents, had started saving for household goods before their marriages. They take credit and spend it on making their marriage ornaments. They pay their instalments by offering tailoring services and making bamboo-cane crafts. For example, a Hindu family in Shantigaon took out a loan and spent it on making her adolescent daughter's marriage ornaments. Now the girl repays the instalments by undertaking tailoring work at her home.

The logic of dowry gifts or giving household goods among Hindus is not same as for Muslims. According to Islamic inheritance law in Bangladesh, a Muslim girl has rights to her parents' property but the Hindu law in Bangla-desh does not permit it. As a result, dowry demand is more widely practised among Hindus than Muslims in this study's research villages. All the Hindu respondents who took part in this study told me that in the Hindu marriages the brides' families must provide gold ornaments, household goods and sometimes cash as well. So dowry demands and amounts are higher among Hindus than Muslims. According to my study data, most Hindu families use or invest micro-loans to arrange dowry payments. For example, Anita, a 22-year-old Hindu housewife married to a barber rationalizes dowry practices in Hindu society thus:

> After marriage a Hindu girl loses her rights to her natal home. It is the custom [protha] of society. Some changes may happen among the edu-cated people but as it is a religious norm of Hindu society most families follow it.

When I enquired whether she supports any changes to this norm, Anita could not say because she does not know the religious rules. Anita is aware that dowry payments are frequently given in her area. She claims that this practice began in ancient times. Both her mother and grandmother brought many ornaments from their natal families. She thinks that without dowry marriage is impossible in Hindu society. Anita thinks that in Hindu marriages the groom's family always demands dowry because they think that in future they may not get anything from the wife's family. Therefore, the Hindu parents first arrange the dowry payment then they start looking for a groom for their daughter. The poor families save a small amount of money over a long period of time in order to arrange dowry payments. From Anita's description, it has become easier for many families to take out loans to fulfil this demand since the inception of microcredit, and then they pay back the credit gradually. Her father gave her some gold ornaments and TK 25,000 in cash as a dowry. Now her husband uses this money for his shop business and Anita also feels good because the husband can support her. Therefore, dowry gifts also work as a safety net in the rural areas. As Oldenburg (2003: 9) also noted, a dowry is a woman's safety net in a setting in which women's marriages are arranged outside their natal villages and where their rights to their natal homes becomes void when they leave for their marital homes.

Although dowry gifts or the giving of household goods is nominally thought as the women's property, there is only a slim probability of the new wife actually establishing her entitlement over this property in the initial stage of her marital life. Generally, before establishing a nuclear family marriage gifts are often used as collective property. In fact, the money for marriage gifts does not come from an individual source, rather it is accumulated from various sources. Usually, in the rural areas a poor family does not arrange all the money for a marriage gift by themselves but they receive help from close relatives and wealthy neighbours. Like the dowry gift, the concept of happiness in the rural area has no validity for individuals. A girl's happiness in her marital home is always dependent upon her relationship with her husband and the other family members of that house.

The issue of dowry vis-à-vis inheritance is important and has been the subject of recent debates among scholars in South Asia. Muslim inheritance law ensures that daughters inherit one half of what their brothers receive (two daughters equal one son), but in Bangladesh the law is 'honoured more in breach than in practice' according to some researchers (Kotalova, 1993: 138; Westergaard, 1983; van Schendel, 1981: 136; Bertocci, 1974). Researchers report that women in Bangladesh are ostensibly entitled to ownership and control of land, but in reality most land is owned and controlled by men. Some scholars argue that land is given to women's brothers for practical reasons. For instance, if women are divorced, or widowed, or separated and remain unmarried, their brothers assume guardianship and provide economic support in return (Gardner, 1995: 29; Westergaard, 1983: 9; Chaudhury and Ahmed, 1980: 8). However, since the law does not uphold women's entitlements to their inheritance by prohibiting the disentitlements of daughters, some scholars view the dowry system as a way of giving women a share of their natal property. Goody considered dowry as 'a type of pre-mortem inheritance' (1976: 6), 'a process whereby parental property is distributed to a daughter at her marriage … rather than at the holders' death' (1973: 1). Tambiah (1973) also held the same opinion, although in a later article he presented a modified version of it (ibid., 1989). On the other hand, researchers have argued that dowry cannot be considered as inheritance or equivalent to inheritance in this way (Agarwal, 1994; Madan, 1989, 1975; Sharma, 1984, 1980; Parry, 1979; Vatuk, 1975). Actually, Goody and Tambiah do not consider the logic behind the dowry systems in the society. I agree with Sharma (1980) and Agarwal (1994) that a dowry, in whatever form it takes, cannot be seen as directly comparable with male inheritance or that a dowry negates women's inheritance property rights. The Muslim respondents to whom I spoke also did not compare dowry gifts or giving *khat-maal* with inheritance property. A young housewife discussed inherited land thus:

> My parents arranged my marriage with my first cousin. My uncle and aunt liked me when I was very little. This liking turned into marriage before I had my first period. On my marriage my parents gave all the

household items. I will also get fifteen decimals of cultivable land from my natal family but not my homestead land, because in our area poor parents generally do not give homestead land to their daughters.

(Afsana, 20 years old)

Women's inherited property rights are often forfeited due to the scarcity of land and hyper-fertility of the households in the study areas. Most of the households have several male children but own negligible amounts of home-stead land, which subsequently gets fragmented among the heirs. As I have shown, in the villages of Zelegaon and Nodigaon only seven respondents (out of 113 married women) owned a small parcel of agricultural land. Conversely, 106 respondents' households have only homestead land (*vita bari*). As a result, when I asked them whether they would give property to their daugh-ters, most found my question irrelevant and replied, 'but where will we get land to give them, as we only have the homestead land on which we live'. However, this does not mean that they deprive their daughters of property rights. For example, Banu's husband died of a sudden heart attack. Conse-quently, Banu and her daughter had to leave her affinal house empty-handed and now she lives at her natal home in a new small thatched hut built with the help of her brothers. Banu promised her brothers that she would not sell this land to others. In return, her brothers have pledged that they will look after her until she dies. The families who have land opine that if their daughters demand land after their marriage they (the daughters) will get it.

Dowry disputes

The respondents of this study have a clear message about giving household goods on marriage irrespective of class and caste: it ensures their daughters' happiness, better treatment, and love in their marital home. It is also a way of demonstrating love to a girl, which intensifies the connections between dif-ferent individuals and facilitates social mobility in addition to social capital. However, most respondents of this study also agreed that giving household goods or dowry places a hefty financial burden on the bride's family:

My family is very poor, so we are now very anxious about our daughter's marriage. She is 16 years old. Her face and complexion are good but no proposal has come yet. We do not know how we will arrange *khat-maal* for our daughter's marriage. You are the rich people [boro lok] so if you help us financially to arrange *khat-maal* for our daughter's marriage Allah will help you.

(Nasibun and her husband)

Now, I have four marriageable daughters aged between 10 and 18, so my condition is awful. Without giving something [i.e. *khat-maal*] I cannot arrange their marriages, but my family has nothing. If Allah does not help me I cannot arrange my daughters' marriages.

(Maya)

Sometimes the groom's family pressurizes on the bride's family to provide a dowry. Therefore, dowry disputes and victimization are also common in Bangladeshi society, and I describe one such case to illustrate the adverse effects of the dowry system.

In 2005 Rukhsana married according to the wishes of her family when she was 18 years old. Her father arranged her marriage with the help of a fictive brother in his neighbourhood. Rukhsana's family owned some homestead land but nothing else. Rukhsana's mother explained the situation thus:

In 2005 we took out a big loan [TK 70,000] from GB so that we could give gifts on our older daughter's marriage. To pay the instalment of this credit, my husband pulled a cart day and night. Every week we had to pay TK 700 to GB as an instalment, which was not an easy task in our rural setting and for a family like us. For this instalment my husband worked in the rain and beneath the scorching sun, and this destroyed his health[2] but we never considered it a great burden since we gave gifts to our daughter and son-in-law to ensure our daughter's happiness in her married life.

However, Rukhsana did not find such happiness in her own conjugal life. Rather, she faced a tremendously difficult situation. During my fieldwork I learnt that Rukhsana was pregnant and staying at her natal home. She already had a daughter who lived with her father. According to Rukhsana, about five months after her wedding her husband started to behave abusively towards her. She found out that her husband was having an extramarital relationship with a woman in a nearby village. As a newly-wed bride, she could not understand her husband's bad habits and sometimes asked him why he came home late at night and where he spent his income. All the while she was subject to violent attacks by her husband. Rukhsana became a mother to a daughter and thought that her husband's behaviour would change as a result, but it did not. After just one year of married life Rukhsana's husband put pressure on her to obtain TK 5,000 from her family. Rukhsana's parents managed to beg TK 2,000 from rich people by telling them about Rukhsana's vulnerable position. Some time afterwards, Rukhsana's husband again demanded TK 4,000 to run a small business and Rukhsana's parents gave TK 2,500 to ensure their daughter's happy conjugal life. However, their efforts failed again. Rukhsana continued to suffer violence at the hands of her husband and fell ill as a consequence.

I felt sorry for Rukhsana when she showed me the injuries to her arm. She showed the upper part of her body to my wife, who suggested that we should help her to obtain legal support. We escorted Rukhsana and her parents to a counselling centre that gives legal aid to poor women. The counselling centre issued a legal summons to her husband and the local union council member. Initially, Rukhsana's husband tried to deny the charges, but when the lawyers showed him the evidence he fell silent. The husband assured them that he would not be violent towards Rukhsana again but she did not trust him. She chose not to return to her marital home; instead she demanded maintenance costs for her children and *den mahar* (bride wealth) from her husband. During my fieldwork we met three times but could not resolve the issue, although the lawyers assured me that they would try to do everything possible to help Rukhsana.

In sum, we have seen how dowry gift-giving or giving household goods as a form of marriage gift is extensively practised in the rural communities of Sylhet in Bangladesh. The microcredit borrowers, irrespective of class and caste, regard the giving of household goods for weddings as a social norm or local practice. Through an analysis of the data it was revealed that gifts act as 'symbolic capital', which provides positive self-images including honour, esteem or recognition, and reconstructs a girls's social and cultural identity when she enters her marital home. Gifts also influence the position of the gift-giver. Gifts create and intensify the social bonds and networks between different families and family members. Parents give household goods as wedding gifts trusting that they will ensure their daughters' happy conjugal lives as well as a better standard of life, and better treatment from their husbands and in-laws. I found that microcredit is strongly related to gift-giving at marriages. The programme has increased the practice of giving wedding gifts, and now many people take microcredit to cover the cost of such gifts. Adolescent girls take credit and make marriage ornaments for themselves. Previously, daughters' families often had to mortgage their valuable property to purchase wedding gifts but now due to microcredit programmes they no longer do so. However, I would like to argue that the way people use credit as a form of dowry gifts to increase social capital is in fact limiting their productive capacities. When credit is used for dowry payments, it reinforces the practice of dowry giving and the role of women as traditional rural Bangladeshi wives rather than their potential as productive individuals. It is an apparent ideological clash between established practice and modern aspirations. The potential of women's position as independent economic agents is in conflict with their embeddedness in patriarchal gender relations.

Notes

1 On this topic see also Uusikylä (2000: 55–60).
2 During my fieldwork I observed that Rukhsana's father was always in bed or sitting in front of his house. When I talked to him he told me that he did not have the energy to work outside the home.

4 Intra-household decision making and conflict negotiation

Women's empowerment through microcredit has become the mantra among development practitioners and scholars, yet there is a vigorous debate among researchers about the positive and negative impact of microcredit on women's empowerment. In this chapter I examine how microcredit relates to everyday intra-household decision-making processes and conflict negotiation capacity within the realm of the conjugal household. My aim is to explore the relationships of women and men, as well as between women themselves, and to understand the equalities and inequalities in the relationships, i.e. who does what; who has what; and who decides. More specifically, in this chapter I answer the following questions: how does microcredit involvement relate to gender roles, women's subordination and participation in intra-household decision-making processes? Does microcredit increase women's confidence, self-esteem and recognition by others within the household? How do women evaluate these changes? How does microcredit relate to women's exposure to violence and fertility behaviour in the household?

Credit decisions, arrangements and income: who is the boss?

Microcredit is a family economic scheme whereby women procure a loan and are responsible for its repayment. Therefore, knowledge about the person who decides to take the credit, uses it, and controls the resulting income is crucial for understanding the changes in gender relations and women's empowerment.[1] As mentioned in Chapter 1, studies in favour of microcredit (e.g. Osmani, 1998; Hashemi *et al.*, 1996; Pitt and Khandker, 1995; Islam-Rahman, 1986, Rahman, 1986a, 1986b; Amin and Pebley, 1994) confirmed that microcredit involvement has a positive impact on women, particularly with regard to their income-generating work and decision-making capacity within the household compared to non-participating women. The problem with these studies is that they mechanically investigated whether women had become 'more empowered' (cf. Johnson, 2005) through microcredit involvement, while limited focus was given to gender relations in which repression and empowerment are entrenched. Apart from this, almost all of the above studies were donor-driven, conducted by economists and largely based on statistical data.

During recent decades, the role of microcredit programmes as a vehicle for facilitating women's empowerment has been contested (e.g. Karim, 2008; Leach and Sitaram, 2002; Rahman, 1999, 2001; Goetz and Sen Gupta, 1996; Montgomery *et al.*, 1996). They argued that women's access to credit reinforces patriarchal norms of women's subordination, leading to worsening gender relationships and disempowerment of women. The aforementioned studies (e.g. Goetz and Sen Gupta 1996; Rahman 1999; Karim 2008) are often cited by critics of microfinance as a proof of its failure to improve women's economic position within their families and societies. According to these authors, women were not the self-directed recipients of credit; rather, they were influenced or ordered by their husbands or male relatives. Despite having no control over their loans, they bear the consequences to the loan centres for the credit repayment burden in their households.

Nevertheless, as in the above-mentioned studies, I also found that most women procured credit on behalf of their husbands or other male family members. I asked the respondents: 'who was first to take the initiative to join a credit programme?' In response to this question, approximately 71 per cent of my 151 female respondents stated that their husbands had suggested that they join the credit programmes, whereas only 7.9 per cent of the women applied for credit of their own volition. About 8.8 per cent of couples took the initiative jointly, and 10.6 per cent of the women were requested by their sons to take credit (see Figure 4.1).

When I enquired who controls credit, the overwhelming majority of the respondents considered this question to be irrelevant. My respondents unanimously pointed out that the microcredit programmes stipulate that credit is only given to women. As a result, if anybody wants to take out a loan he or she has to follow the rules of the credit programme, otherwise it is impossible to procure a loan. All the wives argued that without their husbands how could they take out loans? If a woman takes out a loan herself and gets into difficulties, who will rescue her from the NGOs? They often told me that women cannot do anything without 'a husband formula' (swamir formula chara ekjon mohila choltae pare na). My respondents repeatedly tried to explain to me that the credit goes to the whole family and that the NGOs also see it this way. My ethnographic data suggest that there is a shared, mutual interest in microcredit in the household economy. They do not consider credit as individual property. Rather, they consider it as a collective resource, which is used for the well-being of all the household members.

The household is not simply an antagonistic unit, but it often also involves 'economic co-operation' (Sharma, 1980). The feminist critique of Chayanovian, Marxist and neoclassical household economics views the household not as an abode of altruism and sharing, but of conflict and oppression, as 'a locus of competing interests, rights, obligations and resources, where household members are often involved in bargaining, negotiation and possibly even

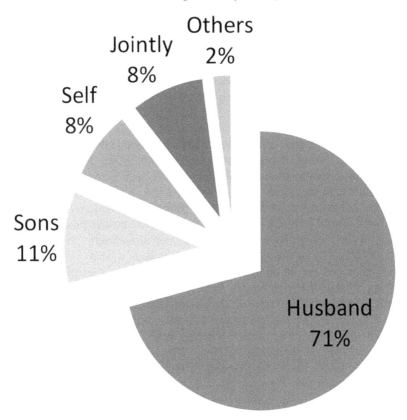

Figure 4.1 Who was first to take the initiative to take credit?
Source: Author's survey

conflict' (Moore, 1994: 87). Sen (1990) in a nuanced way argued that cooperation and conflict occur simultaneously in households, and greater cooperation between husbands and wives is generally desirable. According to Sen,
'the member(s) of the household faces two different types of problems simultaneously, one involving *cooperation* … and the other *conflict*.' (ibid.: 127,
emphasis in the original). Social arrangements regarding who does what, who
gets to consume what, and who takes which decisions can be viewed as a
response to this combined problem of cooperation and conflict (ibid., 1990).
To my mind, the studies by Goetz and Sen Gupta (1996), Rahman (1999) and
Karim (2008) ignored the complementary bond between husband and wife,
and envisaged competing, coercive or conflicting intra-household relationships. In particular, these studies did not appropriately consider gender relations within the household and the wider community, which constrain most
women to take credit for self-investment and compel them to hand over credit
to their menfolk for profitable investment.

The fact that loans are channelled through women by the NGOs does not imply that they are only intended for women's self-managed enterprises. The male household members mostly invest credit because women cannot pay weekly instalments by investing credit themselves. Whenever I brought up the issue that since women were accountable for paying instalments they had to cope with greater mental pressure, this suggestion was rejected. They argued that in the family one person may feel a lot of pressure (*chaap*) or responsibility and the other less; they considered this to be the custom (*niyam*) of society. If husband and wife always calculate who does more and who does less for the family, a viable conjugal life will not be sustained. However, the relationships between husband and wife are not merely rooted in cooperation; rather, they demonstrate complicated negotiations, collective interest, interdependence and episodes of discontent. It is understandable that by participating in the credit programmes wives bring valuable capital to the house that can help their husbands to find ways of increasing their income and to cover family expenditure (collective/mutual interest). Even so, such cooperation does not necessarily mean that it contributes to increasing women's decision-making power, control over resources or that it brings value to and within the household or reduces victimization by their husbands.

Next, I cite a part of an in-depth interview with Gulecha (35 years old) about credit and instalment repayments:

Q: Who suggested that you take out a loan?
My husband suggested that I take credit.
Q: Why did he suggest this?
How else would he be able to collect or borrow money for his fishing business? ... NGOs extend credit through women but they keep our husbands' names in their record books, because the husbands are related to their wives. Even if a husband persuades someone to give him credit, the NGOs suggest collecting his wife's signature for getting credit.
Q: So your husband controls the credit and its income.
You can say so, but I don't think so. We do not think like you.
Q: Are not you accountable for paying the instalment money?
Yes, but this is not my headache [jontrona] alone. When we reduced our food or ate smaller meals (for example, rice with fried chillies) in order to save money for repayments I did not starve or eat less myself, they also faced the same problem.

Some women who took credit and used it themselves stated that before taking credit they first informed their husbands. For example, Fouzia invested credit in her river-dredging business so she took the decision about the matter herself. It is her debt and she pays the instalments herself but before taking credit she informed her husband: 'I took credit from GB and BRAC for the last few years for running my business and for family expenditure. My husband knows that the money I get from the NGOs is useful and that we have to repay the money. I always ask him in advance'. Another respondent said that together with her husband she took and used credit. She did not face any problems regarding credit use and its investment. She considers credit a family matter. Indeed, women are not driven by calculated self-interest. A picture of the interdependence of gender relations emerged from of the statements of most respondents. Whether husbands or sons have asked for or used the credit is not a pertinent question or a source of friction. Rather, these are examples of household altruism. Consequently, the ethnocentric Euro-American notions of personal use and individual responsibility make it difficult to understand how credit is controlled and channelled in families in Bangladesh.

The husbands also explained their position in a similar fashion. They do not see their wives as individuals, but instead refer to women according to their relationship to them. They explained that they take loans through their wives but it does not mean that they alone enjoy the income from the loan selfishly. The credit is used for to care for all the family (stree and santan). The husbands argued that if the NGO staff tied up their wives with string for failing to repay their instalments, it would not only destroy the *izzat-shanman* (honour and respect) of their wives, but would also destroy the honour and respect of their sons and all the family members. The husbands or the sons could not run away, they would have to come to stand beside the wives or mothers. For example, Habiba's husband (a GB and BRAC microcredit borrower from Zelegaon centre) explained:

> Are husbands and wives individual people? What a wife needs in a poor family are two meals each day, clothing, and a life with a husband and children, nothing more. It is only possible if a husband can earn or increase his income. So according to our suggestion, they take credit in their names and hand it over to their husbands. The NGOs know well that by investing credit, husbands can run the family and pay the instalments.

Nevertheless, not all the borrowers are of the same opinion. In some cases, the husbands and mother-in-laws ordered their wives to take out loans. These respondents claimed that as they are the wives of these houses, they have to obey their husbands and mother-in-laws. They have to act according to the wishes of the older family members. A few husbands behaved badly with regard to their wives to getting loans. Nira, a 25-year-old Hindu housewife from a joint family, has had bad experiences. Nira did not directly agree with me that she was forced by her husband to get credit but said that in conjugal life a woman has to accept many things by holding her tongue. Her husband takes loans from GB and BRAC in her name and uses the credit for his grocery business. He handles credit taking and its investment and never talks about these with Nira. Nira has travelled the road in front of her husband's shop many times but she has never entered the premises. Nira asked her husband to buy a sewing machine for her but he ignored her request. Her husband told her it was not needed in the family. Nira told me she is just a medium for taking credit because she never visits the instalments payment centre or feels pressure to pay instalments. It is entirely the responsibility of her husband. The officer collects the instalment money from her husband's shop.

On the other hand, Pearun, a 32-year-old housewife, admitted that her husband had abused her in order to make credit instalments. Her husband instructed her to take out the loan and hand over the entire sum to him so that he could use it for his fishing business. She never keeps a single paisa for her own use. Pearun claims that in order to follow her husband's orders, she got entangled with the programme. She considers paying credit instalments an onerous problem (*boro jamela*) but she is helpless (*oshohai*), because her husband has no other means or capital to run his business.

As we know from the prevailing literature, the interdependence of gender relations within the family is highly unequal in Bangladesh. Despite this gender asymmetry, husbands and wives do not have major conflicts about taking out loans or utilizing them. Similarly to Rahman (1999, 2001) and Karim (2008), I did not find that most women faced patriarchal subordination due to credit involvement. Rather, I found that most husbands took out loans through mutual consent or consultation with their wives. The husbands seldom forced their wives to take out loans due to the assumption that NGOs might not give credit if they found out about it. Prevalent views (Goetz and Sen Gupta, 1996; Rahman, 1999; Karim, 2008) about control of credit or the assumed use of force by husbands and sons to take credit away from their wives and mothers reflects the problematic oriental stereotypes about South Asian and Middle Eastern men in general, than the actual cooperation patterns within the families.

Unitary versus bargaining models of the household

The household is the locus of the decision-making process in Bangladeshi society. Many researchers (Mahmud, 2003; Osmani, 1998; Schuler *et al.*, 1996; Pitt and Khandker, 1995; Mizan, 1994; Amin and Pebley, 1994; Islam-Rahman, 1986; Rahman, 1986a, 1986b) have previously shown that women's access to microcredit leads to increased income under women's control, an increase in women's decision-making capacity within the household, and increased well-being (consumption, health status, literacy, housing) for women and their children. However, whether credit brings actual direct benefits to women themselves in the household environment remains a debated issue (Ali and Hatta, 2012; Karim, 2008; Rahman, 1999; Goetz and Sen Gupta, 1996). With respect to the decision-making process within the household, the dominant view of female microcredit borrowers interviewed for this study is that their husbands (the household heads) are the main decision makers within the households. Sometimes the husbands take household decisions with elder sons or mothers-in-law. In such cases women feel that they are subordinate to and controlled by their husbands. Their husbands often pay no heed to their participation in household decisions or ignore them and take family decisions alone. By investing credit husbands make some money but this does not necessarily have an effect on their wives' daily lives. I found only a few cases of couples reaching household decisions through mutual discussion.

Many women have little or no knowledge about their husbands' incomes. The most important financial decisions are taken by men, who hardly ever consult their wives.[2] In their quantitative study Hashemi et al. (1996) examined the increased likelihood of assets being held in women's names as a result of microcredit involvement. My data raise strong doubts about whether microcredit services help women to acquire or control land or to purchase a house. Baruah (2010) also observed the same phenomenon in her research undertaken in India about the possibilities of microcredit (even credit designated for land and house acquisition) to help women control these assets. Of the present study's respondents, three borrowers bought land with the help of credit but the deeds of the land were written in their husbands' names. The overwhelming majority of my respondents do not believe that microcredit membership has enhanced their capacity to control material resources, increase their self-confidence and bargaining power or decision-making roles within the household. Women can make some minor household decisions independently such as how much or what sort of food should be cooked, borrowing or lending small amounts of money or purchasing and selling eggs, food items, snacks, cheap jewellery, etc. However, these types of minor decision-making options are not completely new for women in Bangladeshi society (Gardner, 1995). For example, it is common practice that women save small amounts of money by selling eggs or vegetables but such small-scale savings are not made on a regular basis. Moreover, women cannot keep these savings for any length of time because they are poverty-stricken and they have to spend the money on family crises.

When the respondents were asked whether they are treated differently by their husbands because they take out loans from microcredit organizations, most said that this was not the case. They do not feel that they have earned more respect in the community nor has their own self-esteem or self-value increased accordingly. Unlike the existing quantitative studies (Hashemi et al. 1996; Osmani, 1998; Pitt and Khandker, 1995; Mizan, 1994; Islam-Rahman, 1986; Rahman, 1986a, 1986b), my study reveals a gloomy picture of women's bargaining capacity and empowerment through microcredit involvement. There follows an extract from an in-depth interview with one of the successful microcredit borrowers from the point of view of understanding women's participation in household decision-making processes. I asked her whether her husband consults with her when he takes family decisions, and she said:

My husband handles everything. Since I am a woman, he does not consult me. He thinks that I should listen to him and obey his orders. I decide how much food or what type of food shall be cooked each day.

But in a sense, it is also decided by my husband because he does the shopping [*bazar kora*] so I have to cook whatever he brings home.

Q: Do you know how much your husband earns from his business?

He does not consult me nor does he talk about the profit, loss or income of his business. Sometimes I ask him but he says that it is none of my business. My duties are preparing food, caring for the children and my mother-in-law, and looking after the house.

Q: When you need something how do you buy it?

This is not a problem. Sometimes I can buy things and sometimes he brings them. If I need money, I tell him.

Q: Does he feel that you are important since you take credit on his behalf?

I do not understand, you can ask my husband.

(Shorola, 25 years old)

Pronoti, a 35-year-old Hindu housewife, added that it is the husband's family (*swamir sangsar*), so whatever it is that her husband decides she is obliged to listen to him and obey for the peace of the family. The husband decides everything according to his own wishes. He never attributes any importance to her wishes and opinions. Pronoti passed the Secondary School Certificate examination but her husband would not allow her to get a job. Pronoti asked her husband many times to let her work but her husband said that she could only get a job in the village. Pronoti wonders where she could find a job in this village. As a result she does not work outside the house. She is now too old to get a government job.

Some women have to consult both their husbands and their mother-in-laws. For example, Hasna (30 years old), a microcredit borrower from Zelegaon, told me that her husband is not a good man. He does not consult her about any household affairs. Sometimes Hasna tries to make her opinion heard but it is very difficult to make his husband listen. Occasionally, he accepts Hasna's opinion but most of the time he does not. The husband often consults his mother but he disregards her wife's opinion. Hasna told me that her mother-in-law frequently pokes her nose into their affairs. She tries to control Hasna. I asked Hasna how the mother-in-law controls her, and she replied:

My mother-in-law thinks that her son rescued me from danger by marrying me. She thinks that she and her son know everything and treat me as if I do not understand anything. She tries to show that she is something but in reality she is nothing. I have to follow my husband's and mother-in-law's decisions otherwise it causes disquiet in the family. If I were to quarrel with them, it might damage our marriage. I am the daughter of another house [*porer barir meye*], so I have no value in this house.

Nevertheless, I also found some respondents who did not think it necessary for their husbands to consult them when making family decisions because of the cultural construction of passivity, appropriate female behaviour, social norms, and tradition in the family. These women have no difference of opinion with their husbands. They think that their husbands are sincere and treat them equally. They can depend fully on their husbands and do not consider themselves to be separate entities. For example, Jesmin's husband told me that he often tries to consult his wife about plans and financial decisions, but she does not like this. 'When a man does not have the ability to take decisions alone, what kind of a man is he?' asked Jesmin.

In his bargaining model, Sen (1990) argues that the outcome of the bargaining process depends on how clearly the person perceives his or her interests and contributions. The outcome will be less favourable to a person (a) if less value is attached to his or her own well-being relative to the well-being of others (perceived interest response); and (b) the smaller her or his contribution to the household economy is perceived to be (perceived contribution response). Sen argues that both types of scenarios are usually biased against the woman of the household. These biases vary from society to society but they are regressive in societies like India or Bangladesh where many women do not perceive their individual well-being in terms of self-interest and where the woman's economic contributions to the household is undervalued.

Sen's argument is correct to some extent for the South Asian context where many women's economic contributions to the household are disregarded. However, like Sen I do not consider that women's lack of perception or incorrect perception of their self-interest are the main barriers for participating in household decision-making or bargaining. With a few exceptions, the overwhelming majority of women microcredit borrowers I interviewed told me that they do not like their husbands to take all the household decisions alone. These women are aware that they are subordinated but they do not legitimize the prevailing inequality of intra-household decision-making processes. Sometimes they question the dominating behaviour of their husbands but often they avoid asking questions in order to maintain peace and keep their conjugal lives on an even keel.

However, as mentioned earlier, some women use loans for their self-managed enterprises. These women use the income from their businesses to pay credit instalments, and often meet their own expenses in addition to other family members' expenses. My study suggests that these women mainly have a strong voice in household decision-making processes and they face little or no subordination within the home. Aysha is an appropriate example of the independent woman.

Aysha: an enterprising woman

Aysha has three daughters and two sons. Her husband Nurul is a fishmonger on a small scale. The household has 10 decimals of homestead land and a few decimals of cultivable land. Aysha has been taking microcredit for 18 years from different organizations including GB, BRAC, ASA, and FIVDB for investing in her business. Aysha observed that her husband's income could not cover the household expenses. His earnings could not guarantee two meals a day. Therefore, one day Aysha talked to her husband about taking out a loan and running a small business. At first her husband was unhappy about this and refused her permission to take out a loan. However, eventually she convinced him, and he consented to her taking out a loan. Initially, Aysha took TK 2,000 from GB and invested most of it in a rice business. She kept back a small amount of money for paying some of the instalments. During the paddy season the price of rice is comparatively low so she bought rice with the help of her husband and then sold it in the lean season when the price is comparatively higher. By doing this Aysha made a profit and her husband appreciated her business acumen. Aysha claims that she knew that she would not fail because her mother was also involved in a family business. Later, when Aysha started another business by using credit her husband supported her.

Aysha has a unique skill for making *nakshi-kanthas* (thick embroidered quilts). Aysha sewed a *nakshi-kantha* and showed it to some of her neighbours with a view to selling it. Her neighbours liked her quilts and they spread the news. Since her mother had been involved in this work for many years she also sent some customers to her. Over the last 18 years, she has been taking credit in order to carry out her *nakshi-kantha* business, thus building up her reputation and recognition in Zelegaon and the adjacent villages. This work enhances her self-confidence and self-esteem. Her wares cross the border of the country. Aysha explained: 'I have a good reputation [naam daak achey] in this area. If you ask anybody about me in this village or the nearby villages people can easily show you my house as a *nakshiwali*. My products are sent to London for weddings there. Sometimes I get five or six requests at a time for a "London-Sylheti" wedding. It is a great achievement in my life.'

Aysha charges TK 3,000–4,000 for each commissioned *nakshi-katha* quilt. The price depends on the type and quality of the work. For heavy embroidery work she charges approximately TK 4,000 per *katha*. Normally, during the winter (the marriage season) she gets more orders (10 to 12) and can earn an ample amount of money. Aysha learned this unique sewing skill from her mother and her mother had learnt it from her mother (Aysha's grandmother). She does not know who taught her grandmother to do this work. Aysha has also taught her daughters to make *kathas* and now they help her. Aysha hopes that in future her daughters will also do this work and thus be able to earn some money for everyday expenses (*hath khorosh*).

Aysha is satisfied with her work and her earning capacity. She is not only happy because of her financial achievement but also clearly recognizes her contribution to the family. As she says, 'Still what my husband has earned can only support half a month's family expenditure'. Aysha asserts that if she relied on her husband's income or was an ordinary housewife like other women in the village she would be a street beggar (*path-er fakir*). She would have to live in a tiny hut and would not be able to afford to arrange her eldest daughter's marriage. Now she lives in a good house and her elder daughter resides in her affinal house with honour and prestige (*maan-izzat*). Aysha has tried to grant all her sons' and daughters' wishes.

Aysha has complete control over her income. She is happy that unlike other women in her village she does not have to ask her husband for money in order to buy things. By selling *nakshi-kanthas* she has built a three-roomed house with brick walls, a tin roof and a mud floor. She has a tube well, a ring latrine, and has acquired some household furniture and bought a 21-inch colour television. She covered all the costs of the marriage of her elder daughter. She has already made some ornaments and saved up some money for the marriages of her two remaining unmarried daughters. Aysha asserts that she is on equal footing with her husband in deciding how the family income should be invested. She participates actively in all family decisions. Before making decisions about her elder daughter's marriage, Aysha's husband consulted her first. Aysha thinks that a woman should have a commitment to something she can do, and stand on her own two feet. In her opinion, cooperation between the husband and wife is important because if the husband and wife do not have a peaceful relationship it will be impossible for a woman to fulfil such a commitment. My impression of Aysha is that she has grown up as a village woman following local norms and practices (*rity-nity*) but at the same time she has astutely created her own path to make some changes in her surrounding structural societal boundaries. This example shows how social structures and individuals simultaneously interact (Giddens, 1984)[3] in the local settings in Bangladesh.

Previously, Aysha's husband accompanied her if she needed to visit a doctor but now she goes with her son. Generally, when she leaves the house to visit her natal family or the home of a relative she asks her husband for permission. She argues that leaving the house without the husband's permission is not good because he is the head of the household. She opines that her husband supports her in every matter: 'Due to my husband's support I changed this household through my intelligence and actions. We take all family decisions jointly. There are neither problems nor conflicts between us. My husband is aware of my intelligence and the contribution that I make, so he cannot ignore me when making family decisions.'

She argues that microcredit has been an important but not a vital factor in her success. She referred to her mother who did not get involved in a credit programme but became successful by dint of hard work and through selling *nakshi-kantha* quilts. She claims that everybody in her area knows she starts work before dawn and continues until well after dark. She has no time to gossip with other women or to visit other houses. For the past few years, Aysha has tried to leave the microcredit programmes because at present it is not important for her to take credit. 'But the NGO officers advised me to remain a customer because they could easily collect repayments on time from me. They would not find a client in this area like me', claimed Aysha.

Like Aysha, some women who used loans for self-managed enterprises including sewing and producing bamboo-cane crafts at home did perceive a positive change in their status. In other words, they are constructing particular class categories or their own identities in the local communities. As Scott (1988) noted, class hierarchies are gendered constructs. These women demonstrated that prior to their participation in the credit programmes they had little say over household decisions, income or spending money but this has changed. Their ability to earn an income independently of their husbands gives them confidence in their own capabilities and a sense of self-worth. Even their neighbours' general attitude changed. They efficiently incorporate their work into the household and women's domain. Consequently, they can also maintain the gender norms associated with women residing in their homes or homesteads areas. They construct their freedom in terms of savings, control over household resources and the ability to spend money on their own. In poverty stricken families, I find that such women's income earning capacity helps to strengthen the bonds between husbands and wives. As a result, their husbands proudly inform me that their wives help them to cover the living costs. Therefore, I suggest that microcredit can increase women's participation in household decision making in rural settings when credit is offered to support the development of women's marketable skills and trading abilities.

Credit and women's exposure to violence

One of the crucial gauges of women's empowerment is connected to violence against women. Studies conducted of rural married women have demonstrated that domestic violence against women is common in Bangladesh. However, these studies produced divergent statistics on rural Bangladeshi women experiencing physical violence in their marital relationships. Steele *et al.* (1998) reported 32 per cent; Khan *et al.* (2001) 43 per cent; Koenig *et al.* (2003) 42 per cent (N = 8,000); Bates *et al.* (2004) 67 per cent (N = 1,200); Hadi (2005) 19 per cent (N = 500), and the Bangladesh Institute of Development Studies (2004) 72 per cent. Some studies have revealed the following reasons for domestic violence: the wife's failure to perform household work adequately; insubordination towards her husband or members of the extended family; and unacceptable interaction with male outsiders. Assaulting a wife physically is seen as a husband's appropriate and justifiable response to all these (Schuler *et al.*, 1996, 1998; Hartman and Boyce, 1983; Abdullah and Zeidenstein, 1982). However, the existing studies have reached conflicting conclusions with regard to the relationship between microcredit involvement and violence against women. Most of the studies argue that microcredit programmes have reduced women's vulnerability to men's physical repression, divorce, desertion and violence (Ahmad, 2007; Schuler *et al.*, 1997a; Hashemi *et al.*, 1996; Khandker and

Latif, 1995; Dreze and Sen, 1995; Schuler and Hashemi, 1994; Amin and Pebley, 1994; Rahman, 1986a, 1986b; Ahmed, 1985). Conversely, Rahman (2001, 1999) in his anthropological study painted a dismal picture of violence against women. He found that GB loans resulted in greater violence against women. Rahman found that only 18 per cent of GB members reported that domestic violence had decreased, whereas 70 per cent claimed an increase in violence and aggressive behaviour in the household. Likewise, Ahmed (2005), Bhuiya *et al.* (2003), Chowdhury and Bhuiya (2001), and Goetz and Sen Gupta (1996) confirmed in their studies that members of microcredit organizations faced higher levels of violence at the hands of their husbands.

Collecting data on gender-based domestic violence against women in rural areas is a difficult task. Most women usually prefer to talk about other women's sufferings, not about violence towards themselves as individuals. When I asked the respondents: 'Do you face violence from your husband such as scolding or hitting (*boka, galigalaj, marpeet*) by your husband?' Most women replied that a lot of husbands in their area scold their wives, use filthy language and sometimes beat their wives, but they themselves are fortunate because their husbands never assault them physically. For example, Nasibun informed me that her husband never physically assaulted her, but when he becomes furious he makes a whining sound. Since her husband is *habla/shida* (simple-minded), he only makes this type of sound. In this sense, Nasibun claims that she is lucky because, unlike other women in her area, she does not face physical or verbal violence. Nasibun says that there are a number of causes for violence against women in her area including short-tempered husbands, economic hardship and the burden of many children, and some men are violent towards their wives in order to get remarried. She observes that women cannot do anything about violence against them – they can only cry or refuse to eat for one or two days because there is nowhere else for them to go.

Another woman added that her husband did not assault her physically but frequently berated her.She hates it when he behaves like this but does not dare to protest because this could make him more furious and likely to assault her physically. She does not know what she would do if her husband were violent nor where she would go:

> You will not find a woman who does not face a husband's scolding in this village. Men's mouth is bad (purushder mukh kharap) in this area. It also happens due to financial hardship. Most people in our area are still poor. The husband suffers from poverty, and so does the wife. It creates problems in family life. When men become angry they often only smack their wives. Sometimes women cannot tolerate this, so they also become angry and start to argue with their husbands. If wives argue or protest about their husbands' rough behaviour the husbands often thrash their wives but they rarely get divorced … Sometimes neighbours and

elders have to come forward to restrain the violent husband forcibly. Actually, a poor woman has nothing except herself.

(Minu, 30 years old)

In Bangladesh conflict between mothers-in-law and daughters-in-law is to some extent common at least before the daughter-in-law becomes a mother herself (Uusikylä, 2000: ,60–61). Some of the respondents stated that domestic violence was perpetrated by both the husbands and the mothers-in-law. For instance, Mayarun (30 years old) told me that her husband is not a good man, and scolds her when he becomes angry. He uses filthy language as and when he likes. He only listens to his mother. Her mother-in-law also abuses her through frequent scolding, back-biting and provoking her son in many ways. Mayarun tells me that it is her mother-in-law's habit to make up stories about Mayarun. Her mother-in-law never ever says anything to her son.

I found that most women feel shame and disgrace when disclosing that they are physically abused by their husbands. The elders (particularly the affines) do not like the wives of their house sharing family matters with other people. Therefore, many informants told me that their husbands only abused them through scolding, quarrelling and sometimes slapping. Nevertheless, some women revealed that they were physically assaulted by their husbands.

My husband is a very bad man (*kharap beta*)

During my fieldwork in the village of Zelegaon I often used to visit the homes of my assistants, Suchona and Azad. One day, I found Azad in a disconsolate mood. When I asked why he was unhappy he tried to avoid the subject, but Suchona urged him to tell me about the problems confronting his younger sister, Pearun. Azad thought for a while and looked at me with a gloomy face. At first, Azad felt ashamed to say anything about the physical violence experienced by Pearun who is a microcredit borrower. Her husband frequently beats her and reproaches her using filthy language. Sometimes it becomes unbearable for her. Today Azad had heard that Pearun's husband had severely thrashed her again.

Pearun has been married for many years and now has six children. Her eldest son is now fourteen years old and in the sixth grade, but her husband has not stopped his violent acts. Azad asserts that Pearun's husband has no shame (*lojja-sharam nei*), and no humanity. Owing to pressure from her husband, Azad's sister has been taking credit over the years, handing it over to her husband for the running of his fishing business, but Pearun gets nothing.

Azad's parents arranged their daughter's marriage to a man living in a neighbourhood near to their village. This is just a couple of minutes' walking distance from Azad's house. When Azad's family arranged his sister's marriage, the whole family was happy. The family did not think that the sister's husband could be so violent. According to the local practice (*niyam*), they provided all the household goods at the wedding to ensure conjugal happiness for Azad's sister, yet she has sunk to a bottomless sea of sorrow. Azad has five brothers, so I asked him whether they try to control Pearun's husband's violent behaviour. Azad replied sadly that Pearun's in-laws are also not good; they do not say anything to their son to stop his violence. Azad's family and some of the elders have asked Pearun's husband to stop behaving violently several times but in vain. When they entreated that the violence should stop, Pearun's husband promised to not to commit any more violent acts with his wife but after a few days he behaved violently again. Neighbours are also well aware of how violent he is towards his wife. Therefore, Azad's family has sought help from the neighbours but they are worried about what would happen to Pearun if her husband divorces her and then remarries. Where would Pearun go then with her six children? Azad's parents are poor, so they cannot support such a large family.

I accompanied Azad to the neighbourhood to the west of the village to talk to Pearun and her husband, but we did not meet her husband because he was at work. The entrance of the house was surrounded by bamboo trees and there were five households on only 15 decimals of land. When we entered the homestead area we saw some children playing in the mud and shouting at each other. One was Pearun's five-year-old son. Azad told his nephew to call his mother and Pearun came quickly and arranged a chair in the bamboo garden for me to sit on. Azad told her to bring tea for us. I tried to refuse but I failed, and she rushed off with a smile. Azad pointed out the households, and informed me that Pearun husband has five brothers, all of whom live there with their many children. The children are always very noisy, so Azad only visits his sister's house occasionally. After making tea, Pearun called us inside her house but Azad told Pearun that we would prefer to stay outside where it was cool and comfortable. Pearun brought us refreshments. Azad told his sister that I had some questions for her about the microcredit programme and her family, and to talk to me openly.

Pearun thinks that her husband as a very bad, short-tempered man (*kharap beta*). He does not like the family or the children. Her husband is in financial difficulties and cannot support the family. However, her husband only thinks about his own belly and food. Sometimes Pearun does not eat herself but instead keeps food for him so as to avoid his malice. Her husband becomes angry over the most trivial matter. He used to sleep until noon and if he was disturbed by their sons he became angry with Pearun. He often thrashed the children and scolded her. I asked Pearun whether her husband behaves badly with her because of microcredit instalments, and she answered:

> Sometimes he does it for this reason. He only wants to get money but he does not take responsibility of paying it back. If I say something, he becomes furious and behaves badly towards me.
> Q: What type of misbehaviour does he show towards you? Does he beat you?
> (She bites her *sarir achol*) Yes (in a low voice), he does what he likes. He

often beats me [mar-peet kore] and my children. He shouts at me and uses filthy language. He does not care about anything. My in-laws are also blind to their son's behaviour; it is their aim to find out my faults, not their son's.

Q: Did you not say anything about the violence to the NGO officer?

It would bring disgrace upon me – what would people say? The bank only provides loans with interest and recovers instalments, it doesn't solve family matters. The officers do not talk about such matters.

Q: So, how do you manage the instalments?

Usually, after shouting at me he tries to manage the money but sometimes he cannot because his income is inadequate. Then I sometimes borrow from other people and sometimes my brothers give me money. Besides, when my brothers give me some money I do not spend it – I keep it.

Pearun informed me that in her homestead area everybody knows about her husband's behaviour but they do not do anything about it. Moreover, some people do not see the faults of her husband; they only ostracize her and try to find out her faults. They accuse her of not being able to pacify her husband and cater to his needs. Pearun's relatives and neighbours sometimes advise her to adjust to her husband. Nowadays she occasionally protests about her husband's foul behaviour. Pearun considers her children as her future security: 'My children are growing up, so I think in future he won't be able to do it because they will reprimand him.' Pearun repeatedly asked where she would go with her children, there is no way to go back and stay with her natal family because they cannot support her. Pearun told me that there is endemic violence against women in her village. Many women are often abused by their husbands and by their in-laws. Pearun believes that she is ill-fated. Allah runs her family. She has no knowledge of the ideal family life, so when her husband orders her to end her membership of the microcredit programme only then she can leave the programme. Pearun rationalizes that her husband has no options without microcredit because there is no other source of money to run his business. Pearun has asked her husband many times to do business with her brothers in addition to his fishing in order to increase his income. They think that if he could increase his income he might not be violent towards his family but he does not pay heed to them, he 'walks according to his own way'.

Pearun thus demonstrated that she faces domestic violence as a result of her husband's financially vulnerable situation and inability to run his big family, although it is not poverty per se that naturally leads to violence but the husband's perception of the situation in a patriarchal society. Domestic violence in the rural area does not follow a uniform pattern. Next, I describe another microcredit borrower who invests credit herself and has a steady stream of income. Unlike Pearun, the following case study exemplifies other aspects of domestic violence in the rural area.

I have much experience of fighting my husband

Fouzia is an angular and hard-faced woman. Her husband Nizam is her first cousin and is about the same as her. Fouzia's father was mainly a fish trader but did not earn enough to meet the expenses of a family of 14. When Fouzia was just 14 years old financial hardship drove her father to arrange her marriage in a different upazila to a man who worked in Saudi Arabia. However, Fouzia could not stay in this marriage. Before marriage she had a romantic relationship with her first cousin. Some months after the wedding her husband left again to work in Saudi Arabia. Then her cousin started visiting her affinal house and seduced her with gifts such as earrings, necklaces and hair ribbons. One night Fouzia clandestinely left her affinal house with her first cousin and then, with the help of some friends, a *mawlana* (religious leader) joined them in marriage. Fouzia's parents eventually accepted her new marriage.

Fouzia now has four children ranging from 12 to 20 years of age. Her first and second sons drive a rented three-wheeler. The second daughter is 19 years old and was married two years ago. The fourth child, a daughter, was studying in the seventh grade at the time of this interview. Fouzia has six decimals of homestead land and 20 decimals of cultivable land in her own name. The family uses a ring latrine. They prefer to use river water for drinking and cooking purposes even though the family has a shallow tube well. Fouzia has been taking micro-loans for the last ten years from different organizations including ASA, BRAC, FIVDB and GB for different purposes. She has been using credit for herself. The river Surma flows just behind her house, so in the winter season she leases part of the river for dredging and selling sand. In order to operate this business every year she has taken out micro-loans and earned some money.

Fouzia has access to social networks and mobility beyond that of her neighbours. For the river dredging business she has maintained a network with various people. Notwithstanding that the river-dredging business is dominated by men, she does not feel ashamed to do business with men: 'If I feel shame how I would run this business? They do their work, and I do mine.' Fouzia must have been a strong woman even before joining the microcredit programme. Her father sometimes also did this work as well as his fishing business, so she knows everything about the dredging business. Moreover, she knows the people, as she operates her business in her natal village. Marriage within the same neighbourhood also puts Fouzia in a strong position to operate the business. According to her, 'Micro-loans from the NGOs may be important but not a decisive factor for me. Now it has become a bad habit because whenever I face an economic crisis I can take money from the NGOs.'

Fouzia also stood for election at the last local union council member election. Thus in her area she is familiar as a *memberni*, although she failed to get into office in that election. She hopes to compete again and win the next election. Fouzia knows how to sew *nakshi-kanthas*. Every year she gets orders for three or four *nakshi-kanthas* and earns some extra money. She had tried marketing her wares but failed because people prefer Jessore-stitch *nakshi-kathas* instead of *Sylheti nakshi-kathas*. Fouzia claims that she alone bears all the expense of running the family. She asserts that her husband makes no contribution to the family so she bears all the responsibilities for the household. Her husband does not care if there is food in the house or not. I asked Fouzia what her husband does, and she replied:

> My husband is a rascal [bodmash]. He is a cook but he has no motive to earn money; he goes to work occasionally. I do not see his income. He just wants to drink tea, smoke *biri* [locally produced cigarettes], eat betel and nuts, and gossip in different houses with women.
> Q: Don't you quarrel with him about these things?
> Is it possible not to quarrel with this type of bad man [kharap morod]? He frequently quarrels with me. He is a lecherous, characterless man. Despite the fact that he has a wife at home he covets other women.

Fouzia built some rooms on her land and rents these out to families. Her husband frequently went to talk to the tenants but Fouzia did not understand his hidden motives for doing so. A few days prior to my data collection, she caught her husband red-handed one night. She found him in bed with a woman. This woman had rented the house only a few months ago. Therefore, the next day, with the help of some other people, Fouzia evicted the woman. I asked Fouzia whether her husband had stopped this relationship. Fouzia thought for while and told me that marriage for love or marriage to escape from the natal house has no peace. At the time, she was young (*obuj*) so she did not understand but now she understands what a blunder she made. People in Bangladeshi society do not view this type of marriage positively.

Fouzia asserts that sometimes she does not give any importance to her husband but sometimes she has to listen to him. She arranged her eldest daughter's marriage without her husband's consent. She found a good boy who also did river-dredging work in her area, so she did not discuss it with her husband. Moreover, she bore all the expenses of the marriage by herself. Showing a scar close to her left eye she said, 'I have much experience of fighting with him.' I asked Fouzia whether the husband assaulted her physically, and she replied:

> What I am saying to you? He frequently quarrelled with me and used filthy language. Sometimes he hit me but nowadays I also do not leave him unchallenged. When I married this rascal I had a peaceful conjugal life for only for a few years then, day-by-day, his real character emerged. He always prefers profligacy and to enjoy my money. He cannot provide anything for the household but he thinks that I must do what he tells me.

During our conversation, her husband came in with a cup of tea. He offered me a cup of tea several times but I refused politely. 'Why do you not drink my tea?' he asked me. Fouzia shouted and said: 'Why do you bother us? I will beat you, and hit your backside with a bamboo stick.' Muttering under his breath he left the house. I asked Fouzia whether she would leave her husband. Fouzia says that despite having a bad husband she has to stay in the marriage in order to guarantee their children's future. Sometimes she has to consult her husband about the children's activities. Now her children are all grown up, and if her husband continues his bad ways the children will get angry and reprimand him. Fouzia agrees with me that society would ostracize her if she left her husband. They will say that she left her first husband, then got married again and now is trying to leave her second husband. Fouzia added that most people in society do not blame men, no matter what men do or what they do to women, they always seek to find fault with the women. Society blames the women. Everyone prefers to cast aspersions on the women. Fouzia thinks that her husband will not leave her because he has no property: 'He did not get any property from his parents' side. He resides in my house and enjoys my property, so where would he live if he left me?'

Regarding other women in Nodigaon, Fouzia says that domestic disturbance between husbands and wives is a daily occurrence but sometimes it turns into physical violence towards women. She sometimes hears brawling between the husband and wife but keeps her nose out of others' affairs. According to her observations, the level of physical violence has been reduced in comparison to the past. I asked her: 'Is it because of women's microcredit involvement?' She replied:

> It is difficult to say, if it is for microcredit or the wife's income I may not face violence. I have inherited property and income before joining in the microcredit programmes but I face violence.
> Q: Because of your income, can you protest against your husband's behaviour?
> Yes, it gives me the power that many others do not have. Most women take credit for their husbands. However, not everyone is the same in society – there are some good and some bad people. Some feel shame and some do not.

Fouzia told me that some men often scold and sometimes thrash their wives because of financial hardship, dowry, number of children, and if they do not find their wives beautiful. She argues that men compare their wives with other peoples' wives, which also creates dissatisfaction among the men towards their own wives. People do not like Fouzia because of her non-subordination to the expected gender roles and the set of behaviours ascribed to women in society. She is regarded as domineering by many other villagers. Fouzia informs me that some people treat her as a masculine woman (*beta mohila*).

Does credit mitigate domestic violence?

The abuse of wives is commonplace in the areas where this study was conducted. Of 137 respondents (with the exception of 14 widows), 48 per cent of women confirmed that their husbands often scolded them, but that they were seldom physically assaulted by their husbands. Generally, the young wives were more likely to be abused by their husbands than the elder women.

I also found that there is a generational difference in the way in which women view domestic violence. Some elderly women justify husbands' violence by stating that the men may be more bad-tempered because they work outside the home with different kinds of people. They earn money and feed the family, so they have right to control their wives or to speak harshly. They think that when a husband speaks angrily to his wife, it is always better that the wife remains silent or does not respond. These women believe that a wife should understand her husband's moods and behave accordingly. As a wife always stays at home, she should be calm and quiet. She should perform all her household duties according to her husband's wishes. Besides, they think that when a men and women live together, there may be some collision but a woman should be patient because it is a great virtue for a woman to have a successful conjugal family life. Many women do not understand these objectives, so they are frequently abused by their husbands.

Some wives do not perceive verbal violence as abnormal. Sometimes the mother-in-law instigates the abusive behaviour of her son by complaining about his wife's disobedient behaviour, back-biting, not taking care of her in-laws and inadequate performance of household work. Even though mothers-in-law are not directly involved in physically assaulting their daughters-in-law, they may play a pivotal role in some bouts of violence because most of the time husbands listen to their mothers.

Violence is not just gender-based. It is also, to some extent, poverty-based. Among the respondents, the borrowers from Zelegaon village were comparatively more poverty-stricken than the borrowers from Shantigaon and Nodigaon. Among 66 respondents (with the exception of ten widows from Zelegaon) approximately 54.5 per cent (N = 36) confirmed that their husbands often scolded them and sometimes beat them. However, in Nodigaon and Shantigaon they numbered 49 per cent and 40 per cent, respectively.

Study respondents had mixed opinions about whether microcredit involvement has reduced domestic violence against women. Abdur Rahim is a microcredit borrower's husband and an old man (*local murubbi*) from Shantigaon who got involved in local arbitration (*shalish*). Abdur Rahim thinks that physical violence towards women in general has declined to some extent because people have become aware of it through watching television and listening to the radio, and they know about government laws. Moreover, people, particularly the victimized women, rarely speak up publicly because of the shame and disgrace it would bring upon them. Rahim does not think that micro-loans per se have reduced violence against women. However, he observed that husbands and wives used to quarrel more frequently about microcredit instalment repayments and he joined these arbitrations but nowadays it seldom happens because the husbands understand well that if their wives do not get credit, they will not be able to obtain funds for their petty businesses, agricultural work or other household activities.

Unlike Rahim, some respondents believe that violence, specifically physical violence, has declined due to the penetration of microcredit programmes in their areas. They argue that microcredit programmes have partially reduced intense economic pressure and tension in the home, so violence towards women has declined in the rural areas. Aysha (see above), who runs a nakshi-kantha business, reported that she does not face any violence because she has an understanding with her husband. She believes that if two parties live under the same roof some altercations may happen, but it should never turn into severe arguments. Previously, there was abject poverty in her area, so she saw that husbands and wives frequently had altercations, which often turned into physical violence towards wives. According to her, when the men have no money to spend and no food in their bellies their heads do not work properly.

About 25 per cent of the study respondents claimed that patriarchal violence (both verbal and physical) towards women has declined owing to the microcredit programmes. The women who invested credit themselves or jointly with their husbands faced less or no violence towards them. Micro-credit involvement has brought about change at the personal level in the form of increased self-worth. At the level of the household, these women are helped by increased resources, which led to declining levels of economic tension and pressure; consequently, they rarely faced violence. About 9 per cent of respondents claimed that microcredit programmes have helped to increase verbal violence against women because the male household members often pressurize women into taking loans but they rarely think about credit repayment instalments. However, most women (65 per cent) do not agree that domestic violence against wives has declined due to the involvement of microcredit programmes. As Jackson (1996: 501) argues, poverty policies (for example, microcredit programmes) may not help to tackle gender issues because the subordination of women is not caused by poverty. The social forces that create poverty are not synonymous with those that create gender disadvantages.

Based on the in-depth interviews, it was found that gender violence has a different logic from poverty. The women attributed various reasons for violence against them such as husbands' financial hardship and frustrations, disruptive children, and dislike. Nonetheless, one of the most important causes they repeatedly emphasized is the inherent flaw or fault disposition of the males in society that does not stem from poverty. My findings suggest that the husbands expressed their flaws through short tempers and by exercising power over their wives. The husbands have often used filthy language against both their wives and their wives' parents when they shouted at their wives. They abuse their wives mentally, verbally and physically. They take advantage of their more powerful position in society socially, culturally as well as religiously. Thus, from my perspective the husbands' fault disposition is embodied in their language, thoughts and actions. When a wife challenges her husband's role it means that she challenges her husband's role, masculinity and position within the family structure. Moore, for instance, notes that 'the relations of domination and subordination which are at the base of gender inequalities within the household cannot be explained as a simple outcome of economic inequalities … gender relations are always involved with power' (1991: 8–9).

Some wives who have independent incomes (e.g. Fouzia) have challenged their husbands' violent attitude towards them but the majority of the respondents seldom protested because if they did their husbands might become angrier and consequently they would have to face even more violence, and in extreme cases the marriage could end. Most women who face violence claim that they tolerate violence by holding their tongues because they believe that women have no standing in Bangladeshi society. Many of the women's narratives demonstrate that women use 'the weapons of the weak'[4] (Scott, 1985) including crying, refusing to eat on one or two consecutive occasions, and not communicating with their husbands. They rarely seek help from their neighbours because of the shame and disgrace it brings upon them. Sometimes the neighbours come forward to help and stop the physical violence temporarily. When a wife faces severe violence, generally she informs her natal family (e.g. Pearun) but such action does not challenge the patriarchal norms and structures of society (Vatuk, 2006).[5] Generally, the natal family and local elders (*murubbi*) or a union council member arranges arbitration to accommodate both parties or pacify the situation. By focusing on the social and cultural values of society, they often advise both parties to adjust. If a woman leaves her conjugal family, her natal family often considers her a burden and frequently blames her. Consequently, the woman also feels guilty.

Fertility practices

Bangladesh is one of the poorest and most highly populated countries in the world. The rapidly growing population poses tremendous challenges for Bangladesh. Its population density (964 inhabitants per square kilometre) is the highest in the world and is a drain on the country's resources. The current population of Bangladesh numbers approximately 164 million, and the population growth rate is 1.34 per cent (UNFPA, 2010; BBS, 2011). In spite of this worrying trend, the Bangladesh Family Planning Programme is considered a global 'success story' (Uusikylä, 2000). The country has experienced marked increases in the prevalence of contraceptive use, from 3 per cent to 45 per cent since the country's independence in 1971 and a significant decline in fertility, from 6.3 births per woman in 1975 to 2.7 births per woman in 2007 (BDHS, 2007; Cleland *et al.*, 1994; MHPC, 1978: 73).

Some researchers have argued that microcredit programmes have reduced women's financial vulnerability, strengthened their position within their families, pulled them into the public arena, and exposed them to new ideas. Thus, they argued that credit programmes may have decreased the desire to have children, increased demand for family planning services and thereby reduced the social costs of fertility regulation for women (Bernasek, 2003). Some statistical studies have already revealed an association between women's exposure to credit programmes and contraceptive use in Bangladesh (Schuler *et al.*, 1997b; Khandker and Latif, 1995; Schuler and Hashemi, 1994; Amin *et al.*, 1994). Schuler and Hashemi (1994) revealed that GB influences contraceptive use by promoting family planning norms and argued that GB model microcredit programmes can play an important role in accelerating a fertility transition throughout the country. The study found that 59 per cent of GB borrowers had used contraceptives compared with 43 per cent of the control group. A subsequent study by Schuler *et al.*, (1997b) found that the GB credit programme still had a positive and significant effect on contraceptive use. The next section of the text examines the way in which microcredit relates to fertility and contraception. Do the female microcredit borrowers in my study areas give birth or use contraceptives in the same manner as in other parts of Bangladesh?

Having a big family as a norm

Zamila (40 years old) is one of the oldest GB borrowers of Zelegaon. Her husband Abul (50 years old) is illiterate. He is a day labourer but frequently cannot find work. The family lives in a small two-room tin-roofed house. The walls of the house are made of dilapidated bamboo matting. Abul has no cultivable land. He owns 24 decimals of homestead land, but can use only 5 decimals because the house was built on a small hill. As a result, the family will not be able use the land to enlarge the house in future either. The family uses a *katcha* (unsanitary) ring latrine and fetches drinking water from their neighbours. Zamila has been taking micro-loans from GB for the last 14 years. Her sons have invested credit at different times in different businesses including vegetables and rice business but have not done well in any of their enterprises. Her husband never used credit because he found it too problematic. The family's financial situation is dismal. Zamila explained it thus:

> We are now caught in a vicious cycle of loans: loans from NGOs, loans from relatives and neighbours. We pay credit instalments through frequent starvation. People misbehave towards us; they use abusive language because we cannot repay their loans on the due date. If I ever take a loan from the NGO it takes a long time to repay. I do not like this situation but what can we do? Now our relatives no longer give us loans. Allah makes us poor; it is not in our hands.

Zamila got married when she was just 14 years old. She gave birth to her first child after she had been married for just over a year. She has never used any contraception, and during the past 26 years of her conjugal life she has been pregnant 13 times, and given birth to ten sons and three daughters. None of her children have completed a primary school education. The first son (25 years old) and the third son (20 years old) are masons, and the second son (22 years old) works as a salesman for a local company and earns only TK 1,000 per month. The fourth and fifth children (daughters) are 18 and 17 years old respectively, and are unmarried. The remainder of her children range between two to 14 years of age. I asked Zamila whether the microcredit NGO officials or other borrowers have ever asked her about family planning methods. She replied:

> For me the main purpose of going to the GB centre is to get the loan. The GB official never talked about this matter. They gave me loans and I paid the instalments. If I could not pay off an instalment I requested that I could pay the following week with a fine. This is the relationship between the bank and me, nothing more.

Zamila is aware that people may argue that two or three children are enough for a happy family but she observed that there are many women microcredit borrowers in her area who have between six and ten children. She said:

> Can you tell me who is more powerful [boro], Allah or the people? Can people create a child? Allah gives us children; they are the gift from Allah. What Allah gives us as a gift, should we spoil [nosto-kora] it? If we do so, it will be a great sin [boro-pap]. I do not think about my sons, Allah will take care of them. What can I do about their futures? Sometimes I think about my daughters because they are of marriageable age but no proposals have come yet. See, my daughters' faces look good.

That her daughters should marry at an early age is important to Zamila but she does not understand why no suitable proposal has come yet. The family decided to give household items when their children married by selling some trees. Allah gives them daughters so they have to love them and be affectionate to them. They never say that they will not give them anything. Zamila does not even let her daughters do any household work because when they go to their affinal houses they will have to work there. Zamila does not know whether or not her husband will give land to her daughters but her elder son said to me that he cannot see where this land will come from. Zamila also could not explain how her 10 sons will reside on this small piece of land. She only says, 'Allah will provide'.

Of the 151 married respondents, Zamila was not an exceptional case. Like Zamila, there were 42 women (55.3 per cent) out of 76 women from Zelegaon, 18 women (48.6 per cent) out of 37 women from Nodigaon, and 13 women (34.2 per cent) out of 38 women from Shantigaon villages who had between five and 13 living children. Women were married off very young in Zelegaon, Nodigaon and Shantigaon villages. I asked all the respondents interviewed for this study how old they were when they were first married, and the mean age at marriage was 16.6 years. Girls' early marriages are still common in Bangladesh. UNICEF (2011: 29) reported that 74 per cent of Bangladeshi women had married before their eighteenth birthday.[6] Table 4.1 indicates the high fertility rate among the female microcredit borrowers in the three study villages.

I found that many women who have large families continue to hope for male children and do not view them as a burden to the family. However, in reality they cannot provide their children with an education or sufficient income-earning opportunities owing to scant resources. Saleha (55 years old) married at the age of 14 years. The family has only 12 decimals of homestead land but no cultivable land. Saleha's husband had a fish business but he died four years ago. The family has been taking microcredit for the last ten years. Like many people in Zelegaon, Saleha's financial situation was not good but this did not deter the couple from bearing one child after another. During 40 years of marriage she bore nine sons and two daughters. Now she has seven sons and one daughter, the daughter being the youngest. Three children died just after birth.

From a young age Saleha's sons have engaged in different types of work according to their abilities, including a fish business, truck and three-wheeler driving, running a small grocery shop, and working in a workshop. They only can write their names. 'For the poor it is not necessary to have a higher education', Saleha thinks.

Table 4.1 Mean number of births and children of microcredit borrowers in my research area

Age groups	Number of living children	Number of births
0–18	1.5	1.5
19–23	1.5	1.5
24–28	2.65	2.8
29–33	4.04	4.68
34–38	4.07	4.52
39–43	5.21	5.68
44–48	5.43	5.76
49 and above	6.38	7.52
Total	4.50	5.00

Source: Author's survey

The cost of gender preference and child mortality

Owing to the gender preference the differential treatment towards boys and girls in rural Bangladesh is almost universal. The 'power of culture' (Miller, 1981: 13) shapes family attitudes towards children and influences the different treatment of children based on gender. I asked the respondents about child preference and the ideal sequence of children born to a mother, and found that the first one should be a son (see also a study carried out in South India by Säävälä, (1997)) in. In Egypt, according to Inhorn (1996), sons bring social power to their families, and especially to women. Begetting male children in my research areas ensure a woman's strong position in her conjugal household. Failure to conceive soon after a wedding sometimes puts women in an awkward situation. If the first child is a daughter, it is considered as bad luck to some degree but when a couple already has two or three sons, another son's birth is never seen as a misfortune in this society.

Old age security or support has commonly been regarded as one of the main explanations and motivations to have so many children in South Asia and in developing societies in general (Säävälä, 1997; Datta and Nuegent, 1984; Cain, 1981; Mamdani, 1972). However, there are other reasons for having many sons in rural Bangladesh including financial support, inheritance and cultural practices. As several cross-cultural comparisons have shown, the son preference in South Asia is found to be strongest in Bangladesh, Pakistan and India, all countries with strong patriarchal structure (Bongaarts and Amin, 1997; Nag, 1991, 1976: 59–60). Moreover, these studies considered a number of factors including patrilineal descent, inheritance and patrilocal residence to explain the preference for sons over daughters. In Bangladeshi society male children are viewed as a source of security or insurance against risk in the face of socio-economic and environmental uncertainty (Ashrafun and Uddin, 2010; Cain, 1977a, 1977b, 1980, 1981, 1983). Like North India, where families strive to maximize the number of sons and minimize the number of daughters in a family (Wadley, 1993; Jeffery *et al.*, 1989: 185–188; Miller, 1981), in Bangladeshi society girls are less desirable than boys. The strong preference acts as a significant barrier to national family planning efforts in Bangladesh (Kabir *et al.*, 1994; Rahman and Da Vanzo, 1993).

Families with daughters can be expected to go on having more children in the hope of eventually producing a son. Some families in my study areas had borne many children as an result of repeated attempts to produce a son. Individual and familial desire for male children was a strong factor influencing the decision by both the husband and the wife not to use contraceptives. Maya (48 years old) married when she was 20 years old. Maya thought that she had married late. She became pregnant after two years of marriage and gave birth to a baby girl, although both her conjugal and natal families expected her to give birth to a male baby. She became a little worried, but did not totally despair. Just after one year she became pregnant again. Again she failed to give birth to a male child. Therefore she tried repeatedly for a male child and in time gave birth to four more daughters. At last, she gave birth to two sons, and now she is the mother of six daughters and two sons.

Maya has to arrange her daughters' marriages, which she considers very difficult. Maya believes that for the poor, a male child is essential. The boy can do everything inside and outside the home. When her husband died their sons were just six and four years old, respectively. However, Maya is happy that Allah gave her two sons. Without male children, who would carry on the family name and look after her in old age? Maya had been taking micro-loans from GB for over 12 years. Her husband died three years prior to the study. He worked as an agricultural labourer, and sometimes on the land. The family was never financially secure and owned only six decimals of inherited homestead land. Now Maya's family is assisted through the government Vulnerable Feeding Group plan and the negligible income derived from the tailoring work of one of her daughters.

A preference for boys was not shown by all women, and some couples wished to have a girl child when they already had sons. Raton and Shorola are Hindus from Shantigaon village and are considered to be successful microcredit borrowers. Shorola (25 years old) married when she was 15 years old. She is now the mother of four sons. At the time of the study, Shorola was trying to conceive again but when I asked her whether she wanted a boy or a girl, Shorola became embarrassed and replied that she needs a daughter. 'Only a girl can understand her mother. My husband also loves girl babies. I should respect my husband's wishes, she explained. As Minna Säävälä discovered through her study of South India:

> A mother without daughters is an object of pity by other women, although a woman without sons is a source of even worse pity. Lack of a son is regarded more as a hardship and failure to fulfil the prestigious ideals of family life and success, whereas the lack of daughters is regarded as an emotional short-coming for a family, especially for the mother.
>
> (1997: 162)

Child mortality is another factor that contributes to high fertility in the rural areas of Bangladesh. Although child mortality has declined overall in Bangladesh, I found some women microcredit borrowers in the study villages who had borne many children to cover the risk of child mortality. One of the group leaders, a 34-year-old Hindu woman, explained:

> I have only a son and a daughter. I have been pregnant five times, but my three daughters did not survive, they died during childbirth. We have been trying for more babies but we do not understand our fate. Family planning is needed for those who have many children, are poverty-stricken and cannot feed their children.

Shoani (50 years old) is one of the oldest microcredit borrowers in Shanti-gaon. She had been taking loans from GB for the past 18 years prior to the study. She married when she was 15 years old. During 35 years of marriage she had been pregnant 14 times and had given birth to 12 children. Five of her children died within one year of birth. In order to the cause of her children's deaths and to avoiding any further deaths she first consulted a *hujur* and drank *pani-pora* (blessed water). However, this did not work; she lost yet another baby during childbirth. Later, a *kabiraj* (herbalist) told her that she was under the spell of an evil spirit (*jiin/bhut*), so she wore a special amulet (*tabiz*) given to her by the *kabiraj* to protect her surviving infants and any future pregnancies and babies. She believes that by dint of the treatment of the *kabiraj* she protected seven out of 12 of her children.

Attitudes towards contraception

Contraception is a decisive factor in controlling fertility. All the respondents stated that they knew of several methods, including the pill, female sterilization, intrauterine device (IUD or coil), abortion, and withdrawal. Nonetheless, this awareness is poorly reflected in the practice or effectiveness of these methods. The majority of the respondents stated that they do not use any family planning control. Among all 151 married women (including widows and divorcees), 66.2 per cent never used any form of contraception. Among the users, 18.5 per cent women were currently using contraceptives, about 10 per cent

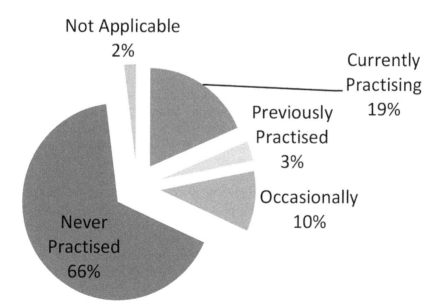

Figure 4.2 Contraceptive practices among the microcredit borrowers
Source: Author's survey

have used contraceptives occasionally, and 3.3 per cent had previously used contraceptives (see Figure 4.2).

Remarkably, none of the men whom I talked to used family planning methods. The wives who use contraceptives had talked to their husbands about contraception but their husbands had not agreed to use contraceptives themselves. However, I found that women were aware of their social-economic situation, in addition to the health and benefits of having small families. With regard to contraception, religious rules, norms and practices are not rigid for them. Indeed, they are rather flexible. Mina (25 years old) originally talked to her husband but he did not wish to use contraceptives. She now takes the pill, although it does not entirely agree with her. Another mother argued that now if they were to behave in the same way as their mothers' or grandmothers' generations, society would not change. She claimed:

> I know our hujurs are against family planning, but if we think about them we cannot look after our family. Every day my family needs TK 200–300 but my husband earns only TK 150. So I asked my husband about sterilization and he gave his consent, so I was sterilized. I was not afraid to do this; I did not look to my husband because I know that the men in this village do not like using contraceptives. I think the wives should take responsibility because if the husbands get sick due to per-manent methods [e.g. sterilization] the family will not be able to function.

Some researchers have argued that women who control money and partici-pate in family decisions have more control over reproductive behaviour (Schuler *et al.*, 1997b). I have already mentioned that only a few women use credit directly but my data suggest that they have also had many children. For example, Aysha who runs her *nakshi-kantha* embroidery business has five children. Fouzia, who has a river-dredging business, has four living children and one who died. Kamrun, who produces bamboo-cane goods with her husband, has seven children. Nazma and her husband run a small hotel shop and they have seven children. Minu, who helps her husband with his grocery business, has four children. Among them only Minu has used family planning methods, but not on a regular basis. As the majority of the study respondents do not use family planning methods, I asked them why they do not use con-traceptives. They attributed a number of reasons for not using contraceptives such as side-effects, husbands' refusal, mothers-in-law's prohibition, and reli-gious rules and regulations. For example, when Zamila (40 years old and the mother of 13 children) came as a wife to her husband's house her mother-in-law prohibited her from using contraceptives by stating, 'Never use any methods, it is not good. Allah gives children, so it should not stop. Family planning is prohibited and sinful in Islam.' Zamila's husband explained to me:

I am a pious man [foreheg-gar manush]. I pray five times and often recite the name of Allah. So I cannot do such a sinful thing [pap kaj]. If anybody does this, Allah will punish him after he dies. You will not find any *hujur* or pious men who permit their wives to use family planning methods. I heard that some people in our village use contraceptives but that is their business. I hope that when my sons and daughters marry they will also not become involved in this sinful act.

My analyses suggest that religious conviction, the negative attitude of husbands and mothers-in-law have a strong influence on fertility practices in the three studied villages. Thus, many women who might be interested in using contraception may not be allowed to do so. Although contraceptives do not always cause significant side effects (Hartman, 1987), the women interviewed in this study who occasionally used family planning methods were often put off using them owing to side effects such as bleeding, headaches and fatigue. These side effects often hindered them from carrying out their household chores. Hashi, a 30-year-old microcredit borrower from Zelegaon village, has two sons and two daughters. She has previously taken the pill but it did not suit her. She explained that if women take oral contraceptives they are aware of the potential problems associated with them. Hashi experienced a number of side effects. Once she had an episode of severe sickness and was admitted to hospital for treatment, for which she had to pay. As a result, she now avoids contraception, and her husband has turned completely against it. Hashi's case shows that it is important for women that their husbands cooperate in family planning matters. However, Hashi's husband is not a good man and did not do so. Hashi told me that she cannot pressurize her husband into using contraception. Instead, she has to respect his likes and dislikes or risk destroying the peace of the family. Ruena (30 years old) added, 'Once I used the IUD but I had severe problems with it. I experienced severe headaches and stomach pain, abnormal bleeding during menstruation, and dizziness. I could not even do my housework. My husband became angry with me. He does not like any problems. So I had it removed by the doctor.'

The family planning workers do not perform their duties satisfactorily among the impoverished, poorly educated women. Access to safe contraceptive methods with comprehensive information on benefits and risks, a full range of reproductive health services, and good medical test and back-up are still limited in rural Bangladesh (Hartman and Boyce, 1983). Unsurprisingly, women who encountered difficulties stopped contraception as soon as possible. It may be less problematic and even less costly to have another child than to have to cope with the health problems (Abdullah and Zeidenstein, 1982). According to Hartman and Boyce (ibid.), family planning workers in Bangladesh often discussed the concept of birth control but did not encourage the women to ask questions. She observed that the family planning workers showed the women pills, advised them how to use them, and talked about the

IUD and about sterilization but they neglected to tell the women about the side effects associated with these methods or how they actually worked.

Sylhet is a conservative region, where social and religious circumstances act as strong barriers against using contraceptive methods. For a few, the religious rules, norms and strictures are flexible but in most cases gender preferences, religious conviction, husbands' and in-laws' prohibitions work against the use of any method to limit the number of children born. These data on fertility practices may provide different results to those of the earlier quantitative studies on microcredit and fertility control in Bangladesh. The other studies were based on larger datasets. However, the point is that my findings are not totally unexpected or worrying, because according to government statistics fertility rates are particularly high in Sylhet. I did not find any connection between microcredit programmes and reproductive behaviour and fertility practices in the areas where this study was undertaken

Notes

1 In assessing the impact of microcredit programmes on women, researchers have used different disciplinary stances and theoretical perspectives on women's empowerment (e.g. Mahmud, 2003, 1994, 1991; Huda and Mahmud, 1998; Kabeer, 1998; Goetz and Sen Gupta, 1996; Hashemi *et al.*, 1996; Pitt and Khandker, 1995; Amin and Pebley, 1994; Zaman, 1996; Mizan, 1994; Islam-Rahman, 1986). The most frequently identified dimension is women's absolute well-being, whereby empowerment is considered to be the process of increasing the welfare of women and girls, indicated by outcomes that are compared with the present status with regard to literacy and schooling, consumption, health and nutrition, labour force participation, contraceptive use, mobility and ownership of clothing and assets. Another dimension is women's relative well-being, whereby empowerment is viewed as the process of improving the position of women relative to men within the realm of the household, and is indicated by women's involvement in intra-household decision-making processes, control over household income and assets, and control over loans, etc.
2 See also Streefland *et al.* (1986).
3 According to Giddens' theory social structures shape individuals. Individuals reciprocally shape the social structure in accordance with what he refers to as the 'duality of structure'. It is thus recognized that although individuals undertake social actions and interactions and use their knowledge in various situations, simultaneously they create and follow rules, and use resources and social relationships that are produced and reproduced in social interactions (1984: 25–6).
4 The concept has been described in detail in Chapter 7 of this book.
5 Sylvia Vatuk (2006) in a study on Domestic Violence and Marital Breakdown in India stated that 'women who are motivated to articulate and tackle tribulations through action, seek help from family, from a religious or community dispute settlement body or from the state, are rarely engaged in an effort to question the patriarchal values of their society.'
6 www.unicef.org/bangladesh/Gender_Paper_final2011Low.pdf.

5 Gender relations and hidden regulatory practice

In the previous chapter we looked at how the relationship between micro-credit and ideas of women's empowerment involves contradictory processes. We learnt that most women take credit on behalf of their husbands or other male relatives, and that men are the main users of credit. Generally, when a female borrower transfers her credit to non-family members she tries to hide this information from the NGO staff, but the transfer of credit to the husbands, sons or son-in-laws is not done covertly. The NGO officials usually know about it and do not view it negatively. As women are not the main users of credit it must be asked why NGOs offer credit through women instead of men? Is credit through women a regulatory practice? Taking Foucault's concepts of 'power', 'discipline' and 'docile bodies' as a formal structure of analysis, I examine how microcredit exploits women's vulnerable position in society and furthers the NGOs' capitalist interests. Earlier studies revealed that women microcredit borrowers do hand over credit to men but paid little attention to why they do this instead of using it for their own purposes. In this part of the study, I shall delve into those aspects of gender relations, both within the household[1] and in the wider community, which prevent women from using credit and from taking credit for themselves.

Tracing the shadows: why women cannot use credit

Many observers of Bangladeshi society conceptualize women as a homo-genous and subordinate category in terms of marriage, religion, property rights and employment practices, and treat gender relations as static (Rozario, 1992, 1998; Kotalova, 1993; Mandelbaum, 1988; Blanchet, 1984), but not in the broader social context. Sarah White (1992: 11–26) criticized international development aid for affecting economic and political relations within Bangladesh and also for treating Bangladeshi women as a homogenous category. She argues that Bangladeshi women are often considered as a 'problem' that needs solving, but are also a potential source of productive labour when correctly utilized and motivated. Similarly to Third World women, Bangladeshi women are associated with powerlessness and passivity. They are presented as passive and miserable victims of their own culture, particularly as a result of patriarchy. They are not perceived as agents who are able to manipulate circumstances to their own advantage or form a strategy with the resources they possess. White rejects the passive focus on 'female status' and favours the active emphasis of women's power. Thus, according to White (1992), the notion of the 'contested image' is useful for understanding the discourse on gender in Bangladesh. However, I concur with Gardner (1995) that compared to men in many ways rural women in Bangladesh are subordinate, dependent and have fewer opportunities to control their circumstances and strategize their available resources to their own advantages.

Of my 151 respondents, only ten women (6.6 per cent) and four women and their husbands (2.6 per cent) were involved in income-generating activities (such as the production of bamboo-cane handicrafts goods, the rice business, grocery, tailoring and embroidery) in addition to household work. Women who invest credit themselves have much in common: some have acquired skills, some are widowed, some of their husbands also do the same work, and some have married within their respective natal village. The majority of the respondents (93.4 per cent) did not use credit for their own purposes. When I asked Rahima, who has been involved in the GB microcredit programme for 18 years why this is the case, she replied:

> What will women do with credit? Can you tell me where women will use credit? Is there any place or scope in the village for women to invest their credit? There is no work for women in the village. In this village, women do household work and the men work outside of the home. Women cannot do business in the market place. It is shameful [*lojjakor*] for women. It is men's work.
> Q: Why, can't women invest credit in growing vegetables and poultry farming (such as ducks and chickens)?
> It is not possible for women to pay the weekly instalments through the sale of gourds, papayas and eggs [*lau-kodu, pepe, dim*]. Despite the fact that my husband had a fishing business in the market, we faced huge difficulties to pay the weekly credit instalments. Now my sons also face the same difficulties. The men use credit in various businesses including fishing, vegetables, groceries but they also get into deep water trying to pay the weekly instalments.

Whenever I brought up the issue as to why the majority of women do not invest credit themselves, my respondents cited a number of crucial factors, including gendered norms and the division of labour, patriarchy, women's lack of marketable skills, traditional economic limitations and the pardah[2] system, all of which may obstruct women's income-earning opportunities, restrict both their choices and ability to carry out business in the marketplace and their autonomous decision-making capacity. These factors lead to their dependence on men.

The majority of the study respondents (93.4 per cent) spend their days at home carrying out chores such as cooking, cleaning, childcare, fuel processing, poultry farming, and so on. Most observers of Bangladeshi society (Todd, 1996; Gardner, 1995) also arrive at the same conclusion that women in rural Bangladesh work extremely hard within their homesteads. Despite the fact that women spend nearly all of their time carrying out household activities, their input has received little attention. Since women's work is seen as part of the normal household activities it is considered as having no remunerative monetary value.

Many studies have explored how women in rural areas do agricultural work but no women microcredit borrowers in this study ever participated in agricultural work in the field. Gardner's (1995) observations from the same region support my findings about women not working in the field. I found that a few women in the village of Zelegaon once worked as earth-cutters (*mati-kata sromik*) due to severe economic hardship. Since the work beyond the homestead domain is culturally and religiously undesirable for women, most women avoid such work and will deny ever having done this kind of work. They considered this work as disgraceful for rural women. Suchona, a microcredit borrower from Zelegaon, sometimes worked as an earth-cutter:

Yes, I once faced severe financial difficulties due to the sudden death of my husband, so I worked as an earth-cutter. I have experience of how people evaluate women when they see them working outside the home. People treated me as a lower category [chotolok] poor woman; they thought that as I have neither husband nor elder sons I am obliged to do this work. If a woman does work at the roadside or in the fields people treat her as a brazen woman ... Suppose that a woman has a young daughter, and she works outside the house, she will find it very difficult to arrange her daughter's marriage. I think it is better for women to work in the homestead area.

The gendered occupational structure is omnipresent among the microcredit borrowers of the villages studied. The rigorously applied gender-specific roles limit women's work to household activities. While the men are expected to undertake agricultural or other income-generating activities, women of all ages agree that their daily role is to carry out typical household chores for the benefit of the family. As a result of the prevailing patriarchal structure and gender-specific roles in Bangladeshi society household responsibilities fall to women. This may also cultivate 'the deepest sense of what one is' (Goffman, 1977: 315). Thus, rural women prefer to introduce themselves as housewives.

As mentioned above, some of the respondents are involved in income-generating activities in addition to household chores but generally these women identify themselves as housewives. They work at home or in homestead and to a large extent they are unable to challenge the traditional gender norms or boundaries and relations of the wider community through their work. The innermost feeling of most of the women is that housework is designated for women. Occasionally, some of the husbands help their wives but it is unusual in the rural setting for a man to do household chores. The gendered division of labour in production and economic activities affects the way credit is used. As Montgomery et al. pointed out: 'Women borrowing cash and generating cash income tend towards a contradiction of existing norms' (1996: 99). Local patriarchies and social status shape allocative behaviour and constrain women's access to income-generating activities (Kabeer, 1996, 2001).

The respondents often claimed that although the NGOs channel credit through women they never specify that women must use credit for themselves. They argued that in fact NGOs give credit to a family. Often women justify this gender division of labour by referring to the customs and traditions of Bangladeshi society and the distinction between indoor and outdoor work. They argue that women should occupy themselves with household chores (*ghor-sangsarer kaj* or *ghorer kaj*) or work indoors (*bitore*), while men should focus on outdoor work (*bairer kaj*) as they are the sole breadwinners and are responsible for generating an income for the household. Social norms discourage and even prevent women from working outside of the home, and restrict their presence in public spaces, ideologically characterizing them as dependents and men as breadwinners (Agarwal, 1997: 16). According to Islamic law, 'Man is the earner and woman is the server of man' (Cain *et al.*, 1979: 407). Islamic law 'clearly states that men and women have their own spheres of activity: a scheme of functional division in accord with their respective natural dispositions and inherent physical and psychological qualities and characteristics' (ibid.). Many women microcredit borrowers consider the existing gender role as follows:

> Women must do household work. We have always known this. Parents do not like their daughters to work outside the house before marriage and following marriage neither the husbands nor the in-laws (*shashur-shashuri*) like the housewives (*ghorer bou*) to work outside the house. As children grow older they do not like that mothers to work outside the house because it brings social disgrace to the family.
>
> (Minara)

Another woman added:

> Our society has some rules [niyam-niti] for men and women. It is very important for a woman to perform *pardah*. No husband wants his wife to work in the fields. If anybody supports this idea he must answer to Allah. The NGO officers are well aware that the women cannot use credit themselves, so when they give credit to a woman they ask about her about her husband's income and that of other family members.

The gendered division of work may be relaxed due to special circumstances, local understanding of class and status hierarchies. For example, when I asked Abdur Rahim (a microcredit borrower's husband and a financially well-off man from Shantigaon) whether women from this village work outdoors he stated:

> The women from poor and lower status families may sometimes leave the homestead area in order to work but in my area I do not see them working in the fields or by the side of the main road. Women from good and financially well-off families [bhadra-ghorer *meye manush*] always try to adhere to the *pardah* norms and *izzat-shaman* [honour and status] of the family. They never work in the public space [*barir baire*], it does not look good. People do not view it positively.

The female micro-borrowers and their husbands often describe themselves as poor (gorib-manush) but they do not view themselves as *chotolok* (people of lowly status). As Spivak (1996: 339) points out, the subalterns are the creation of the elite. During my fieldwork in the village of Zelegaon, I talked to some women who sometimes brought their goats to the roadside in their *para* where they collected arum leaves and straw. They considered such tasks as household work (sangsarer *kaj*). They argued that due to the needs of the family/household sometimes women from poor families have work outside the house otherwise the conjugal household will not run properly. However, they claim that they generally work within the same bari. Among the respondents there is a broad consensus that work within the homestead area is dignified and suitable for a woman. They explained that occasionally they work outside of their hamlets when the male household members are unavailable, absent or unwell. It is considered indecent for a housewife to work in the fields or by the roadside as it destroys the family's status and honour.

Women's acceptance of the gender division of work is not always a direct manifestation of patriarchy but rather a sign of adherence to status, norms, and familial and communal codes of conduct. Female demeanour acts as a decisive factor to the construction of male honour throughout South Asia, the Middle East, and the Mediterranean (Abu-Lughud, 1986; Pitt-Rivers, 1977; Schneider, 1971; Dobkin, 1967). As Henrietta Moore wrote, 'Women are the guardians of male honour, and because of this, they themselves need to be guarded' (1988: 107 cited in Gardner, 1995: 218). Fruzzetti (1990: 125) notes that the status of the male family members is reflected in women's status, but reciprocally women's code of conduct also serves men's status. In fact, women use the *ghor-sangsarer kaj* to refer to everyday family life, household duties, and domestic work as a broad sense of *sangsar*. According to Fruzzetti, it is 'the world of everyday life encompassing locality, relatives, and sentiments' (1990: 129). My ethnographic data suggest that outdoor work or work undertaken beyond the household domain in the rural communities does not harmonize with social traditions, social customs and the concept of the housewife (*ghorer bou*). Gender disparity is deeply rooted in social culture, as reflected in the respondents' statements:

> I do not need to work outside. I need two meals in a day and to live with maan-sanman [honour and prestige].
>   Allah makes us poor but it does not mean that I have to do work outside the home. If it is necessary I will eat one meal in a day, but I will not work outdoors. What will people say if I work with men by the roadside or in the village market?

Only a few of the microcredit borrowers have broken the gender-based segregation of labour and become the sole family breadwinners. Fouzia has a river-dredging business behind her house, Aysha produces and sells *nakshi-kanthas,* and widows Kamrun and Mayarun produce bamboo-cane handicrafts in their household domain, as well as looking after their families. However, all the respondents agreed that outdoor work such as agricultural production beyond the homestead, care of cattle and other livestock in public areas, fishing in the river, selling items or doing business in the village market or the weekly bazaar are exclusively jobs for men. I asked Fouzia how she runs her river-dredging business, and she replied that in order for her business to function she employs workers. Her business involves lifting sand from the river bed and selling it. Sometimes she faces problems, but she finds positives in the fact that her father was also involved in this business. As she married within her native village she knows everybody. More importantly, the river runs just behind her house. She wears an *urna* (a piece of cloth worn by women to veil their head and face), so that nobody can criticize her for immodesty. She explains that rural people do not like their wives or daughters working outside the house. Fouzia points out that most women in her area have no skills or knowledge so they could not use credit for themselves. Some women can do embroidery and tailoring but they cannot get work in the village. I asked her how women use credit, and she said:

> NGOs only give credit through women but they do not consider how women might use the credit. If they offered some training then women could take credit for their own use and produce something in their homestead areas. Moreover, the men should change their attitude towards women in society. Our husbands think that their wives must stay at home and take care of his children and other members of the family.

The pardah system in the rural area has governed the economic mobility of women and structured inequality through limiting access to the public sphere such as local markets, agricultural fields. As mentioned above, the homestead domain is by and large considered a female sphere. The manifestations of *pardah* may not be static but most scholars refer to it as a complex social institution, which is ideologically, economically and sexually linked to the division of labour. It restricts women's movement and economic autonomy, and imposes and corroborates the domination and dependence of women upon men (Gardner, 1995, 1998; Sharma, 1980; Jeffery, 1979; Cain *et al.*, 1979; Papanek, 1973). Paradoxically, separating the male and female domains of economic activity strengthens their interdependence. Ideas of female modesty also imply that women require protection and shelter from men (Jeffery, 1979: 13). It is clear that rural women cannot imagine themselves as traders or business women. They believe that the marketplace is for men to run their businesses.

Pardah in the research area is physically expressed by the use of a *burqa* (full veil), an urna, or a *sarir achol* held across the face and head. In their studies carried out in Pakistan and Sylhet, Bangladesh, respectively, Farida Shaheed (1998) Gardner (1998) observed that like other religious practices, *pardah* is integrated into women's everyday routines and practices. Although it is difficult to draw boundaries between 'religious' and 'social' practices of Muslim ideology (ibid.), for the microcredit borrowers *pardah* is more a social/cultural practice than a religious one. When I asked the microcredit borrowers interviewed for this study whether they always prayed five times a day, most said no. They explained: 'If you are poor good things do not always come to mind.' However, when I asked whether they adhere to the *pardah* system they all replied that when taking trips outside the village they wear the *burqa*, and in the village at the very least they cover their heads with their *sarir achols*. In public discourse, this practice relates to women's shame and honour. Women are criticized if they do not practise *pardah*. I learnt that to the female microcredit borrowers *pardah* does not mean merely covering the body or head or lowering one's eyes, but also the internal state of modesty, purity and honour which dictate the boundaries of their relationships with men who are not members of their family. Fouzia, from Nodigaon village frequently travels alone in connection with her river-dredging business and claims that she does not always wear the burqa or *urna* in the correct manner but that does not mean that she is irreligious, shameless or immodest. According to Fouzia, 'suppose that I always wear the *burqa* but my mind is not pure while I am wearing it, what if I were to conduct an illicit relationship with a man – would there be any point in wearing the *burqa*? It is important to ensure that one's mind is pardah. In our society some well-off women wear expensive *burqas or urnas* to display their wealth – they are not always good people.' Another woman who works as a domestic assistant stated that 'there is no value in wearing the *burqa* if women are not conscious of their modes of behaviour, and the manner in which they conduct relationships with men'.

Women's geographical mobility is, to a large extent, closely related to local understanding of religion, social class, status, age and also place of residence. In comparison to the female microcredit borrowers from Nodigaon village (which is situated near to the peri-urban area and next to the main road) have more geographical mobility in comparison to the borrowers from Shantigaon and Zelegaon. The mobility of the Muslim female microcredit borrowers is more restricted than that of the Hindu women. Women from poor families who cover their heads with their *sarir achols* move around freely within their *bari* or sometimes from one *bari* to another as easily as financially well-off women. Elderly women may travel alone more freely beyond their own neighbourhood without loss of status compared to other groups such as young girls, newly married women and middle-aged women.[3] Nevertheless, the phenomenon of women moving and interacting outside the home has to some extent increased due to the improvement in road communications, the introduction of mobile phone networks, and the involvement of the NGOs. Rural women usually visit shopping centres, the doctor or the parental home with their husbands or sons, but nowadays some women also visit their parental homes alone in the event of an emergency. I observed that after veiling themselves with an urna or *burqa* women go to the roadside shops or to the city and share three-wheelers with strangers, but they avoid the weekly bazaar. As a result they cannot directly sell their products in the bazaar, which is the best place for selling their wares and getting the best price. Similarly, some widows produce bamboo-cane goods but as they have no male family members they cannot sell their products in the market place. Consequently, buyers (or middlemen) visit their houses in order to purchase their products but unfortunately they do not pay fair prices.

The micro-loan system is structured by a neoliberal ideology, which at the individual level includes the cultivation of the rational economic actor who is logical, goal-oriented, and makes strategic choices about a variety of directions, strategies and tools with which to respond to the problems and challenges in his or her surroundings, and in ways that make intelligent use of existing resources (McDonald, 1999; Gordon, 1991). As a result, a major disjuncture takes place between microcredit policy, practices and the inherent structure of local female borrowers. Micro-loans rely heavily on strict repayment schedules (see Chapter 7 in this volume). The individual borrower is responsible for ensuring that repayments are made on time. I suggest that most women do not take credit to invest themselves owing to gender-specific norms, their lack of marketable skills, investment capacity and technical knowledge. Most poor women are afraid to take loans to invest themselves because they are concerned about their inability to pay the weekly instalments. Microcredit practitioners claim that by organizing and providing financial assistance in the form of credit to rural women, they can help to nurture responsibility, earning potential, independence and confidence. I argue that because micro-loan programmes do not offer any training for women to acquire business skills, self-confidence and positive self-image, they fail to prepare women to confront the challenges of credit investment in rural areas. Encouraging women to take loans without imparting entrepreneurial skills translates into keeping women in their prevailing state of economic vulnerability and social marginalization instead of turning them into economic actors and part of the mainstream economy.

The respondents often lamented that barely profitable businesses, largely traditional income-generating activities such as livestock-rearing, selling eggs, producing vegetables such as gourds and papaya in the homestead areas do not yield sufficient profit for paying the weekly instalments. Some respondents informed me that they operate a tailoring business from their homes but the demand for tailoring activities in one rural village is not enough to pay instalments. As a result, credit has the potential to trap women in a cycle of indebtedness. Research suggests that microenterprises owned by women are the most successful in alleviating poverty when economic opportunities exist (Jain, 1996; Todd, 1996). However, women's access to income-earning opportunities or entry into public domain businesses (for example, the local bazaar) and also transgressing gender-specific norms and culture make it difficult for most women in rural Bangladesh.

Microcredit programmes have ignored or discounted the accepted gendered practices, the reality of women's lives and the larger infrastructural conditions that impinge on the ability of women to invest credit in the rural area. They are not looking to change the gendered practices and norms but to integrate women into the existing sociocultural structures. Goetz and Sen Gupta (1996: 59) argue that women's exclusion from markets is perhaps the greatest constraint to their productivity. It means that they lose control of a critical phase of the production process and are unable to make informed assessments of market demands and new productive opportunities. Although I agree with the authors on this point, in my opinion improving women's access to markets is not in itself a sufficient condition for women to use or invest their credit. With the exception of a few (ten out of 151 married women in this study), most women have no marketable skills. Consequently, both the development of training and marketable skills in handicraft production, embroidery, sewing and tailoring, and the provision of access to the market are crucial for the optimum use of microcredit by women. The NGOs could also help the borrowers to sell or market their products to ensure that they receive fair prices for their products. There would be even greater potential for change if women were offered training in more lucrative fields such as the provision of solar technology, information and communications technology (ICT), waste management and mobile telephony. Initiative is needed to increase women's awareness, and to alter the sociocultural and structural constraints as well as the gender norms in society because in many cases women's inefficiency is maintained and reinforced by these sociocultural beliefs and gender norms. So far, the microcredit programmes of Bangladesh have not taken any initiatives to address the above issues, thus most women cannot use credit or they do not feel comfortable taking credit for their own enterprises.

Credit for women as a covert regulatory practice

The GB credit programme in Bangladesh initially offered credit to men and women alike, and had the foresight to ensure that at least 50 per cent of its clients were women (Yunus, 1997). Until 1984 membership was fairly evenly distributed between men and women (Hossain, 1988), but in the mid-1980s the bank changed its policy and began to focus on women. BRAC's micro-credit policy has also concentrated on women. At present, about 97 per cent of GB borrowers and 98 per cent of BRAC borrowers are women. Commenting on the long struggle to ensure that GB's micro-loans reach women rather than their husbands Muhammad Yunus stated, 'Grameen has come a long way since then. Now Grameen lends money to husbands, but only through the wives. The principal borrower remains the wife' (Yunus and Jolis, 1998: 91). Commenting on the rationale of the GB programme to focus on women, Yunus argued, 'Women go through hunger and poverty in much more severe ways than are experienced by men. Women have to reside in their homes and handle the family with virtually nothing to manage with. Given the opportunity to fight against poverty and hunger women turn out to be natural and better fighters than men' (1994: 40–41). In fact, Yunus's arguments and those of the World Bank are intertwined: investing in women is critical for poverty reduction, it speeds economic development by increasing productivity and promoting a more efficient use of resources; it produces significant social returns, improves child survival and reduces fertility; and it has considerable intergenerational payoffs (World Bank, 1994: 22). However, in reality most women do not take credit to invest themselves, rather, they take credit for their men who are able to invest it in local settings and are able to derive an income from their businesses that supports the entire family. The NGOs are also aware that men are the main users of credit, so why do they give credit through women instead of giving it directly to men? Is credit channelled through women to ensure a covert regulatory practice?

Through ethnographic research Rahman (1999, 2001) and Karim (2008) investigated the reasons for which NGOs provide credit through women. According to Rahman (1999, 2001), although GB has argued that its 'public transcript' is poverty alleviation and gender empowerment, there is a 'hidden transcript', which is the patriarchal and hegemonic exploitation of poor women by men and even by wealthier women. Similarly, Karim (2008) analysed the role of gender in the expansion of globalization and neoliberalism in Bangladesh. In particular, she showed how Bangladeshi rural women's notions of honour and shame are instrumentally appropriated by microcredit organizations in the advancement of their capitalist interests. In my opinion, the issue still needs more detailed investigation. While analysing my study data on why NGOs provide credit through women, I found that the respondents repeatedly noted their restricted geographical mobility, structurally weak position and social passivity (i.e. shyness, shame and modesty) in Bangladeshi society. For grounding my analysis, I briefly discussed Foucault's concepts of power, discipline and docile bodies.

In Foucault's view, power and visibility are entangled, these cannot be detached: 'Power is exercised by virtue of things being known and people being seen' (Foucault cited in Townley, 1993: 520). For Foucault, people under constant surveillance have a tendency to internalize that gaze, transform their behaviour and question their identity in order to be consistent with a given social norm (Dryburgh and Fortin, 2010: 96). What is significant about the panopticon, an architectural model of an ideal jail which aimed at close surveillance that was invented by Jeremy Bentham at the end of the eighteenth century, is that it aims to stimulate individuals to exercise surveillance over one another. To make this possible, it is necessary to create an environment of constant surveillance for giving the impression to the targeted population that somebody is always monitoring them. Surveillance is omnipresent in different institutions and places of contemporary society. In fact, Foucault mentions that surveillance and disciplinary technology are oriented towards the human body and seek to control and discipline it and to create good citizens. He argued that the purpose of disciplinary social institutions and surveillance mechanisms are to produce 'docile and useful bodies' (1977: 231). For Foucault 'a body is docile [and] may be subjected, used, transformed and improved' (ibid.: 136). Thus Foucault's work on discipline shows how the body is socially produced through regimes of knowledge and power (*dispositif*) [4] and is therefore a cultural, rather than a natural, entity (McNay, 1999: 96).

Aroti is a local union council member from Shantigaon village. She had been taking credit for the past eight years from GB and also BRAC. At a glance her financial circumstances and education (she attained tenth grade) are better than that of many other microcredit borrowers. When I asked Aroti why NGOs give credit through women, she told me without any hesitancy that:

> The main goal of NGOs is to lend money with interest and recover it on the due date. So the NGO personnel are well aware from whom they collect their instalments without difficulty. NGOs in my area do not get involved with other activities. NGO personnel never discuss why they give credit to women. When sanctioning a loan, they demand the wives' names so the husbands use their wives' names in the loan applications. Sometimes people also use their sisters' or mothers' names.

Aroti thinks that there are two reasons for which NGOs give loans through women: first, to increase family income; and second, NGO staff can easily contact women. Over the years she has noticed that women are afraid of the NGO officials and understands the reasons for this; they also obey the NGOs rules and regulations. When I asked her if she also feels shame and fears the NGO officials, she replied:

> To some extent, I am different from the others: I live in my native village and I am also a union council member in this area. I work with both men and women, but if I failed to pay the instalments or did not follow the NGOs' rules, they will say this woman does not keep her word. If that

happened, it would bring great shame upon me. So, I have to be careful to maintain my own esteem. Actually, NGOs execute their activities according to the rules; we are only taking money from them with interest.

Unlike Aroti, only a few women pointed out that microcredit is given to women to promote women's status in society. For example, Fouzia asserts that banks give credit to women because 'when a woman earns money through the use of credit, she can easily spend it on herself and in support of her family. She can talk loudly in the house. It gives her strength of mind.'

The majority of this study's respondents agreed that microcredit NGOs offer credit through women because women's mobility is restricted. Women are tied to the home. This indicates a sense of belonging, which develops through the 'rites of passage' such as birth and then marriage. Their addresses are fixed: they either remain with their natal families or in their affinal families' houses. The NGOs record both addressess. 'They keep our fathers' [*baba*] and also the husbands' [swamir *bari*] home addresses,' claimed Chayarun. Microcredit organizations, the guarantors and the group leaders can easily find out where women are located, track their movements, and keep them under close observation or even constant surveillance, which is not always possible in the case of men. They explain that if a man does not make a credit instalment payment by the due date, he can easily escape from harassment by the loan collector by taking shelter at the house of a relative or friend in other area. However, if the debtor is a woman, she cannot go into hiding because she has to care for her children and family. Women inter-viewed for this study asked where they would go if they left their husbands, families and children. Moreover, they asked that what people would say if a woman were to run away. Thus, by giving credit through female microcredit personnel can easily avoid difficulties in recovering credit. The following statements exemplify women's views:

> The men always work outdoors; they do not remain in one place [kono *thikana nai*]. It is very difficult for the NGO staff to find them and recover any unpaid instalments. Women are always at home.
>
> (Chayarun, 35 years old)

According to Amina:

> The banks do not give loans to men because they fear that they might not find the man when the instalment is due. In giving credit through women the officers do not face any difficulties, although they cannot search a woman [mohilader *khujte hoy na*] in order to recover any instalments.

However, my respondents also claimed that women are more sincere and trustworthy than men. For example, Minu thinks that NGOs give credit through women because women do not waste the loaned money. According to Minu, women try to use credit through the agency of their husbands. Women always think how to pay their instalments on the due date. However, men waste money by chewing betel and smoking cigarettes or idling. Minu argued that the NGOs believe that women invest the loans properly, and thus increase the family income. As a result, the NGOs can easily recover their credit.

It is important to consider the prevailing social norms, cultural values and rural women's modesty and passive characters. The attributes of shyness, submissiveness, shame and modesty (*lojja-sharam*) are deeply embodied in the values of society.

The study respondents explained that if a woman talks loudly or does not maintain *shalinota* (modesty or decorum) people may speak rudely of her and call her a 'man-woman' (*beta-mohila*) for example, or they may say that such a woman lacks shame and is brazen. They argue that local women possess a more acute sense of shame and modesty than men. The news of a woman's transgression in a local rural setting rapidly spreads throughout the community. If a woman experiences rough behaviour from an NGO official or if an NGO official scolds a woman in front of other women owing to her failure to pay a credit instalment on the due date, it causes great shame and disgrace for that woman. In order to avoid this, women always try to pay their credit instalments in time. Most commentators on Bangladesh agree that shyness, shame, modesty, submissiveness are closely intertwined with women's position and status in rural Bangladeshi society (Rahman, 1999, 2001; Kotalova, 1993; Abecasis, 1990; Kabeer, 1998; Mandelbaum, 1988; Feldman and McCarthy, 1983; Arens and Van Beurden, 1977). Even though Islam advocates the equal status of men and women, some of its practices and behavioural restrictions contribute to the gender gap. As Feldman and McCarthy (1983: 951) note, the Islamic dictum for women to be 'shy and have shame' has lead to the rule of showing reverence to the elders by being quiet and keeping one's head covered in their presence. Having shame refers to appropriate behaviour in relations with others so that a wife does not jeopardize the prestige of her husband's family. Society demands that women 'act in accord with their own ascribed behavioural code' (Kotalova, 1993: 85).

Rahim (52 years old) is married to a microcredit borrower from Shantigaon. He told me that the women in his village and the nearby villages are modest and humble (*lojjashil*). Until just a few years ago neither Hindu nor Muslim women uttered their father-in-laws' names in front of their husbands. For example, if their father-in-law's name is *suruj* (sun), a woman would never say *sujja utache* (the sun rises) rather they say *aftab utache* (*aftab* means sun in Bengali). Rahim observes that some changes have occurred in Bangladeshi villages due to the influence of television and the media but women's humility is still prevalent in village life and is considered to be a very important attribute for a woman (*lojja narir vushun*). Rahim argued that as locals the NGO officials are also conscious of the submissive character of women. They find women easy to handle, which might not be the case if they had to deal with men.

In fact, shame and modesty are an integral part of being a woman in rural Bangladesh. To some extent all Bangladeshi women aspire to these codes of behaviour, which regulate their demeanour and voice in their daily interactions; they are learned, taught and are not 'detached from the body' (Bourdieu, 2002: 218) or thoughts. In rural society a woman's shame and modesty can be observed in many ways such as in her manner of sitting, talking, laughing, movement, bodily gestures, and the lowering of her eyes etc. They are maintained through personal behaviour and often define how women should conduct themselves. For example, if a woman gossips, laughs, or talks loudly or makes direct eye contact or quarrels with strange men people generally treat her as a shameless or immodest woman. Owing to shame and modesty a woman must 'exert some control over the guise in which [she] appears before others' (Goffman, 1975: 28). As a result, shame and modesty restrict women's ability to bargain or negotiate their rights with men.

Izzat (honour and respectable behaviour) is another important quality that is frequently referred to by rural men and women. Anyone can gain or maintain it to a greater or lesser extent. However, the microcredit borrowers interviewed in this study generally used the term in the sense of honour, code of conduct and respectable behaviour. The female borrowers fear the loss of honour when they are spoken to harshly by the NGO officials in front of the other borrowers, in the event that they are late with their repayments, and are accused of not keeping their word. By channelling credit through women, micro-lending NGOs draw the whole family into the programme because if a woman loses her honour it destroys the honour of the whole family.

According to Karimunnesa:

> When I found I was in disgrace [be-izzat] I cried in front of the all borrowers at the centre. I had failed to pay the instalment. The official said, 'You didn't think previously when you took credit. Now you cannot keep your word. You are a liar.' A man would not cry but I cried because of this humiliation.
>
> Q: Did you argue with the official?
>
> No, it was my fault that I had failed to pay the instalment. So I spoke very little to the official. Had I done so it would not have increased my honour or prestige, instead people would have said that I had no shame, rather than feeling ashamed that I had argued with the official.
>
> Q: I hear that some women do argue with the officials.
>
> Not all women are the same; some women may do, but I do not know. Honour is important to everybody. If I do not maintain my honour carefully, nobody will do so on my behalf.

The study respondents stated that they accept the prevailing rules of the NGOs because they have no alternative. They take the loans, so they are bound to conform to the rules attached to those loans. In other words, by providing credit micro-lending NGOs have earned the legitimacy to exercise their power over borrowers. Being poor and uneducated, women fear the NGOs' rules and most respondents believe that they have no power to change them. The respondents often recounted that women are comparatively soft-minded (*norom moner*). 'NGOs know that women are gentle and timid so they can handle women easily. If an NGO's officials were to treat them roughly they would avoid getting involved in direct altercations,' Fouzia claimed. Some other studies (Rahman, 1999; Goetz and Sen Gupta, 1996) also noted that NGOs workers feel easier to work with women than men. In her research on GB members Helen Todd (1996) notes that 'mainly in response to increasing repayment problems within the male centre, the GB project began a shift towards recruiting mainly women members.'

However, most respondents acknowledged that before approving loans, the NGO officials question all the female applicants about their demographics including their husbands' occupations; male household members' occupations and the value of the family's income. Women are asked if their husbands or family will be able to repay the instalments. Even if a widow makes a persuasive case to obtain credit, the NGOs maintain records about her, particularly in respect to her financial status as well as the combined income capacity of her family members. As a result, if a female borrower defaults, her family members cannot avoid the issue but are obliged to release her from her debt. Thus, both GB and BRAC have triumphed as the banks for women and are able to ensure a recovery rate of approximately 98 per cent thanks to society's gender norms.

In his article 'La Domination masculine' (1990), Bourdieu draws upon his ethnographic research carried out in Kabylia, Algeria, to illustrate the paradigm of symbolic domination, namely gender inequality (1992: 170). In this study he showed how 'masculine domination imagines a natural, self-evident status through its inscription in the objective structure of the social world', which is then embodied and reproduced in the *habitus* of individuals (McNay, 1999: 99). Bourdieu views masculine and feminine as the most significant features of social division. I do not believe that the gender *habitus* women find themselves in the rural area is totally static, but we have seen how some cultural practices, social norms and values, moral obligations and codes of conduct are intertwined in the daily course of women's interactions, social position and status in Bangladeshi rural society. These practices are widely accepted, and fall into the arena of the uncontestable. At any given time, in any given society, some of these practices would fall in the realm of what Bourdieu terms doxa (that which is accepted) as a natural and self-evident part of the social order, which goes without saying or contestation (the 'undiscussed, unnamed, admitted without argument or scrutiny') (2002: 167–70). Society also promotes these practices in its activities. As a result, they reappear constantly in women's 'manner of standing, speaking, and thereby of feeling and thinking' (ibid.: 93–94). Thus, not everything is contested: there has to be a common system of intelligibility, a meaningful order in difference as grounds for sociocultural life (Sahlins, 1994: 386).

Theoretically, by offering credit to women, microcredit NGOs have taken the initiative to change women's position in society but most microcredit borrowers' statements indicate that microcredit-providing organizations in reality offer credit via women due to their restricted geographical mobility and their cultural features of passivity and docility. Such female character-istics help NGOs to control, mould, discipline, socialize and conduct surveil-lance of female borrowers, and to exercise their power over female borrowers in order to create useful bodies, or 'good citizens' (Foucault, 1977). In other words, they become a group of good borrowers who by maintaining complete repayment histories are helpful for the furtherance of the NGOs' capitalist interests. From the Foucaultian point of view, I argue that microcredit is not necessarily an emancipatory intervention for poor women. Rather, it operates as a form of governmentality that appropriates the entrenched kinship net-works and gender norms. It increases the penetration of power into the indi-vidual and social body of the Third World through disciplinary power and technologies (see Chapters 6 and 7 in this volume).[5]

Notes

1 In Bangladesh a household (*ghor*, literally house) is based around the physical division of rooms and eating arrangements: people who eat food from the same cooking pot (*deg*) are considered to live in one *ghor* (Gardner, 1992).
2 *Pardah* is the religious and social practice of female seclusion.
3 On this subject see also White (1992).
4 Foucault (1980: 194) uses the term *dispositif* (apparatus) to refer to a 'thoroughly heterogeneous ensemble' of discursive and material elements. A dispositif consists of 'discourses, institutions, architectural forms, regulatory decisions, laws, adminis-trative measures, scientific statements, philosophical, moral and philanthropic pro-positions'. According to him, the dispositif is not simply the collection of elements, but rather the dispositif itself is the 'system of relations … established between these elements'. The relationship between the various elements can be conceptualized in terms of knowledge (discourse), power and subjectivity.
5 On this subject see also Morgan (2001).

6 Competition and the new reality of microcredit

The microcredit sector in Bangladesh witnessed rapid growth under the framework of neoliberal policies in the late 1990s. In early 1990 there were 59 microfinance NGOs; by 2006 the number had reached 2,000. This rapid growth was largely instigated by some big NGOs including GB, ASA and BRAC. NGO activity is mostly concentrated in the rural areas where most of the poor people reside. In 2010 Muhammad Yunus mentioned that 80 per cent of the Bangladeshi population had access to micro-lending programmes.[1] Donor funding has become increasingly concentrated into a small group of large NGOs. For example, of the 1,250 NGOs receiving international assistance in 1999–2000, the three largest NGOs, BRAC, ASA and Proshika received more than 72 per cent of the available donor funds (Kabeer *et al.*, 2012). The increasing concentration of donor funding into a small group of large NGOs has been reinforced and accelerated by the commercialization of the sector.[2] That commercialization has increased competition among microcredit organizations and has led to competitors establishing new branches in the same locality where an incumbent already exists and is actively serving its clients. Rhyne (1998) and Christen and Darke (2002) conjectured that a more commercialized industry is better able to serve the poorest members of the community, since the profit motives of the organizations helps them to be more efficient and more willing to seek out new areas of expansion for their business. On the other hand, Armendariz de Aghion and Morduch (2005) and McIntosh and Wydick (2005) pointed out that the existence of competitors in the market weakens microcredit organizations in two respects. First, it lessens borrowers' incentives for repayment. These incentives importantly depend on the threat of being denied access to further credit in the case of default. Second, owing to the lack of well-functioning credit bureaux, borrowers might take out multiple loans. In such cases, the level of debt can become so high that borrowers are unable to make repayments. This chapter is an ethnographic account of what happens when multiple credit organizations offer loans simultaneously in the same locality. How do microcredit organizations compete with each other for the same clients by appropriating neoliberal policies while also targeting richer clients for profit to strengthen their own sustainability?

The role of credit in competitive business

I began my investigations for this chapter by asking GB micro-lending officials how they perceive the GB microcredit programme against a background whereby a number of competing programmes offer similar amounts of credit in the same locality. Kalam, an area manager who has worked for GB for 22 years, stated that generally the different organizations were not interested in each others' programmes. The official recounted that after GB began its activities other microcredit organizations began to offer micro-loans in Shantigaon and attempted to poach GB's clients. However, this backfired and resulted in panic among the competing organizations. According to the GB official, some GB borrowers had taken out loans from other organizations but did not see any return on their credit investment, and as a result these borrowers fell into debt.

GB has been offering micro-loans in the Shantigaon area since the early 1990s, and there are now two centres in the village. Both the GB area manager and branch manager informed me that although originally there was only one GB micro-lending operation in the village another centre was opened in a different part of the village owing to increasing demand for loans. They claimed that the village economy had changed because of infrastructural development in this area. As a result, people have become less indolent. Instead, they want to improve their circumstances and credit has become very important in realizing these goals. I learned from the officials that previously GB gave credit only to those people who met the bank's specific criteria (see Table A.1) but unofficially these prerequisites have changed. The officials purported that nowadays the bank generally does not give credit to any family that possesses a colour television and a refrigerator, but my data do not support this claim (see below).

I observed that the GB officials no longer follow GB's sixteenth decision (see Table A.1) which states that GB always strictly maintains a concrete measureable definition of its target group of rural landless poor who own less than half an acre of cultivable land or assets with a value equivalent to less than 1.0 acre of medium-quality land. In response, the area manager became annoyed and asked me, 'Are you talking about the micro-lending business of 1980s or 2010s?' I realized that nowadays the sixteenth decision is flexible in order to serve the credit organization's own business interests. The NGO personnel who work at the field level have their own strategies and prescriptions to run their business. There are no hard and fast rules regarding the giving of micro-loans; it all depends upon the field situation. The field assistant knows whether an applicant is creditworthy, and whether that applicant will repay the instalments. The NGO officials are pragmatic about the way they conduct their business. Why give credit to someone who might be unable to pay the instalment?

The GB officials were quite clear that the priorities of the microcredit business lie in adherence to market principles. For instance, one official stated,

'The GB micro-lending programme is not a charity. The bank is ready to give credit to people who are able to pay the instalment, but not to those who cannot.' In other words, the GB credit programme in the studied village emphasizes individual collateral rather than the group collateral mechanism. The official argued that if GB operated the credit programme in the same way as it did during the 1980s, people would no longer take loans from it. Consequently, GB would be forced to leave the business. Other microfinance organizations would enter the market and plunder people's money. He claimed that today, despite tough competition in the market, the condition of GB in Bangladesh was better than that of the other credit organizations. From his point of view, the GB officials are benevolent towards the poor, and they say that they are trying to help the local people. The official declared that GB micro-lending officials conduct this profession on a humanitarian basis, whereas the attitudes of the other microcredit programmes in the rural area are mercenary because they are only interested in making a profit, and now borrowers see through this. Howver, the official was not prepared to divulge the names of such NGOs.

I asked BRAC officials for their views about the other several microcredit NGOs operating in the same locality of my research areas. It was noteworthy that a branch manager without any hesitation said that after 10 years of working as a micro-lender at the village level he believed that microcredit is merely a business operation. According to the official there are many different types of business in Bangladesh, and microcredit is one of them. In his view, the rural people had few or no options for obtaining financial capital. Previously, they took loans from the *mahajan* (traditional money-lenders) with high interest rates that varied between 100 and 200 per cent. As a result of taking loans from the traditional money-lending business the great majority of the poor were forced to lose their land or other valuable assets, and sometimes they lost everything. Now people do not lose their properties, thanks to the NGOs' microcredit. The official claimed that the traditional informal money-lending business has disappeared and has been replaced by the NGOs' structured and codified money-lending business. Borrowers perceive the NGOs' micro-lending business to be more sophisticated than the traditional money-lending system. NGOs do not charge exorbitant interest rates and, more fundamentally people can repay the loan through instalments.

I asked if microcredit as a business ultimately could benefit the poor and help to reduce poverty. My respondent said that access to microcredit programmes helps borrowers to buy small ornaments, household goods, or overcome some of their financial difficulties and deal with unanticipated crises temporarily. The official agreed with me that nowadays a number of credit organizations offer credit at the same time in the same area, and as a result the microcredit business has become competitive. I considered Nodigaon village to be a pertinent example of such practices and informed him that there are only 98 households in the village but a number of microcredit organizations including GB, BRAC, ASA and the FIVDB all operate micro-lending facilities. Consequently, most of the households in this village were involved in one credit programme or another. Since it is possible to get credit easily, the financially well-off people take the opportunity to get credit. The respondent added that none of the micro-lending NGOs strictly adhere to the rules of credit lending owing to the competitive nature of the business. In other words, if they were to adhere to the rules they would lose clients (i.e. the borrowers), which would put in jeopardy the sustainability of the organizations in villages. As a result, many micro-lending programmes currently engage in two major activities: disbursing loans and recovering the payment instalments. Previously, BRAC divided the borrowers of my research areas into two groups: the dabi (the financially weak group) and the *progoti* (the financially well-off group) but they no longer paid importance to this distinction. The two groups have merged into one and all the borrowers were treated in the same way.

Another BRAC branch manager in my research area stated that BRAC started its microcredit programme in his area only four years ago. Before this a number of NGOs such as GB, ASA and FIVDB already operated micro-lending facilities in his area. I asked him which credit organization had the largest number of clients in the area. The official believed that ASA had the strongest organizational base in the area and GB the second strongest. Although BRAC had commenced its lending programme at a later date, its operation had already reached some remote areas not yet targeted by other microcredit programmes. As a result its client base was expanding rapidly. The official explained, 'Now people can make comparisons and work out which NGO is for the poor people. People like the BRAC microcredit programme, not the programme belonging to kabuliwala.'[3] He explained further:

> The GB micro-lending operation is simply a *kabuliwala*-type business. It only knows how to make a profit and not how to help the rural people. However, BRAC employees always try to discourage clients from becoming permanently bogged down in debt. Instead, we advise people to take credit, use it, and then leave the programme. GB, on the other hand, tries to ensnare its clients with debt year in and year out.

According to the official, in the GB micro-lending programme a borrower is allowed to take out more credit when she has paid only half of the instalments of her original loan. Now the main goal of many GB borrowers is somehow to pay 23 weekly instalments and qualify for a further loan. As a result, GB borrowers get entangled with micro-loans. The official claims that the GB micro-lending system cannot help borrowers to become self-reliant and reduce their vulnerability. The credit histories of GB clients reveal that borrowers have been entangled with micro-loans for many years. The official pointed out that the promoter of GB often claimed that the GB-model credit system is a 'magic bullet' that alleviates poverty, but nobody asks why the poor clients of the GB get caught up in a cycle of debt year in and year out.

The official suggested that GB should abandon this *kabuliwala*-type business. He claimed that whereas a lay man can understand the interest rate of the BRAC micro-lending programme which is made clear in the BRAC credit instalment book, nobody can understands GB's interest rate mechanism.

However, the official also pointed out that the microcredit business, be that GB, ASA or BRAC, survives by dint of the strenuous efforts of the field-level officials. Their duties include business expansion, client recruitment and loan recovery. Although they put in long hours daily their remuneration is modest. The official told me that GB salaries are better than those offered by BRAC. Although BRAC achieves huge profits annually, unlike GB it has yet to implement a national salary scale. The BRAC official lamented the fact that that despite a good service record the BRAC head office had transferred him from a suburban location to this rural area. The official recounted some grievous events that had taken place during his working life. A few years ago his father died but he did not get the news because he was working in a very remote area and nobody could contact him before the funeral took place. A couple of years ago, he worked in the river basin area of Jaintia, Sylhet, where he had to cross a number of rivers by a small boat. One day, having collected loans from various centres and he was crossing a river in order to get back to his office, but the boat sank in the middle of the river owing to strong currents. He swam to the river bank losing his shoes and other possessions in the process, but managed to keep hold of the instalment monies because he had to deposit the funds in the office.

The BRAC official and I visited one of the organization's remote village payment centres so that we could meet the borrowers there. The official was worried about some clients' behaviour because they are often late to pay their instalments and waste time. In this instance, the official had to deal with a borrower who had fled with his family some weeks previously without repaying his loan. The concerned official did not recover the credit. However, the client had returned to the village, and so the official could meet the family to recover the loan. I enquired how he would collect the credit from the man, and he replied:

> I have already convinced that client. I have decided to give him a fresh opportunity by sanctioning a new loan. As a result, I can cut all the outstanding dues, and the family will know that we are good people.

This official had previously criticized GB for its kabuliwala-like transactions, which trap borrowers into a cycle of debt. In reality, this official also played the same game with BRAC borrowers. Indeed, competition among the micro-lending organizations in the same locality leads to unhealthy competition, arbitrary action, manipulation of the lending market, and a lack of transparency in objectives and practices. I believe that this official's attitude is similar to that of the traditional money-lenders who are often portrayed as 'coldly preying upon their clients, luring them deeper and deeper into debt, and finally sucking them dry of surplus, savings, property, and liberty' (Rudner, 1994: 36). As mentioned above, both GB and BRAC currently adhere to a self-sustainability paradigm. Rushing to self-sufficiency has forced the micro-credit organizations to be at odds with their original mission and, consequently, has serious and negative repercussions on the development work, as other researchers in Bangladesh and elsewhere have suspected (Dixon *et al.*, 2007; Wright, 2007; Ahmad, 2002, 2003; Milgram, 2001).

Owing to competition and self-sustainability, micro-lending NGOs have created patronage relationships with clients so as to recruit new members, motivate existing members to continue their membership in the programme and collect instalments smoothly. Shorola's husband Raton has taken loans from GB for the past 16 years and in that time has run a successful and profitable three-wheeler business. Now he owns three three-wheelers. However, some borrowers accused Raton for working as a broker for GB. By maintaining good relations with the NGO and increasing his access to credit and other benefits, he intentionally appeals to other rural people by saying that they should take loans from GB because they are poor. As a result, their son will get a job with the NGO in the future. If people try to leave the programme Raton persuades them not to do so by telling them that if they leave the programme they will not be able to get credit from the NGO in the future. Sabiah's husband, Mehedi, a microcredit borrower from Shantigaon, informed me that many people question Raton's true motives and furthermore they are now helplessly caught up in the NGO's credit-debt cycle.

Competition among the NGOs in the study villages is well known among the borrowers. Habiba (38 years old), a local primary school headmistress and a BRAC microcredit borrower from Shantigaon village, explained that GB, BRAC and ASA all compete for the same clients in the Shantigaon area to maximize their lending profitability. She observed that NGOs entice all villagers to join the programme, except for the very poorest, by making use for the last five or six years of the 'spin' that the scheme is designed to alleviate poverty. Owing to such competition, many borrowers have double or triple membership in different microcredit organizations. According to her, the rich people take credit in order to expand their business activities, whereas the poor people take credit from one organization so that they can pay the instalments to another organization. She argues that some people's credit engagement is dubious. For example, one of Habiba's office colleagues (Urmi, 45 years old) had been taking micro-loans from GB for 17 years and from BRAC for four years, but Habiba does not understand why Urmi needs the credit. The poor illiterate people seem to not understand the advantages and disadvantages of taking credit, so when they take out a loan they usually get caught up in the credit-debt cycle.

Suchona, a GB microcredit borrower and the group leader of Zelegaon village, has keen observations on the transition of the GB micro-lending business in her locality: 'In Zelegaon a number of microcredit organizations now provide credit, so GB has stopped caring about rules and regulations because borrowers could go to another NGO and as a result GB would lose its clients.'

Like Suchona, most borrowers frequently report that both GB and BRAC are now reluctant to follow their own rules and regulations. Helena recounted that when she took out a loan from GB some 18 years ago, the official told her to learn all of GB's sixteen decisions so that she understood the NGO's rules, but now GB officials make no comment about the decisions. The officials merely advise borrowers to take more credit and to increase their instalments (*shomoy moto ksiti dao*).

However, some female borrowers appreciated the present trend evident in microcredit organizations. When interviewed, most of the respondents demonstrated that due to the presence of multiple credit organizations in the same locality they can get easy access to credit. Jesmin, a microcredit borrower from Nodigaon village, is pleased that there are a number of NGOs in her area because she can take credit from BRAC for herself and from ASA for her nephew. According to her, 'If only BRAC operated here it could follow many rules, which it currently ignores.'

NGOs are institutions with organizational cultures, ideological commitments, and competing or sometimes contradictory priorities embedded in complex processes of local, national and international events (Fisher, 1997; Petras, 1997; Edwards and Hulme, 1996). NGOs operate in complicated fields of action in which they are not only the actors (Biekhart, 1996). They must balance multiple agendas as they attempt to secure their own survival (Cosgrove, 2002). From the discussion above we have seen how microcredit organizations compete with each other and evaluate their own and their opponent's activities to enhance their positions at the field level. The microcredit NGO officials use different types of capital and techniques to secure their survival or to get hold of more capital. Owing to this competition, these organizations interact and share information with each other either very little or not at all. For example, if a GB official is asked about the location of the BRAC centre in the same village, he will not give an exact answer or may even give out misleading information. He might say, 'Oh, I know this organization is operating a microcredit programme in this village but I do not know the exact address of the centre or how many borrowers they have. Moreover, I am not interested in finding out about that organization. They do their work and we do ours.' As a result, it is very difficult to gauge accurately how many multiple borrowers there are in the same locality.

While it is true that as there are several NGOs in the same locality people now can take a loan from different micro-lending programmes, the borrowers denied this fact. When I asked the GB borrowers in one of my research areas whether they take credit from other organizations, they strongly denied having done so. However, I collected data from BRAC from the same area and I discovered that the opposite was true. Take, for example, Alapi, a very poor microcredit borrower, who informed me that she only took credit from GB. However, when I collected data from the BRAC centre located in the same village she was registered as a member there too. Eventually, Alapi told me that she originally took credit from GB but she failed to pay the instalments because her husband suddenly fell ill, so she then took a loan from BRAC to enable her to pay the instalments to GB and to cover some family expenses.

Among the 38 GB borrowers at the Shantigaon centre, I found ten borrowers (26.31 per cent) who have taken credit from different credit programmes simultaneously. While I was unable to ascertain the exact number of multiple borrowers in the villages of Zelegaon and Nodigaon I estimate that the proportion is no less than 15 per cent. Among them there are some borrowers who were obliged to take credit from one organization in order to avoid defaulting to another organization. As a result, the level of debt became so high that borrowers were unable to make repayments (cf. Casini, 2008). Financially well-off families such as school teachers, rural doctors, household members living abroad, successful business people, or those who have own large amounts of land generally maintain multiple memberships. A few researchers (Chaudhury and Matin, 2002) have considered the issue of overlapping multiple memberships and have tried to ascertain the reasons behind it and the consequences for households. They estimated that 15 per cent of all borrowers take out loans from more than one microfinance institution. They concluded that often the occurrence of an unexpected crisis was the main reason behind households taking out multiple loans from different microfinance institutions. Charitonenko *et al.* (2004) found that some microfinance institutions in Bangladesh have experienced a decline in their loan recovery rates due to rising client desertion rates associated with increased competition. I did not hear that the loan recovery rates had declined dramatically in my research areas. The NGO officials in the study villages claim that their recovery rates are between 98 and 100 per cent. However, the analysis of my data suggests that competition among microcredit organizations at the local level has led to 'mission drift'.

Mission drift and diffusion

Dichter and Harper (2007) argue that the microfinance industry is 'coming of age'. The maturation of the microfinance industry has been accompanied by claims that the industry is abandoning its mission to serve the poor. Woller *et al.* (1999) and Woller (2002) held the opinion that mission drift occurs when a microcredit organization abandons its poor customers. Without eschewing this idea, I argue that mission drift takes place when microcredit organizations compromise their mission on poverty alleviation by implementing the goals of market-driven commercial organizations of capital accumulation. The NGOs simply provide money in the manner of traditional money-lenders without offering or giving any training to develop borrowers' skills which might alleviate their poverty. Before launching into this discussion I will focus on how microcredit organizations in the studied villages deselect the poor and attempt to cultivate the financially well-off families as their clients.

All the group leaders in the three studied villages confirm that the micro-lending organizations often try to avoid the poorest people who have no businesses or steady incomes because they fear that there may be problems in recovering instalments. Likewise, they also claim that such people avoid credit programmes because they are concerned that they will not able to repay the loan. I asked Suchona (the centre leader in Zelegaon) how GB prevents the poorest people from taking loans, and she replied:

> Every week, GB members come to my house to paying their instalments and/or to take out new loans. The bank always tries to avoid lending to the poor but I sign in support of the new applicants and often assure the GB official that I know the applicants and their financial situation. Through this information, I try to testify that the applicants are able financially to pay the weekly credit instalments. However, sometimes applicants take offence at me when their applications are rejected by the official. They do not understand that I do not control everything.
>
> Q: I know that there are many poor people who get credit, isn't that the case?
>
> Yes, actually those who are in business are rarely denied access to credit. Sometimes I do not sign in support of poor borrowers because they might not be able to pay the instalments. It is a credit taker's duty to pay instalments.

Microcredit NGOs are trapped in a neoliberal orthodoxy, which prioritizes blind adherence to market principles, although most people who live in the rural areas are not located in the mainstream market economy. Obviously, it is hard for a borrower who has no existing business to produce sufficient profit to pay credit instalments within one week of receiving a loan. As a result, the NGOs exclude the poor from the credit programmes. The exclusion of the poorest people from microcredit programmes in Bangladesh is acknowledged in a number of studies (Ahmed *et al.*, 2006; Matin and Hulme, 2003; Hulme 1996, 2000; Kamal, 1998). What fascinated me is that the NGO officials rarely acknowledge this fact. They astutely avoid the issue by stating that credit is offered to all poor people.

There were not many well-off families in the study villages, but most of them took part in microcredit programmes. Muhammad Yunus argued that financially well-off clients outnumber poorer clients in any credit scheme. He always insisted that his programmes are exclusively dedicated to the poor: 'In the world of development, if one mixes the poor and non-poor within the format of a single programme, the non-poor will always drive out the poor' (1984: 57). Yet there continues to be a gap between the rhetoric and practice at the field level.

Mayarun, a microcredit borrower from Zelegaon, shared her experiences of how her applications for loans were rejected by GB without any grounds. In her account, her husband was a day labourer but he did not get work every day and her family led a miserable life. Mayarun observed that some of her neighbouring women took credit from GB and invested it in producing bamboo-cane crafts. As she is familiar with this work, she talked to her husband about taking out a loan and doing this work. Accordingly, she talked to the group leader and requested the GB official for a loan amounting to TK 5,000. However, the GB official repeatedly refused arguing, 'You are very poor and old. Your family has no business nor regular income, so we cannot give you credit. You will not be able to pay the repayment instalments.' Mayarun told me that in pursuance of her interest, she appealed to the GB officer, modestly touching his hands and legs (*hath-paa dharay*) but the official turned her down. However, she did not give up. Eventually, the group leader and two other borrowers reassured the official by saying that 'if Mayarun is not able to pay the instalment, we will bear all responsibility for repaying the credit'. Now Mayarun pays her instalments without any difficulty. Mayarun believes that the official dislikes poor people who have no good businesses or incomes. Rather, they prefer rich people who do not need loans in the first place.

A similar episode occurred in Shantigaon. Kamrun is one of the oldest GB borrowers in the village Shantigaon. Two years before we met, her husband suddenly died. As a result, she ended up in a financially terrible situation. Over the years, Kamrun and her husband had taken out loans to make bamboo-cane crafts. They always paid their instalments by the due date but following her husband's death, GB no longer wanted to give her credit. Kamrun claimed that when her husband was alive they always paid instalments on time even if it meant going without food, but now the bank is no longer interested in helping her. Kamrun and a male relative requested a new loan in my presence, but the GB official and some other borrowers gathered there pretended not to hear. In Chapter 2 I mentioned the lack of solidarity and collective identity among the borrowers, so in this case by using his discretionary power the patron (the NGO official) either sanctions or denies the biggest window of capital (i.e. credit) to the poor.

Alapi is one of the oldest microcredit borrowers in Shantigaon. She has served as a group leader and contributed to the development of the centre. Her family lost everything due to debt and is now homeless. During my fieldwork, I witnessed Alapi and her husband entreating a GB branch manager to sanction a new loan of TK 50,000 in order to buy an old three-wheeler and a small patch of homestead land to build a house. They tried to convince the official to loan them the money by saying that they have a big tree, which they can sell in order to repay the instalments. Moreover, they strived to assure the GB official that after buying the land they would hand over the deed of the land to GB as security on the loan. Despite these entreaties the official paid no heed to them.

NGOs have a preference for rich people

Abdur Rahim had been taking micro-loans through his wife from the BRAC microcredit programme in Shantigaon. Rahim studied up to tenth grade (but failed to obtain his Secondary School Certificate), and his wife studied up to fifth grade. Rahim has three sons and a daughter. The daughter (20 years old) studied to tenth grade and got married two years before to our meeting. His eldest son too had failed obtain his Secondary School Certificate and was running a stationery shop. The second and third sons were studying in the twelfth and eleventh grades, respectively. Rahim had been working in Saudi Arabia for about ten years and returned to Bangladesh five years ago. At the time of our meeting he had 88 decimals of homestead land and 120 decimals cultivable land. He owns a big L-shaped tin-roofed brick-walled house. Visitors can easily see that his house is more opulent compared to the other houses in Shantigaon.

When I visited the house Rahim welcomed me into his living-room. There he has two sofas, a wardrobe, a desk in the corner and a single bed with a nice bed cover and pillows. On the wall there hung a clock, a big photo of the holy Kaba and some Islamic calligraphy. The living-room was neat and clean, and Rahim was well dressed. He wore a white striped *lungi*, and an ash-coloured *panjabi*. He uses henna to colour his beard. When I began to talk about his family's microcredit involvement, he said modestly, 'You are my guest [mehman], so first you must take something to eat and then we will talk.' Rahim's eldest son brought in tea and handmade pita (a type of cake). After eating the snacks, he offered betel leaf and said, 'Please taste it, it is from my garden.' In front of his house there is a large garden where he cultivates fruit and vegetables. Indeed, everything reflected his high social and financial position. Rahim did not forget to inform me about his position in Shantigaon: 'I am the secretary of a mosque and a co-operative in this *panchayat*. My elder brother is the headmaster of the only high school in this area. My maternal grandfather stood as a candidate for the local union *parishad* election twice during the Pakistan period under President Ayeb Khan's basic democracy.' As Rahim is actively involved in the local *panchayat* and mosque, his wife does not speak to strange men, so he talked to me on her behalf.

Rahim confirmed that his wife takes out micro-loans but he agreed with the NGO that his wife only signs for loans and he receives the money. Rahim's wife does not go to the centre for weekly instalments. The NGO's loan collector takes the instalments from his son's shop. Rahim thinks that the NGO needs to invest its money safely and it will not face any problems in recovering money from people like him. He claimed that currently many NGOs provide loans; they have a lot of money so anybody who believes that they can pay instalments can easily get a loan. I discussed Rahmin's family's microcredit involvement with him:

Q: How long have you been in the microcredit programme and how many loans have you taken out?

I have been taking micro-loans for the last five years. I have taken out loans three times from BRAC. First, I took out a TK 50,000 loan, a second for TK 50,000, and a third for TK 100,000. All the loans have been invested in my eldest son's stationery shop.

Q: Can you tell me who actually should take out the loan?

Who wants to take the burden of credit on his shoulders? Many people have no alternative. In our village, most of the inhabitants' financial circumstances are similar, so who will help whom? In this sense, credit is a good option or a source of capital, but I can say that anybody who has a daily income can take credit, otherwise not. If poor people who have no daily income get involved in the credit programme they will be unable to leave it. The financially well-off families may do something with loans but not the poor. So the poor should try to avoid them.

Q: To whom do NGOs prefer to give credit?

NGOs do business in such a way that they understand from whom they can collect instalments without any difficulty … they do like rich people.

Rahim rationalized that he certainly needs credit because now he has no work and no savings. He took out loans to set up his son's business. He stated that if he had given all the money to his son by selling his land, the boy might not have appreciated the value of the money. He might lose his business and think that it is not a problem because all he has lost is his father's property. Now the son understands that it is the NGO's money, not his family's money. The son himself has paid the instalments, covered his everyday expenses and sometimes contributed a little to the family.

While I was talking to Rahim, the GB branch manager for that area visited his house to ask what I was doing there. The GB official said to Rahim, 'I know you take credit from BRAC but why not from my organization? You can also take a loan from our organization. Your sons do business near to our office, so please come to our office.' The underlying theme appeared to be that it is acceptable for people to get into debt. The official soon left Rahmin's house but after his departure Rahim criticized the official: 'Do you understand the NGO's official's motive? The NGO officials appear as a new form of kabuliwala in the rural areas. Like the kabuliwala, the NGO officials encourage people to take credit and in doing so they ensnare them in debt.' It is revealed that when power relations are hierarchical and asymmetrical, the subordinate people develop forms of action that are hidden from the direct surveillance of the power holders (Scott, 1990).

I asked Rahim why people take out loans if microcredit-lending NGOs operate as kabuliwala. Rahmin believes that rural people are to some extent bound to take credit because they have no other viable source of finance. The agricultural land belonging to many people in the Shantigaon area is too low and wet for productive cultivation. These people live in adverse conditions and experience natural calamities such as floods and droughts. He mentioned how many peasants' crops had been destroyed that year because the monsoon season rainwater had not yet drained away from the paddy fields, so people are compelled to take credit for their day-to-day needs. He claimed if anybody were to visit Shantigaon for a few weeks, they would see why the NGO-*kabuliwalas* move here to invest their monies. If people stopped to think about the advantages and disadvantages of credit programmes, who would feed them? As the government does not operate any form of welfare benefit for the poor, microcredit-lending NGOs have emerged as a monopoly, which takes advantage of and profits from rural poverty.

People might cast their evil eyes on our property

Samirun is considered to be one of the most successful GB borrowers in Zelegaon. She married when she was about 13 years old. Samirun has three children aged between eight and 11 years old, and all go to school. Samirun's household has 270 decimals of homestead land, which will be split between four heirs (Samirun's husband and his three younger brothers). The family has no cultivable land but intends to buy land in the near future. The family lives in a two-storey brick-built house. There are four bedrooms on each floor, three bathrooms, a kitchen and a living-room. In the living-room there are two sofas, a tea table and a display cabinet containing a number of items. When Samirun talked to me she wore a cotton sari, gold bangles on her wrists and a necklace and earrings. Samirun's mother-in-law is a widow but she wears a red sari, which is unusual for widows in rural Bangladesh. She looks happy and content with her life. All this indicates Samirun's financial standing in the village of Zelegaon. Samirun's husband now runs a *sattering* business (which provides building and plastering materials such as wood, bamboo, etc). Previously, her husband lived in Saudi Arabia, and now her three brothers-in-law (her husband's younger brothers) work in the Middle East.

According to Samirun, she had been taking microcredit for six years from GB and for three years from BRAC. First she took TK 10,000 from GB and financed her husband's rice business. Then she took out a GB loan and invested in a cow. Now she was paying instalments on TK 10,000 of GB microcredit and TK 100,000 of a BRAC micro-loan. Samirun declared that her husband knows how to run a business and make a profit. Therefore, her husband advised her to take money from NGOs so that he can invest it in his business. At the time they were able to meet their everyday household expenses of about TK 400–500 and pay the weekly credit instalments by using the proceeds from their business. They will take another loan to expand the business. Samirun's husband has already discussed it with her. I enquired whether they actually needed the credit, and she explained:

> It is true that our family has sufficient income because every year my brothers-in-law have sent remittances and my husband's income is also

good. So in fact we do not need credit for our day-to-day living expenses. However, we take credit to expand our business. As most of the people in this area take credit from different NGOs, what is the problem if my family also takes out micro-loans? Most people of this village are not financially well-off, so if we do not take out a loan the people in our area will be envious of us. They will become covetous of our property and wealth. They may cast their evil eyes [chokh *pora*] on our family. If we take out a loan people will think that we too are in a crisis. It is difficult to understand people's motives, but the fact is we are obliged to take out a loan.

Samirun does not feel the need to go to weekly credit instalment meetings. Her husband's *sattaring* business is located near the group leader's house so sometimes her husband pays the instalments and sometimes the officials collect them directly from her husband's business premises. When I enquired whether the official mentions the weekly credit instalment meeting, Samirun replied that 'The bank needs instalments on a due date and we pay it on time. The NGOs officers are well aware that we do not need them [microcredit organizations] but they need us.' When I talked to Samirun her husband was also present, so when I asked her who most deserves loans, Samirun's husband replied that credit should not be given to people who do not have skills, or a good business or who lack an everyday income. He observed that many poor people in his area take credit and bear the burden of that credit for many years but cannot do anything about it.

In this chapter I have sought to demonstrate that targeting rural people as beneficiaries of microcredit loans has turned rural Bangladeshi people into assets for microcredit programmes. Competition has led the microcredit NGOs to take more complicated action, including unprincipled competitive practices, in addition to embracing activities that are contradictory to the principles of microcredit. Competition obviously has opened up manifold options for the borrowers, but for the NGOs such competition to ensure their own economic survival has meant abandoning their objectives such as poverty alleviation and women's empowerment. It has led to people becoming multiple borrowers, which might be advantageous for the financially well-off families, but for the poor it has meant becoming mired in ever more debt. As a result of their current desire for financial sustainability NGOs of the three villages studied prefer to lend to the financially well-off families, those who have good businesses and a steady income stream. Despite this practice, the majority of their clients are still rural poor people.

Notes

1 See the debate between Yunus and Vikram Akula entitled 'Microfinance or Loan Sharks' at the Clinton Global Initiative. Available at: http://blogs.cgdev.org/open_

book/2010/09/akula-v-yunus-commercial-microcredit-justprofit-or-unjust-profiteerin
g.php.

2 As Devine points out, the pattern of favouring the large NGOs reflected pressures
on donors 'to scale up successful development operations, reduce burdensome
transaction costs, decrease NGOs' reliance on donor money and initiate a process
that would secure financial sustainability' (2003: 230).

3 The *kabuliwalas* were traders who came to Bengal from Kabul, Afghanistan during
the British colonial period to conduct the fruit business in addition to running
money-lending businesses with high interest rates.

7 Market rationality, power relationships and resistance

In this chapter I focus on credit arrangement and enforcement, and the resistance of microcredit borrowers in the villages under study. I examine power relationships and the implications of imposed institutional discipline, the governmentality of microcredit organizations, and the vulnerability of microcredit borrowers. Credit, which is disbursed to promote self-employment and increase household incomes, is approved through set of social and economic enforcement mechanisms which I refer to as 'disciplinary technologies'. By applying Foucaultian theoretical ideas to disciplinary power and govermentality, this chapter contributes to the debate on how NGO loans ensure that borrowers behave in a consistent with market rationality and achieve the micro-lending NGOs' profit enhancement at the expense of the poor client's profit. In order to understand power relations within the framework of microcredit programmes, following Scott's notions of 'hidden resistance' and 'weapons of the weak', I analyse the microcredit borrowers' forms of resistance and how they widely criticize microcredit programmes' rules and procedures when not under the direct surveillance of NGO officials. The interrelation between structure and agency is explored by showing how some clients manipulate the NGOs' rules to their own advantage.

Repayment interest rates

The broad support for micro-lending is based on the supposition that devolving development to the lowest tier of society, 'the people', is not only a sound initiative but also a moral imperative. The essence and desirability of microfinance rests on its ability to ensure a 'win-win' proposition.

The fatal criticism made about microcredit programmes is that micro-lenders grant loans at a higher rate of interest than the government and commercial banks. Referring to the development of microcredit NGOs, Muhammad Yunus declared that such institutions had been developed to combat the traditional money-lenders, and should not become traditional money-lenders themselves. This implies that higher rates of interest are not part of a pro-poor poverty alleviation policy. Furthermore, it may enable many poor clients to gain access to the credit programmes. However, in reality the effective annual rate of interest for a small loan of GB and BRAC credit is about 32 per cent (Karim, 2008). In 2011 the Bangladesh government took the decision that the micro-lending NGOs can charge an interest rate of up to 27 per cent. However, the country's leading charities and micro-financiers expressed strong reservations about this decision and suggested that the rate should be fixed at 30 per cent. The rate of interest of micro-lending organizations is still lower than the interest rate levied by the traditional rural money-lenders (*mahajan*) who have no common fixed rate of interest. In practice, these rates vary between 100 and 200 per cent. Moreover, these rates are not approved by the government so they have neither institutional nor standardized interest rates to carry out their business.

I asked the borrowers about the negative aspects of microcredit pro-grammes. Many borrowers were concerned about the excessively high interest rates charged by both GB and BRAC. Nevertheless, when I asked them about the exact rate of interest, they did not give clear-cut answers. Some claimed that it was 18 per cent while others stated that it was 25 per cent or more. The respondents generally agreed that their husbands or other elderly male members of the household knew what the rate of interest was. Raduni, a GB member from Shantigaon, was not entirely sure how much interest GB charged. She stated that it was very difficult to understand the exact rate of interest from the credit instalment book. In her opinion, 'the NGO officer is clever', because he only mentions the total value of the loan and how much one has to pay. She believes that because rural people are illiterate and simple, they do not understand these figures but she suspects that the GB is cheating her. She explains that she pays more than 20 per cent in interest. Moreover, whenever she applies for a loan, she pays an application fee, and sometimes if she is unable to pay the instalments, she is fined. Thus, she argues that all these factors should be taken into consideration when calculating the actual interest rate levied by GB.

Another woman, who at the age of 45 years is one of the oldest members of the GB and BRAC microcredit programmes in Shantigaon village, added that some borrowers are aware that both GB and BRAC charge high interest rates but they know they cannot do anything about this, since such matters are decided by the heads of the organizations. She said:

We need credit so we must comply with their rules. Otherwise the chances of obtaining credit will become slim or we will not get any credit at all. If you ask clients about the interest rates charged by GB or BRAC you will not hear any complaints. Nobody is prepared to take such a risk because they are afraid of not getting loans in the future.

Micro-lending NGOs usually quote a flat interest rate, not the Annual Per-centage Rate (APR), or effective interest rate, which is the accepted banking standard in the developed world (Augburg and Fouillet, 2010). Flat interest means charging interest on the full or principal amount of a loan, rather than on a diminishing balance. The practice of flat interest rate charging is usually rationalized by the perception that it is easier to calculate than that of a declining balance interest. According to Augburg and Fouillet (ibid.), while this sounds honourable, the reality is often quite different. The bottom line is that customers are frequently deceived by the use of flat interest rates, which, depending on the terms of the loan, can result in an actual interest rate that is twice as high as the headline figure. In the villages under study, most of the members (95 per cent) know that the NGOs charge interest on the capital amount but they do not know about how the instalment payments are calculated because the loan-providing organizations do not explain it clearly to them. I asked Hafiza, who has been a member of the GB microcredit programme in Zelegaon for the last 18 years, whether she knew how GB charges interest, and she said:

> I know that GB always charges interest on the total loan [*ashol takar upar*]. As a result, GB makes a big profit. I cannot explain how the calculation is made, but my eldest son can explain it to you. The loan officers only tell me how much money I have to pay in weekly instalments and give instructions about paying the instalment money on time. We take credit because we need it. There are no other ways to borrow money. Who will lend us money otherwise?
> Q: Why can't you go the other microcredit NGOs?
> You do not know; they are the same. Once I took credit from another bank [NGO] so I know it. Nobody likes the poor.

Karimunnessa takes a somewhat different view: 'I know that GB charges interest on the principal amount [capital amount] of the loan but this is how GB works. Complaining about this will not be of any benefit.' She once asked about the mechanism of credit interest rate calculation but the official said that he only follows the NGOs rules. So if she wants to take money from his organization, she has to follow the regulations. Karimunnessa strongly believes that the GB officials are aware that they are unjust [insaf *korsena*] towards the borrowers, but she believes that nobody cares about the poor except Allah.

Sabiah's husband Mehedi (a microcredit borrower from Shantigaon) explained to me the mechanism of how GB and BRAC levy exorbitant interest rates on their borrowers. He said that both GB and BRAC charge interest on the principal amount of the loan. If a borrower takes out a loan for TK 10,000, then the following week the borrower has to pay TK 1,000 as the first instalment, and the NGO is still owed TK 9,000 from the principal loan. From a rational point of view, the NGO should only charge interest on the outstanding amount of money owed (in this case TK 9,000), but in reality the NGO charges interest on the total principal amount of money, TK 10,000.

Most of my respondents agreed that what micro-lending NGOs claim as their rate of interest is incorrect, as in fact they charge an outrageous rate of interest. However, some borrowers have rationalized the rate of interest and instalment payment calculation. They purported that the bank (GB or BRAC) gives them one loan at a time but collects money through a series of instalments, so charge more. Furthermore, the bank comes to the people in the village, rather than the people going to the bank.

GB is prepared to disburse loans for buying three-wheelers, for example, but in the case of large loans the loan disbursement officials keep the land deed (*jomir dalil*) as a security deposit at the GB office, which in turn secures repayments and increases repayment rates. As land is considered as a particularly valuable resource, when an individual takes out a loan by giving his land deed, he is especially careful to keep up with his repayments. When a new bigger loan is sanctioned the borrowers do not get the full amount of credit, because the NGO keeps about 20 per cent of the loan as security, so only 80 per cent of the loan is actually disbursed. The borrower cannot use the full amount they borrow which in turn induces them to take out multiple loans (see Chapter 8 in this volume). Even though it is argued that the GB model of microcredit business is run on a collateral mechanism that entails trust, taking deposit money and keeping land deeds as security indicates that GB does not trust its borrowers.

Based on these findings, the present study establishes the fact that most borrowers in the villages studied are unaware or have insufficient knowledge of the charges they are paying and the process (interest on the principal amount of the loan) through which GB and BRAC charge interest on small loans. The micro-lending NGOs do not feel that it is necessary to clarify their enforced true rates of interest. As the power relationship is unevenly in favour of the lenders it is unsurprising that micro-borrowers surreptitiously criticize microcredit NGOs' rules. Elizabeth Jelin, an expert on microcredit in Latin American, is correct in perceiving NGOs as 'private-yet-public organizations that do not have a built-in mechanism of accountability' (1998: 412). I would like to argue that the rate of interest on small loans is not rational at the local level because it only ensures the NGOs' own sustainability and profit enhancement at the expense of its own clients' advancement. It could even be argued that a low rate of interest actually reduces the NGOs' financial sustainability. Nevertheless, I think that the NGOs can increase the number of borrowers, which in turn expands the total credit investment of microcredit programmes and may give some sort of boost to the economic viability of the NGOs. In addition, the NGOs can search for other sources of capital.

Disciplining the developmental subjects and instalment collecting bank

The basic principle upon which GB and BRAC run their micro-lending operations is the same throughout the region, namely that having taken out a loan each borrower must repay the total amount of money owed in 46 weeks' worth of instalments. Both organizations focus on efficiency and effectiveness and consider borrowers as not only in an ideal market situation but also as active market subjects, who can easily invest credit, produce a quick profit and start paying instalment one week after they have taken out a loan by using part of the profit produced from the credit investment. Based on my findings, it is shown that many borrowers who take out loans without having an existing business or a steady income pay instalments from capital money sums, not from any profit they make and thus fall into a debt trap. As Mehedi observed, the NGOs are keen to entice people to take out loans so that they can change their lives but they do not show the borrowers how such a loan could change their lives for the better. Mehedi asked:

> Can you tell me if there are any short-cut mechanisms to change peoples' lives in the rural areas of Bangladesh? Where will people invest money in a village? Is it possible to make a business profitable within one week and pay instalments out of that profit? ... the NGOs are strict about repayments but not about how people use the loans. They do not give borrowers a period of time to work out how best to invest the loaned money.

Mehedi observed that microcredit NGOs do not want borrowers to leave their programmes. It is impossible for a borrower to leave a programme, because the NGOs threaten the borrower by saying that if they leave the programme they will not get credit in the future if they need it. Thus, poor people try to continue their membership in order to not lose the possibility of obtaining loans in the future. According to him:

> On the one hand, cigarette companies caution that smoking harms people's health but this does not make a tobacco company halt production. On the other hand, people know that smoking is bad for them but they continue to smoke regardless. The difference between the microcredit programme and a tobacco company is that the microcredit programme never says that credit is bad but the tobacco company does. If someone starts smoking it is difficult to stop, but by the same token if someone gets involved in using credit it is difficult to desist as the borrower gets sucked in.

Fines are an integral part of micro-lending programmes in the villages studied. A fine is imposed if a client fails to pay their weekly instalment, interest or monthly savings. Likewise, if a borrower wants to pay part of the full amount of an instalment, the official will not accept it. Ill health, family problems, death, or natural disasters are not accepted as excuses for not paying instalments on time. Generally, if a borrower fails to pay their instalments on time, they will face harsh behaviour from the loan collector as well as the other group members, particularly the guarantors. The guarantors, some active members of the centres, and the officials try to make the client understand, so as to collect the money. If a borrower regularly fails to pay the instalment on time, the group tries to recover the whole outstanding amount from that borrower step by step, and then the microcredit official uses his or her discretionary power to expel the borrower from the group. Expulsion from a microcredit organization is particularly undesirable for a borrower, because that borrower often loses the option for obtaining future loans. Like Rahman (1999), I too observed that in response to group pressure sometimes borrowers go to their neighbours to borrow money in order to pay the instalment and avoid fines.

The rigidity of GB's rules concerning the regular repayment of weekly instalments is reflected in the microcredit borrowers' sentiment that 'a borrower must to pay their instalment before going to the funeral' (*mora ghore rekhey kisti dao*). Suchona is an active member of the GB credit programme. As a result, she has detailed knowledge about the clients, their activities and the advantages and disadvantages of the GB micro-lending programme. She shared her experiences with regard to the repayment of weekly instalments as follows:

> Clients are bound to pay the instalment even if it means that their dear ones' dead bodies lie unburied in the house. I can recall a sorrowful event in my life. I have been taking credit from the bank for the last 18 years but I was forced to pay the instalment within a day of my husband's death. So you understand GB's attitude about the collection of instalments. Actually, the bank's main goal is not to help the poor but to run a money-lending business. I cannot leave GB because all the banks are the same, and we have no room to manoeuvre.

A borrower is rated according to her record of weekly instalment payments. A good borrower maintains a policy of repaying all her instalments over the required period of 46 weeks. A centre without defaulters is described as a 'good centre' (see also Rahman, 1999). The branch manager and the loan collecting staff play a crucial role in daily operations. The officials' duties revolve around the day-to-day activities with the borrowers. They must focus on collecting instalments and client recruitment. A defaulter is not only bad for herself; she is also bad for the NGO officials. As a high loan recovery rate ensures good prospects for the officials, they do not even follow the government holiday system. Both GB and BRAC's staff told me that in this profession there are no set office hours and no holidays. As a result, they cannot dedicate time to their families and household work. A Hindu branch manager described his experience:

> I only take a few days' holiday each year, so I have to cut all my social relationships because I cannot attend any ceremonies. During the time of *puja* (a Hindu religious festival) I only get two days of holiday and during that time I meet my mother and other relatives. As it is not possible for me to visit them, they visit my house.

Both GB and BRAC staff have to be available in the field in order to be able to collect weekly instalments on the due dates, and sometimes they stay until midnight in the villages. The microcredit officials in the villages researched argued that they do business with rural people who belong to the subsistence or below subsistence economy, so if they do not collect instalments from the borrowers on the due dates they may spend that money on that day. If, for example, a borrower spends her weekly instalment money, the following week she will be obliged to pay two weeks' worth of instalments on the same day, which will be very difficult for that borrower. In fact, the notion was very clear that most borrowers in the villages studied are financially extremely vulnerable, despite the fact that they get involved in credit programmes for many years. I discovered that about 52 per cent of borrowers in Zelegaon and 44 per cent of borrowers in Shantigaon had been involved in the microcredit programmes for at least ten years prior to my study. The mean period of microcredit involvement of the borrowers of Zelegaon and Shantigaon was about eight years and in Nodigaon it was about four years.

The GB and BRAC microcredit officials claim that if they are flexible rather than rigid with respect to the collection of instalments it would create a perception among the borrowers that defaulting is acceptable; consequently, the discipline of the organization would break down and therefore the business would not work. Moreover, the officials have to ensure that loans are collected on the due dates because they themselves are accountable to their superiors. They have to update the accounts every day, so they are not prepared to accept excuses from defaulters. According to the programme's chain of command, the zone managers pass on their objectives to the area managers, who in turn pass them onto the branch managers and the branch managers to the field-level assistants who are expected to impose strict disciplinary and repayment policies. The field-level assistants then pressurize the clients and group leaders. Through these hierarchical governing processes micro-lending NGOs instruct borrowers and establish power relationships. As Foucault wrote, 'Power must be analyzed as something which circulates, or rather as something which only functions in the form of a chain. It is never localized here or there. … Power is employed and exercised through a net-like organization' (1980: 98).

Microcredit organizations recruit young energetic men instead of women and elderly men. It is a glaring contradiction that most microcredit borrowers are women, whereas most NGOs are staffed by young men in the areas that I studied. I visited two GB and two BRAC branch offices but found only one woman, Farida, who worked for BRAC as a loan collector at the field level in one of my study areas. I spoke often to Farida. I asked her whether she liked her profession, but she laughed and said that she had completed her bachelor's degree and was seeking a good job but could not find one. Her husband works in a Chinese restaurant but his income is not enough to run the family. Farida does not like her present job but she cannot find another. Every day she has to walk for hours and cross bamboo mate-shifts over canals to collect instalments from different centres. Farida's profession makes her life very difficult because she cannot spend time with her two-year-old daughter who stays at home with a maidservant. Farida is obliged to collect instalments even during thunderstorms, scorching heat and torrential rain. She regards the rainy season as the worst time because the roads become muddy and partly flooded. According to Farida, she is always stressed because she must keep the instalment money safe from pick-pocketers and thieves. Sometimes she experiences abusive language. She asked me to help her to find a job in a school.

I visited the branch office of one of the NGOs many times with a branch manager. One day the official tactfully drew my attention to another official and said, 'Look at that official's appearance'. The official was dirty and seemed to be distressed. When I talked to the official I found him frail and absent-minded. The official joined this profession a few years before the branch manager but as yet had not been promoted. Nobody knew when this would happen. I was to hear from the field-level officials that microcredit organizations generally tend not to retain the services of ageing field officials. According to the branch manager, there is only one short cut to promotion within the micro-lending profession – efficacious field-level supervision or monitoring. I learned from him that frequent monitoring makes borrowers more responsible and creates the habit of credit repayment. If an officer can maintain door-to-door networks with the local people and ensure client discipline through stringent surveillance with the help of the group leader in addition to having dependable borrowers, he will undoubtedly succeed in this profession. These characteristics ensure a high number of borrowers, or clients, and a corresponding high rate of loan recovery. The official proudly informed me that the recovery rate of the branches under his supervision is 100 per cent. My interviews revealed that the success of microcredit rests on two basic principles: client discipline and institutional discipline. I can apply Michel Foucault's notion of disciplinary power to analyse the rigorous rules, surveillance and instalment collection activities of microcredit NGOs. In Foucault's view, 'discipline'[1] makes individuals and perfect disciplinary mechanisms would make it possible for a single gaze to see everything all the time (1977: 170–173). These disciplinary 'technologies' do not depend on punishment or intimidation, but are applied through apparently 'innocent' aspects of institutional life:

> 'time-tables, compulsory movements, regular activities, solitary meditation, work in common, silence, application, respect and good habits. Ultimately, what one is trying to restore by this technique of correction is not much a judicial subject ... but the obedient subject, the individual subjected to habits, rules, orders, an authority that is exercised continually around him and upon him.'
>
> (Ibid.: 128–129)

I do not believe that the microcredit borrowers interviewed for the present study live in a windowless prison. Nevertheless, my ethnographic data and observations indicate that microcredit NGOs have emerged as a major plank of neoliberal governmental strategy to discipline local developmental subjects in order to make them behave in a particular manner, i.e. that they should repay their credit instalments on the due date. Enforcing the neoliberal developmentalist policy through close surveillance of microcredit programmes has in fact contributed to the closer integration of Third World people into the world capitalist system.

Many of my respondents said that whenever they fail to pay their instalments the NGO staff scold them in front of the other borrowers in the centre. Consequently, they feel inferior (monta *chhoto hoye jai*) and depressed; their social honour is knocked into the dust. The women said that their hearts are broken due to unbearable pain. They are ashamed to show their faces. Owing to the NGOs' disciplinary technology and govermentality for recovering weekly instalments, all the people in the villages studied are very familiar with two concepts: the kisti (instalment) bank and the *taka toler* bank (money-collecting bank). The expression 'kisti day' is familiar to all the villagers, but I do not consider it as an indicator of awareness. Due to the rigidity of the microcredit NGOs goal being solely the collection of instalments, borrowers now see the microcredit organizations as the *kisti* (instalment) collecting bank. Instalment is entangled with the everyday lives of the borrowers and has entered their existing social relationships (see also Karim, 2008, 2011; Rahman, 1999). Since the borrowers are neighbours, they often ask each other if they have arranged their instalment money. Instalment regulates the borrowers' behaviour because most borrowers feel pressure and tension about arranging the instalment money. As one microcredit borrower of Shantigaon village said to me, 'Before instalment day, if you observe closely, you can easily see that most borrowers' faces are gloomy and upset. If you come to my shop, you will find many men who feel dejected.'

Richard Rosenberg argued, 'Can micro borrowers pay high interest rates? … [Microfinance institutions] charging very high interest rates almost always find that demand far outstrips their ability to supply it. Most of their customers repay their loans, and return repeatedly for new loans: this pattern demonstrates the customers' conviction that the loans allow them to earn more than the interest they have to pay. … Thus, there is abundant proof that poor people's tiny businesses can often pay interest rates that would strangle a larger business. Still, this proposition strikes many as counterintuitive' (CGAP, 1996). The above statement illustrates that there are poor borrowers who are able to pay high interest rates, but it shows a failure to understand more deeply how the poor borrowers pay their instalments. The following statement from a microcredit borrower exemplifies borrowers' views:

> Instalment is similar to the pain [*prosob bedona*] experienced by a woman in childbirth. When a client takes credit he feels happy, just like a

child-bearing mother [gorvoboti *maa*], but when he starts to pay the instalment he feels excruciating pain. In order to meet the repayment of instalments borrowers are involved in different types of credit relations such as one client giving a loan to another client with added interest to ensure payment of the instalments.

When discussing the weekly instalments the majority of my respondents said that they face many difficulties in paying the instalment money. There is a constant shortfall between their incomes and expenses. Most of the respondents often claim that they have no lucrative businesses or jobs that produce sufficient profit (*labh*) to cover the cost of food and weekly instalments. Therefore, instalment strongly regulates consumption (such as eating less and starving) and the everyday lives of the poor. Here, some borrowers describe their hardship:

> How can I explain it? We pay the instalments through fasting. I buy rice to eat but when I go to cook it, I change my mind because I am afraid that I won't be able to pay the instalment. So I sell the rice for the instalment payment. It has become a habit.
>
> (Zamila is 40 years old and has been taking loans from GB for more than seven years)

> Dear me, do poor people have a life? We spend our lives in sorrow and difficulties, and kisti is part of them. Instalment destroys mental happiness. Have you seen a two-mouthed snake? It bites people by using both mouths at the same time. If you fail to pay even one instalment the NGO officials and the group bite you from two sides, and the next week two kisti payments bite you again like a two-mouthed snake.
>
> (Ryna, 30 years old)

Most borrowers feel mental pressure, tension and suffer from a lack of sleep. They claim that they do not sleep at night due to worrying about the difficulty of paying the instalment:

> I always feel tense [*chinta*] about paying the instalment. Failure to pay the kisti brings disgrace [bay-izzat *kore*] upon the family because everybody knows about it and the family feels depressed from a social perspective. So, we eat less and pay back instalments.
>
> (Karimunnessa)

Some researchers, e.g. Wright *et al.*, (1997), have argued that savings deposits bring worthy benefits for low-income households, letting them create assets to use as collateral, to reduce consumption instability over time, and to self-finance investments. However, some of my respondents declare that while they pay instalments by suffering starvation or under-consumption, there is no logic in trying to save also. They see this endeavour as a burden, which eventually entangles them with the programme over time. Usually, the poor microcredit borrowers calculate how many instalments they have completed and how many they have to pay. Instalments are a daily burden for poor borrowers. The payment of an instalment gives them respite and they briefly feel better. Paying an instalment decreases the daily tension, but does not mean that the borrower will not take credit again because the future is gloomy and uncertain for the poor in Bangladesh. They do not have much control over their lives.

McDermott (2001) interprets microfinance as a positive neoliberal strategy for global wealth accumulation. However, my study supports the argument made by Townsend *et al.* who view microfinance as a relatively dangerous strategy, 'which draws the poor into the market, imposes on them the responsibility and the costs of their own gains and risks, and often charges them fees to pay the wages of the NGO staff who run the programmes' (2004: 875). Out of all 151 respondents, only 29 per cent of the households meet the instalment payments from profits they made, so the remaining 71 per cent of the borrowers manage their instalments by dint of under-consumption, using capital and taking loans. In fact, one-third (33.1 per cent) of the borrowers manage their payment of their weekly instalments through under-consumption (see Table 7.1).

The borrowers always try to pay off their loans because of the disciplinary enforcement. However, the micro-lending NGOs are strict about repayments but are not concerned as to whether the credit is invested in such a way that helps income generation and reduces poverty among borrowers. I concur with Goetz and Sen Gupta (1996: 56) that extraction of resources from the household economy and the diversion of funds from consumption for the repayment of loans can cause further impoverishment for the poor borrowers.

In this chapter I have argued that mission drift does not only occur when a microcredit organization no longer provides affordable credit to the poor. Rather, it is more likely to take place when microcredit organizations simply provide credit (e.g. traditional money-lenders or traditional financial

Table 7.1 Sources of instalment payment

	Profit % (N)	Capital % (N)	Under-consumption % (N)	Loan and others % (N)	Total number of respondents
Zelegaon	21 (16)	35.5 (27)	38.2 (29)	5.3 (4)	76
Shantigaon	36.8 (14)	26.3 (10)	31.6 (12)	5.3 (2)	38
Nodigaon	37.8 (14)	18.9 (7)	24.3 (9)	18.9 (7)	37
Total	29.1 (44)	29.1 (44)	33.1 (50)	8.6 (13)	151

Source: Author's survey

institutions) and work like commercial organizations towards the achievement of financial goals and sustainability. The microcredit NGOs' officials are engaged in loan disbursement, the recruitment of new borrowers and close monitoring of instalment collection in the field, but they do not give any training or suggestions about how to use the credit. The BRAC officials openly admitted that BRAC's micro-lending division no longer offers any training for its clients. GB officials claim that they still offer some training to the borrowers to improve their lives. The officials informed me that GB offers midwifery training to some of the women in Shantigaon centre. The group leader also confirmed that GB arranges some training and meetings (*kar-moshala*) designed to help the borrowers in the presence of the official at Shantigaon centre. However, when I asked the borrowers in the villages studied whether they had received any training from GB, none of them appeared to have done so. I heard again and again from my respondents that the microcredit officials only advised them to 'pay back your weekly instalments on the due date and take out new loans'.

Rahima stated that 'they (GB) write down many things in their *kisti* book but no officer talks about these'. She claims that about 18 years ago when GB started its operations in her village, it provided borrowers with a pamphlet and told them to learn the 16 decisions (see Table A.2). However, as the villagers are illiterate they could not read these decisions. According to Rahima, when GB came to her village, it spread the idea that it would foster revolutionary change (*bishal porivotton*). No family would have to face poverty anymore but now the villagers know that this is just worthless rhetoric. In recent years Rahima had not heard any of the GB officials mention the 16 decisions, nor had they called a meeting to discuss the villagers' problems and prospects. The villagers recognize that all the banks (micro-lending organizations) in the rural areas of Bangladesh function as money- or instalment-collecting banks. My findings strongly support the study by Montgomery on BRAC in Bangladesh, which reported that present day Rural Development Programme staff are more likely to perceive themselves (and be perceived by members) as 'policemen' and debt-collectors (1995: 11). Owing to commercialization (profit and efficiency) and competition, I argue that microcredit organizations in the areas that I studied have deviated from community mobilization and have suffered from greater emphasis on cost recovery, charging for services, and professionalized staff relationships. As a result, people treat these organizations purely as money-lending business organizations from which anybody who has the ability to pay instalments can get loans with interest.

A few respondents explained that if someone takes out a small loan without an existing business, this amount will be insufficient for them to start a new business. Small loans are often used for daily needs. In contrast, if a client takes out a big loan he will face severe difficulties to pay the instalments because in rural areas it is very difficult to make sufficient profit from the investment of credit. Indeed, the size of the loans, the weekly instalment procedures, and the rigid timelines represent serious limitations for the expansion of business projects that are generally risky and do not usually produce quick returns. Ito (1999) also reached the same conclusion: the GB model micro-loans are not intrinsically conducive to starting up a new business.

In this section I have shown that microcredit NGOs are not immune from neoliberalism, opportunism and self-interest. On the one hand they want to change the condition of the 'developmental subjects' (cf. Morgan, 2006) and on the other hand they also want to increase their own power and/or wealth in order to advance their own agendas. Most of the respondents' narratives of this study express the same phenomenon, namely that their incomes have never matched their expenses, which contributes to borrowers being constantly under adverse conditions of tension, insomnia and hunger. The borrowers are obliged to demonstrate their allegiance to micro-lending NGOs' governmentality, rules and regulations; otherwise, they must to face fines, harassment and lose the possibility of obtaining future loans. I argue that both competition and market-oriented principles have redirected the activities of microcredit programmes into simply sanctioning loans and recovering instalments. Under the neoliberal regime, the micro-lenders and their clients become involved in asymmetrical partnerships: creditors and debtors. In a review Bastelaer (1999) concluded that a re-creation of the traditional patron-client relationship between the micro-lending officials and the borrowers constitutes vertical social capital, which operates to strengthen the credit discipline of the borrowers. However, Bastelaer avoided describing the nature of this relationship, which is undoubtedly based on unequal distribution of power. The promotion of such an uneven relationship has obviously incurred a cost.

The weapons of the weak

In the previous section it was established that the microcredit organizations heavily regulate the everyday lives of most of the borrowers, but do not directly control their behaviour (see also Karim, 2011). Some clients also exploit the opportunities or manipulate the rules for their own ends. The poor people who are involved in the credit programmes are too weak to resist directly the commands of the NGO staff. Instead, they develop covert forms of resistance, which include not only speeches of protest but also a range of practices and alternative social spaces where they can express their dissidence. In what follows I will provide examples to show how the microcredit borrowers manipulate the NGOs' rules to own advantage, and criticize microcredit policies and procedures without coming into direct confrontation with the NGO staff.

The bloodsucker and the *kabuliwala*

One day I stood in front of a small grocery shop in Shantigaon while waiting for a three-wheeler to take me to the city. During this time I talked to the people sitting by the roadside. The shopkeeper informed me that his wife is also a member of the BRAC microcredit programme. The GB branch manager of Pujabazar passed us on his motorbike. As he did so, an elderly man said, 'The bloodsucker [raktha *chusha*] is passing'. As mentioned previously in this volume, some respondents referred to the NGO officials as kabuliwala but I had not heard the expression 'bloodsucker' before. I enquired why he used this term. Initially, he was reluctant to do so, having assumed that I was an employee of one of the microcredit-providing organizations. However, I explained the purpose of my research and that I am not part of an NGO. The man said, 'How did the official manage to get this bike? Where did he find the money to buy it? He got it from all the money they collect from us. They are carrying out a new type of money-lending business [*mahajani sudh babshaw*] for exploiting the poor people. We are the stupid people who do not understand anything.'

He told me that previously only a few people (local money-lenders) lent money at an outrageous rate of interest in the village. The poor people were afraid to borrow money from the traditional money-lenders because if they did and could not to pay the money at the specific times it would cause trouble and they would lose their land or other assets. According to him, people do not understand this new type of *raktha chusa* business. He claimed that the NGOs and some of their followers try to make people comprehend that if people take credit they can pay it through a number of instalments (*olpo-olpo kore*). Therefore, there is no pressure on clients, but this is not the case. He argued that if a person is drawn into this system he will understand how it spirals up and compels poor people to the meshes of debt year in year out. He believes that the microcredit NGOs earn huge profits without giving any benefits to the poor. Hence, the NGO officials can afford motorbikes. According to his observations, nobody does well in his area by borrowing money from microcredit organizations. He used to be a member of the GB micro-loan programme but after paying off the instalments he swore that he would never take out a loan from the NGOs again. He avoids the bloodsuckers.

Later I found out that one of his family members still maintains a savings account in GB for ensuring future loans. I realized that the power of the capitalist system and the position of the micro-lending NGOs in the poor economy are strong. It is not easy for the poor people in rural Bangladesh to evade such a dominant economic power relationship.

Subversions of rules and transgressions

As mentioned above, a major condition of micro-loans is that they are sanctioned to individual borrowers for immediate investment in entrepreneurial activities for generating income. The borrowers are obliged to invest the credit in their specific productive activities within seven days of receiving a loan. However, the difference between the official and actual use of a loan has been noted in many studies (Karim, 2008; Rahman, 2001, 1999; Todd, 1996). Below, I will show how micro-loans have emerged as a mechanism not for only the NGOs but for also for some participants to improve their own position. I found that some borrowers breach the rules of the microcredit programmes for their own benefit.

In every business there there is scope for deception

Rahima was a member of the GB microcredit programme for 18 years. She bore three sons and four daughters. Her husband died six years ago. There are now six people living in her household, including two sons, one daughter, a daughter-in-law and a grandson. When I met her the household had no fixed daily income but required approximately TK 150–200 daily to eke out a living. Rahima's eldest son led a separate conjugal life; the second son was not working regularly but occasionally he provided some income for the family through various activities. The third son drove a rented three-wheeler. The family had no cultivable land; they had 20 decimals of homestead land, which was to be split between Rahima's sons and the sons of her brother-in-law (husband's brother). Rahima will not get any land from her natal family because they have no land.

Rahima was encouraged by her husband to take credit from GB. At first she took TK 2,000 and handed it to her husband to be invested in his fishing business but he was not successful in this. She took credit repeatedly from GB and handed it to her husband for his fishing business but there was no improvement in the quantity or quality of her meals or daily life. Four years ago she had stopped taking micro-loans because she could not pay the instalments owing financial hardship. However, she rejoined the programme in order to help her sons to run a grocery business but her sons lost money in this business. In order to repay instalments on the loan she had to sell her gold chain. Again, her sons pressured her to take out more credit for them to invest in the rice business but they did not succeed in this business either.

Meanwhile, she had taken TK 137,000 from GB, which she loaned to her first cousin (*chachato bhai*) so that he could buy a three-wheeler. Now her cousin gives her TK 2,040 every week towards the instalment, but according to the deed Rahima will get an additional TK 10,000 from her cousin as interest or profit. I asked her whether the GB staff know that she handed over the loan to her cousin, and she replied:

> The GB officer does not know anything about the business between my parallel cousin and me. He thinks that I have invested this micro-loan in my son's three-wheeler. At present the officer does not monitor the way in which borrowers use their credit. The Grameen Bank does business with us and we do business with the bank, so what is the problem? The official only demands weekly credit instalments at the due time, and is happy if he gets it accordingly.

Rahima rationalizes her stance more clearly by claiming that in any business there is some room for falsity. According to Rahima, no one can run a business and make a profit without telling lies. She argues that GB has been doing exactly that to her for the last 18 years. Rahima stated:

> What do we get from this GB business? Nothing! Does GB feel our pain? So, why would we tell the GB official everything? Every week the GB official comes to my house but never asks me what I ate today, nor does he ask whether I can pay the instalments. How do I spend my days? What future can my children expect? Or why am I giving a marriage dowry?

From Rahima's point of view the NGOs only do business and charge high interest rates but never heed borrowers' problems. To her way of thinking, despite the fact that there are many problems in taking out loans from GB; they have to go there because they can pay the money through a number of instalments and this is not possible from other sources. They can get credit within a short time and the micro-lending banks are close at hand. These are the benefits they provide to the borrowers, nothing more. She perceives that none of the poor in her locality have changed their economic fortunes through GB loans because floods, droughts, and unemployment are their constant companions. So she says, 'Poor people play a losing game. Even so the GB never considers this. It never thinks about the borrowers' situations. So I do not think it advantageous to inform GB about the new business that I have set up with the help of microcredit.'

The bank is busy with its interest. Why aren't we?

Hasna joined the bank in the early 1990s and since that time she has taken out some 13 loans from the bank for her husband's tube well setting business. However, her husband has not been successful. He has had to pay penalties on several occasions because he had failed to do the work properly. As a result he gave up this occupation and invested a micro-loan in a three-wheeler business run by a woman in Sylhet city area. Moreover, he was also employed as a cashier for this three-wheeler business. The businesswoman had arranged one new and three second-hand three-wheelers by renting them out to drivers on the condition that each driver pays her TK 400 daily as a hire fee. If the drivers were able to afford TK 100,000 each would be able to buy their respective three-wheeler from her. Therefore, the drivers deposited money with the businesswoman to pay for their respective three-wheelers. A year later, the businesswoman fled with a three-wheeler and TK 100,000. As the drivers could not trace the woman, they have filed a lawsuit against Hasna's husband since he worked as the cashier. The police arrested Hasna's husband, and this plunged the family into a financial crisis. Hasna had to arrange a GB instalment payment and also had to pay the lawyers to enable her husband to be released. During the study period Hasna's husband obtained bail on the condition that he would pay compensation amounting to TK 100,000 to the drivers, after which the drivers would withdraw the case. Therefore, Hasna took out TK 100,000 as a micro-loan on top of her previous GB loan of TK 30,000. According to the lending rules, the bank official was not supposed to sanction a loan for such purpose, but he was able to circumvent the rules and provide the money. I asked Hasna whether the GB official knew that she was not going to invest the credit productively, and she stated:

> We did not say anything to the official but he may have guessed the reason. The bank staff only emphasizes the need to pay the dues. So if he knew of it, then this was not a problem. He needs instalment money, and we are obliged to pay it. GB has many rules about giving credit but do they follow them? No, so if we do not follow them, what is the problem? It is my moral obligation [faraj *kaj*] to help my husband, and not to follow the rules of the bank. If I had followed the bank's rules, my husband would have had to stay in prison.

The microcredit borrowers covertly but consciously criticize the system. Their criticism can be considered as an act of 'covert resistance'. Why is the microcredit borrowers' resistance neither open nor united? Here I turn to James Scott's notions of hidden resistance (1990) and weapons of the weak (1985). In his research in a Malaysian village Scott documented the everyday forms of protests and boycotts of subordinate groups. He reported that oppression and resistance were omnipresent. By focusing on obvious historic 'events' such as organized rebellion or collective action we fail to notice the subtle but powerful forms of 'everyday resistance'. Scott emphasized the lack of consensus in social situations of domination. According to Scott, the subordinated groups are aware of inequalities and their consequences. They clearly understand they are dominated, and by whom and how. However, far from consenting to that domination, they initiate all sorts of subtle ways of living, talking, gossiping or joking about, resisting, undermining, and confronting the unequal and power-laden society in which they live. Scott observed, 'Most of the political life of subordinate groups is to be found neither in the overt collective defiance of power holders nor in complete hegemonic compliance, but in the vast territory between these two polar opposites' (1985: 136).

Scott (1985, 1990) considered the Gramscian notion of hegemony and criticized this notion of overstated dominance. Gramsci (1929) perceived hegemony as a 'material' and 'political' concept. He began his observations on Italian history with reports concerning the history of the 'ruling' and 'subaltern' classes. He wrote, 'The historical unity of ruling classes is realized in the state, and their history is essentially the history of states and groups of states. However, it would be wrong to think that this unity is simply judicial and political. Though such forms of unity do have their importance too, and not in a purely formal sense. The fundamental historical unity, concretely results from the organic relations between state or political society and civil society' (ibid., 1971: 52).

To illustrate the 'passive resistance' of subordinate groups in society Scott introduces the concepts of public and hidden transcripts. When power relations develop through extreme hierarchy and asymmetry, subordinate people build covert forms of action and alternative social spaces where they can articulate their dissidence. In such spaces, as in the backyards and alleys, in the invisible shapes and shadows, in what Scott (1990) calls hidden transcripts, a sense of dignity and autonomy vis-à-vis domination and power is built and protected. These are the protoforms of politics, the 'infrapolitics of the powerless', through which dignity and a sense of community are constructed. Insofar as these are low-profile forms of resistance and hidden, it becomes difficult to recognize them and distinguish them from apathy and subservience. He refers to the activities of subordinate groups as a hidden transcript. According to Scott, 'Every subordinate group creates, out of its ordeal, a hidden transcript that represents a critique of power spoken behind the back of the dominant' (1990: xii). To him, hidden transcripts characterize the discourses that take place offstage, beyond direct observation by power holders. So the hidden transcript is derivative because it consists of those offstage speeches, gestures and practices that confirm, contradict or inflict what appears in the public transcript (ibid.: 4–5).

Chapters 6 and 7 explored the way in which the majority of the respondents repeatedly criticized the strict credit repayment policy, fines and interest rate calculation procedures of the microcredit programmes. The respondents criticized the interest rates imposed against a small loan made by the microcredit-providing NGOs, which are comparatively higher in comparison to those offered by the government or private banks. Since a microcredit organization simply provides a loan with interest and then collects it through a number of instalments, the overwhelming majority of the borrowers treat micro-lending NGOs as money-lending business organizations or as instalment-collecting banks. Rahim characterizes micro-lending officials as *kabuli-wala* and a Bangladeshi peasant calls them *raktha chusha*. What fascinated me was that the respondents never expressed their grievances in front of the credit-providing officials. The microcredit borrowers do not openly challenge the system because they have no alternative options to circumvent this strong capitalist system. Neither do they have any alternative detailed ideas for improving microcredit programmes. Moreover, the usual question asked by the borrowers was: 'Who else will lend to us?' There are some borrowers who manipulate the rules, work as money-lenders and rationalize their activities. They often argue that like the microcredit NGOs they also do business for additional incomes. The hidden resistance of microcredit borrowers may not be sufficient to alter the existing one-sided power-laden relationships between the NGOs and their clients. Even so, the borrowers rationalize their surreptitious activities and criticisms, which give them some pleasure. Through their criticism they may have created the first condition for open resistance even if open resistance has not yet been manifested.

Note

1 According to Foucault, 'Discipline may be identified neither with an institution nor with an apparatus; it is a type of power, a modality for its exercise, comprising a whole set of instruments, techniques, procedures, levels of application, targets; it is a 'physics' or an 'anatomy' of power, a technology' (1977: 215).

8 Credit relations, vulnerability and empowering debt

> I firmly believe we can create a poverty-free world, if we collectively believe in it. In a poverty-free world, the only place you would be able to see poverty is in the poverty museums. When school children take a tour of the poverty museums, they would be horrified to see the misery and indignity that some human beings had to go through. They would blame their forefathers for tolerating this inhuman condition, which existed for so long, for so many people.
>
> (Muhammad Yunus[1], Nobel Peace Prize Acceptance Speech)

The main aim of microcredit intervention is that it can improve the economic condition of the poor, enhance their quality of life in terms of housing and consumption, possibly boost savings in the long run, and provide a safety net in the event of family catastrophe or create the potential to invest in other income-generating activities (see Table A.1 and Table A.2). Muhammad Yunus believed that poverty can be eliminated from the world if there is a vision that poverty is unacceptable. Policymakers and programme organizers are keen to learn the extent of the economic impact of microcredit on borrowers and society as a whole. Although researchers assembled evidence to suggest that microcredit enables millions of people to 'pull themselves up by their bootstraps' (Smith and Thurman, 2007: 205), in Chapters 6 and 7 of this volume we saw how the relationship between microcredit and poverty alleviation entails contradictory processes. In this chapter I investigate why people take out micro-loans year after year despite the many disadvantages it has for them. Following the entitlement approach portrayed by Amartya Sen, I explore and analyse in detail the mechanisms through which poverty forces many poor households into using credit year after year thus becoming further mired in debt. My study also provides insights into who benefits from credit and why.

Resources, vulnerability and insecurity

Rural people share vulnerabilities, which can best be described through the concept of insecurity which I explore in this chapter. This concept covers the complexities and constraints in poor people's lives that compel them to join microcredit programmes. The term insecurity has been applied in various contexts but it is chiefly linked to food insecurity (Chattopadhay, 2007). A theory of social vulnerability that is related to food insecurity has been drawn from debates about human ecology, expanded entitlements and political economy. Social risk allows the assessment of exposure to harmful perturbations, ability to cope with crises, and the potential for recovery (Bohle *et al.*, 1994). The idea of vulnerability is crucial to structuring the discussion of food insecurity in marginal spaces. Robert Chambers (1989: 1) described two aspects of vulnerability: an external side of risks, shocks and stress to which individuals or households are always subject, and the internal side where there may be insufficient resources to cope without damaging the situation of the household.

However, the definition of vulnerability still remains unclear. Dilley and Boudreau (2001) pointed out that during the late 1980s and early 1990s the general notions of vulnerability were refined for specific analytical purposes. For example, experts concerned with disaster management emphasized the need to identify the magnitude of the damage to economic assets in addition to the damage sustained by the affected population. Food security experts conceptualize vulnerability in terms of a measure of how much poor people slide towards a state of food insecurity or famine-like conditions or actual famine itself. In his entitlement approach to hunger and poverty, Amartya Sen challenged the belief that famine, drought and food insecurities are solely due to supply-side functions (Sen, 1981, 1982, 1987, 1992, 1999). In his analysis of famine, Sen writes that:

> Starvation is the characteristic of some people not having enough food to eat. It is not the characteristic of there being not enough food to eat. While the latter can be a cause of the former, it is but one of many possible causes ... food supply statements say something about a commodity (or a group of commodities) on its own. Starvation statements are about a relationship of persons to that commodity ... [these] translate readily into statements of ownership of food by persons. In order to understand starvation it is therefore necessary to go into the structure of ownership. Ownership relations are one kind of entitlement relations. It is necessary to understand the entitlement systems within which the problem of starvation is to be analysed.
>
> (1981: 1)

His views reflected a paradigm shift from a 'natural causes of hunger' model to 'socially and economically created systems of hunger and poverty'. Sen highlighted how a lack of access and effective demand became entrenched in social, economic and political relations. Entitlement, according to him, was 'the legal means available in a society, including the use of productive possibilities, trade opportunities, entitlements *vis-a-vis* the state, and other means of acquiring food' (ibid., 1981: 53). Sen (1999) also considered that a number of concrete factors were significant in determining a person's or a family's ability to acquire goods (including food) and services: *endowment* (i.e. the ownership of productive resources as well as wealth), *production possibilities* (i.e. the available technology as well as people's ability to make actual use of it), and the *exchange conditions* that exist through production and trade, which determine the consumption set available to a person with a given endowment.

Sen (1981) described the failure of entitlement to cover subsistence needs as the key cause of starvation and death by famine. According to him, 'a person may be forced into starvation even when there is plenty of food around if he loses his ability to buy food in the market, through a loss of income (for example, due to unemployment or the collapse of the market for goods that he produces and sells to earn a living)' (ibid., 1999: 161). Sen (1981) considered two types of entitlement failure: *direct entitlement failure* and *trade entitlement failure*. He identifies direct entitlement failure as a slump of entitlement to below subsistence needs due to a decrease in the food produced for one's consumption. Trade entitlement failure is a decrease in entitlement below subsistence needs owing to a worsening in disparity between the commodities that one sells and the food that one needs to buy. Agarwal (1994) observed that in the context of rural poor families, the key determinants of exchange entitlement are ownership of land and access to employment benefits and other income-earning means.

The concept of vulnerability that I use here draws on the above concepts of insecurity and entitlement. I use the term vulnerability because I believe it captures best the economic stress, illness, poverty, or food insecurity of the poor microcredit borrowers in the three villages studied.

Credit relations and poverty alleviation

This section is based on three narratives which outline in detail the interviewees' financial position, reasons for taking out loans, and use of loans. Each client's loan history, income and occupation are important to illustrate how microcredit is linked to the economic conditions and actions of the borrowers at the local level.

Narrative 1: debt begets debt

Suchona is a microcredit borrower who worked as a centre leader for the GB microcredit programme in Zelegaon in the early 1990s. The GB programme in Zelegaon operated its weekly instalment collection activities out of Suchona's house. As a result, she was especially aware of the advantages and disadvantages of the microcredit programme.

Suchona was married off to a family acquaintance when she was 15 years of age. Her natal house is located in the same upazila, approximately 4–5 kilometres from Zelegaon village. Like many elderly people in the village neither she nor her husband were educated, although Suchona now knows how to write her name. She told me that these days most women in Zelegaon know how to write their names, because they learned to do when taking out loans from different NGOs. Suchona has five children aged between ten and 20 years. Due to financial hardship she rented out a room in her house to BRAC for TK 300 for providing primary school education but she regretted that her first three sons had not received an education. Poverty as well as their reluctance to study had prevented them from being educated. The fourth and fifth sons (aged 13 years and ten years at the time of my data collection) were studying in the seventh and fourth grades.

Suchona's household has a *katcha* toilet, which is shared with two other households and is used by 25 people. Some years ago they had a ring toilet but it sank into the mud. They have no money to make a new ring toilet. Suchona and her neighbours share a shallow tube well from which they fetch drinking and cooking water every day. Suchona informs me that her household has no cultivable land.

The family has 20 decimals of homestead land, which was jointly (joutho) inherited. The homestead land was subsequently divided equally between her family and her brother-in-law's family (her husband's eldest brother). I asked Suchona how she will divide up her share of the homestead land between her five sons and brother-in-law's three sons and two daughters, and whether her *vabi* (sister-in-law) will give any land to her two daughters. Suchona became silent and thoughtful and was unable to answer. However, her brother-in-law's eldest son, who is now a father of four children, explained that land disputes are now a regular occurrence in Zelegaon, because most homestead lands are jointly owned. Therefore, the division of homestead land often leads to arguments and fighting. The man added that two days ago the heirs of Ajma's uncle were involved in a fight in which sticks were used (Ajmal is the husband of Nasibun. She is a microcredit borrower from another *para*). Suchona did not know whether her sister-in-law will give any land to her daughters but she was worried about the changing economic structure of Zelegaon. It has become common for people who have left the village and moved abroad to work to return and purchase homestead land from the poor with their remittance money. Suchona considers the example of Samirun, another GB microcredit borrower from Zelegaon, who bought a huge amount of land (240 decimals) from poor people. Samirun was also trying to buy cultivable land. Likewise, outsiders have bought most of the cultivable land from the poor for their own purposes. As a result, the poor are increasingly becoming landless and impoverished.

Suchona first took TK 2,000 as a micro-loan from GB about 18 years ago. She took out further loans from GB to support her husband's business and to eke out a livelihood. She believed that if GB gave credit to men she would have never have become involved in the programme. I asked her who takes credit in her area, and she replied:

Most people take out loans; you will find only a handful of people who have no current income, business or young sons and they are the ones who do not belong to the programme.

Suchona informed me that despite the fact that for the past 18 years GB had operated only one centre in Zelegaon, two months prior to our meeting, Eti, a member of her centre, joined with 20 other women to establish a new centre. According to Suchona, the women did this because they live in a different *para* and it is difficult for them to make the journey to Zelegaon. Moreover, it is very difficult to service 90 members in one centre.

Suchna's family has never been financially well off. When she came as a bride to this family she discovered that the family had always struggled to make a living. The family had a few decimals of cultivable land, and her husband was the sole breadwinner but his income was insufficient so they were always poor. Like most of the villagers her husband was a fishmonger, but due to financial hardship a lot of the time he could not run his business. As a result, the family gradually sold off their cultivable land. Previously, the local money-lenders had lent money to the poor people at a rate of 100 to 200 per cent interest. With no other alternatives available to them the poor took money from the traditional money-lenders. Her husband also took money from them but found it difficult to discharge the loan. This caused a family dispute. Suchona argued that taking money from the local money-lenders was always problematic. If people failed to repay the money they had borrowed, the local money-lender called for village arbitration (*panchayat*) in order to collect the money. Such incidents frequently ended in violence. As a result, when the GB micro-lending officials offered credit they enthusiastically took the opportunity to accept it.

Suchona explained that there was always a disparity between her family's income and expenditure, so she always had to take out a loan to pay the instalment on the previous one. However, she became seriously impoverished following the death of her husband died seven years prior to our meeting. At that time the family often went many days without food. In order to provide one meal a day for her children Suchona worked on the land (*mati kata srawmik*) with other women in different places within the upazila. Every day she earned TK 35–40, which she used to buy rice. Sometimes she worked only for 2 to 3 kilogrammes of wheat, but every month her household was in deficit. During those times she took out small micro-loans for household necessities. She often faced serious obstacles to pay the instalments on the due date. I asked her whether the GB officials were unkind to her at that time, and Suchona claimed that they often behaved roughly with many borrowers including her, but even so the villagers still needed them. According to her, when the villagers had serious problems GB came to the village and supported them. They lent money to the villagers so that they could earn a livelihood. She pointed out that if the borrowers complained and as a consequence the bank was to leave their village they would face greater difficulties. She argued that the bank had saved them from the local money-lender. Now, however, the situation has changed. Over the past few years a number of NGOs have established themselves in this village and now the villagers can choose between GB, BRAC, ASA, Gameen Shakti and FIVDB.

When I interviewed her Suchona was paying instalments on a GB loan of TK 70,000 which she used to build a house. Previously, her family lived in a tiny ramshackle house which was not rain-proof, so during storms rainwater poured in through the roof. Her sons persuaded her to take out a loan and build a new house. Suchona's new house has three rooms, and is tin-roofed with unplastered brick-built walls and a mud floor. In one of the rooms there is a dilapidated wooden bed where Suchona sleeps. There is a small display cabinet in which she keeps some cups, rice dishes, plates, spoons and a bowl. There are some benches and chairs, and also a small second-hand colour television. Suchona informed me that two years ago her sons pressurized her into taking out a TK 5,000 loan from ASA in order to purchased this television. She keeps the benches and chairs because GB borrowers and the official use this room for sanctioning loans and collecting instalments every week. There is a small kitchen area in the corner of the room. A number of string clothes lines were strung across the room. She hoped that within one year she would arrange her first and second sons' marriages and demand furniture and other domestic items as marriage gifts for the house. Inside the second room there was a coarse mat made of bamboo slips on the floor on which her sons slept at night. In the third room there was a very old platform wooden bed in which Suchona's *chacha shasur* (her husband's paternal uncle) spends his time. The man is old, simple-minded and a bachelor. He cannot earn money to support himself, so he is entirely dependent on Suchona's family. Although the man has a share of the homestead land of this family, he does not contribute to the family income any way. I observed that he was not treated well and that he is distressed about the way he is treated.

Despite the fact that Suchona's family now own a brick-built house funded by a micro-loan, which contributes to Suchona's symbolic capital (honour, prestige), she was unhappy because her sons often have to suffer to pay the instalments. Suchona claims that her eldest son now drives a rented three-wheeler. Each day he pays TK 400 to the owner of the three-wheeler, and most days his earnings only cover his rent. The second son has followed in his father's footsteps; he sells fish and runs the family. However, the son suffers from severe stomach pains and frequently is unable to work. The third son was learning electrical work for which he receives TK 200 per month. I asked Suchona how she intends to divide this three-roomed house among her five sons, and she replied, 'it is in the hands of Allah'.

Suchona claimed that her family has not been able to overcome their financial hardship. The family has no savings. Her family takes credit and tries to provide a daily subsistence. It is difficult for her to discern any difference between her family's financial circumstances before and after she started taking microcredit. Like her husband, her son takes out loans to run the fishing business. She thinks that the main problem with fishing is that it is seasonal and only provides an occupation for six or seven months of the year. Business is very sluggish during the rainy season because fish are not available at that time. When her husband ran this business he spent the rainy season idle. At the time her son was also facing the same problem. So during those 4–5 months her family was in a miserable situation. During the rainy season Suchona's family is in a miserable situation. More importantly, during this time not only does the family spend all the business capital but also has to take out additional loans to cover the cost of food. When the fishing season starts again the family is forced to take out yet another loan in order to run the business. Thus, the family is stuck in the credit programme year after year. I asked Suchona if her family could now at least obtain food on a daily basis:

> Yes, in this sense there is a difference. Just a few years ago my family experienced dire poverty; you cannot imagine it. My family faced severe difficulties to arrange a meal a day sometimes. Now we can have two meals a day. But now my sons are grown up and they do some work. In spite of this, sometimes we deliberately cut down on the number of meals that we eat in order to pay the instalments.
>
> Q: Is there any difference in terms of what you were able to eat before you joined the credit programme in comparison to what you eat now?
>
> The quality of food is the same. If we wish to eat a big fish or buy clothes for the Eid ceremonies, we cannot because food and clothing are very expensive now. Before the microcredit programme we ate arum leaves or fried arum roots [kochu *pata* or *lata vaj*]) with dried fish or small edible shellfish [ghura *chingri*], fried potato [alu *vaji*], or mashed potato [alu *vorta*], mashed aubergine [begun vorta] or fried chilli [pora *morich*] with rice and we eat those now too.
>
> Q: Do you think your sons will do well from GB loans in future?
>
> How can I say? We have nothing.

Suchona's family is not an exceptional case in Zelegaon. Most of the villagers are poverty stricken. The poor people in Suchona's area are always in debt. According to Suchona, while the rich people take out new loans for some project she takes out loans for food or for the payment of outstanding dues (*amra loan deye loan mari*). None of the families in her village have become self-sufficient (*sabolombi*) through the microcredit programmes. Poverty forces the villagers to take credit. Sometimes people invest their credit in a grocery or vegetable business, or they use it to cover the cost of medical treatment, and recently they use it for the three-wheeler business. She informed me that one could now take out TK 200,000 to buy a three-wheeler by putting down TK 60,000 as a deposit. Some women now run this business by using microcredit: they take out TK 100,000 for the purpose of buying a three-wheeler but in reality they secretly hand the money to their relatives and keep the interest of TK 10,000 themselves.

In rationalizing the microcredit programme, Suchona viewed GB as a good source of capital. She argued that because most people in her area are poor it allows them obtain large amounts of money and to be able to pay all the instalments. The richer people in her area were more enthusiastic about getting credit than the poor. When GB first arrived in Zelegaon, the *mullahs* did not like people taking credit from the bank but now they themselves also do it. At the end of my interview with Suchona I asked her what were the main limitations of microcredit involvement. I learned from her that debt begets debt in a poor locality and that it is very difficult for the poor to free themselves from debt. As Suchona said:

> The GB credit system sucks borrowers into a wheel of debt; the wheel of debt never stops. The wheels of a rickshaw or a bus stop once in a while but the wheel of GB debt always goes round. So, if one gets caught up in this wheel it is very difficult to get free.

Narrative 2: credit to overcome unanticipated difficulties

As the above case study shows micro-loans are used to meet everyday needs in a poor locality. It also shows how microcredit borrowers from poor localities are caught in a spiralling debt trap. In the following case I will explore ways in which the lives of people in poor households run in a cycle that not only brings material impoverishment, but also further limits the options for escaping the cycle.

Nasibun's household is one of the poorest households among the microcredit borrowers in Zelegaon. Owing to poverty her eldest daughter (16 years of age) left school after completing the fifth grade and was hoping to be married but no proposal had come yet (*ghor ashena*). The second son, who did not attend school, was 14 years old and worked in an electrical shop. The third son was 12 years old and studied at a free *madrasha* (Islamic) school in the fifth grade. The fourth son was seven years old and disabled. Nasibun's household had 12 decimals of joint homestead land. Her household may get six decimals of land which will be divided among the heirs. The heirs frequently get involved in disputes about the division of this land but cannot reach an agreement. When I enquired how the land will be distributed, Nasibun did not give me a definite answer. She just said it was an ongoing problem (*vishon jamela*). Two days before my data collection a violent fight broke out. Nasibun informed me that none of the parties had yet proceeded to litigation.

Nasibun's husband is a simple day labourer who has no fixed income. As her husband is mentally retarded, he cannot always find work. The family needs at least TK 100–150 to pay for two meagre meals per day but cannot obtain this amount of money. Her husband provides some income for the family through various activities including planting paddy rice, harvesting rice on other peoples' farms, and also by selling small fish. Nasibun pointed out that her family had been in deficit on its expenditure so she got involved in microcredit membership. She had been taking micro-loans from GB for ten years prior to our discussion. However, before that she had not joined this programme because she did not have the ability to pay the instalments. Her natal family, which come from the same village, tried to help her when they could despite being poor themselves. Everybody encouraged Nasibun to take out loans and give money to her husband to run a small fish business. Consequently, Nasibun requested the group leader and the GB official for credit. She assured the GB official that her husband would invest this credit in his small edible shellfish business in the local market. However, according to Nasibun, her husband did not run his business properly. As her husband is not good at doing arithmetic, he does not charge the correct price. Nasibun took out a second loan in order to pay for some household loans. During the past seven years, she has continually taken credit for family expenses, her son's treatment and her husband's seasonal business.

Nasibun's disabled son cannot walk or use his hands properly. Every month she has to take him to the Sylhet Osmani Government Hospital for treatment for which she must pay. Six years ago she took out a GB loan of TK 5,000 and spent all of it on the boy's treatment. Nasibun did not know how long she would be able to continue his treatment. She was also unsure whether her ailing child would be cured. Nasibun herself also suffers from goitre (abnormal enlargement of the thyroid gland) disease, but cannot get treatment because it is too expensive. I asked her whether microcredit helps her family financially, and she replied:

> My family does not do anything. We manage to survive [*teekay aache*] and live hand to mouth. Every day we struggle to provide two meals [*dui bela vath*]. When we face severe difficulty, we can use credit for family expenses.
>
> Q: How do you provide the instalment money for the credit programme? What can I say? Allah helps the poor. Even though I am sick I do some work in people's houses. I seek help from different people and people also help my ailing son. This is the way we spend our lives … Once I took credit, then paid some instalments and then took out another loan, and life goes on in this way.

Domestically the family was deeply mired in poverty. The household occupies a tiny ramshackle house to which a rain-proof tin roof had only recently been added but the walls were fenced by old bamboo slips. Inside the house there is a crumbling, cheap wooden bed, a clothes hanger, and some old utensils. Nasibun possessed two *saris*: one bought a few months prior to our meeting; the other was torn. Nasibun's household used a *katcha* (unsanitary) lavatory and had no tube well. Nasibun fetched drinking water from a neighbour's tube well. I talked to Nasibun in the doorway of her shack. She said, 'I have no chair in my house to offer you to sit on'. During the conversation, her sick child pestered her for food. Nasibun went into the house and returned with a handful of musty rice (*vath*) with dried chilli (*pora morich*). The boy sat on a *piri* (small wooden stool) and with the help of his sister hungrily gulped down the food. I enquired whther this was a normal meal in Nasibun's house. She said that it depends on the season, but normally arum leaves and roots fried with dried fish, fried or mashed potato, pulses (daal) and dried chilli with rice are the staple food of the family. They also eat the small shellfish sold by her husband. I enquired if the credit programme would improve her way of life. She became silent and could not answer. Although Nasibun has been taking micro-loans for several years, she does not think that microcredit could give her household a bright future. However, without the credit programme she could not see how else she would manage. She mentioned that at present the village people would not like to lend money to her family because previously she could not pay the debts as promised. Moreover, most households in her village were poor and struggled to support themselves so they were unable to lend money to others. Some people are financially well off but they do not lend money either. In this sense, the GB loan is advantageous; she can pay it back over many instalments.

As a senior member of the microcredit programme, Nasibun was able to take out TK 170,000 as a micro-loan, of which she gave TK 150,000 to her nephew (her sister's son) to buy a three-wheeler. The rest of the loan she used to buy a tin roof for her house and pay her son's medical expenses. Nasibun repaid TK 2,550 as a weekly instalment. To cover this her nephew gave her TK 2,500 every week. In addition, her nephew was to give her TK 7,000 in interest. I asked her what she thought of this new money-lending business. Nasibun is positive about her present investment because previously she was treated harshly by the officials when she failed to pay the weekly instalments. In this case, Nasibun was able to pay her instalments easily. In addition, by lending the credit money to her nephew she was getting some additional income, which would benefit her family and cover her son's medical expenses. I enquired what would happen if the GB officials were to find out about her activities. Nasibun replied, 'What is the problem for GB? I am alone in doing this? Nowadays many members are doing the same. I am honest so I have told you about it, but the others would never tell you'.

Domestic and financial uncertainties are common events for Nasibun's family, and she did not expect microcredit to resolve all her future problems. As her household is very poor, she will be happy if her sons are able to provide two meals a day and if she can arrange her daughter's marriage with ease.

Narrative 3: You cannot survive by another's oil

The third case study concerns a microcredit borrower who is regarded as a successful microcredit borrower in Shantigaon and the nearby villages.

Shorola is a Hindu housewife and a long-term microcredit borrower of the GB and BRAC programmes based in Shantigaon village. Shorola has four children. Shorola's family has seven decimals of homestead land, a rain-proof tin-roofed house and an annual income of about TK 160,000. Shorola's husband Raton is very familiar to all the microcredit borrowers and the micro-lending officials in Shantigaon. Everybody considers him to be a successful microcredit borrower. When I first visited the Shantigaon centre, the GB official introduced Raton and his wife to me as an example of successful borrowers. However, 16 years ago their lives were not good. Raton left school after completing the eighth grade owing to his parent's financial difficulties. Like the rest of his family he pursued the *chira-muri* business. In the early stages of this business, he borrowed money from the local traditional money-lenders at their usual high interest rates; as a result, his business was not profitable. Consequently, he left off this profession until early 1998 when GB the micro-lending operations were mushrooming in the Shantigaon area.

Raton first took out a micro-loan of TK 5,000 through his mother to run his *chira-muri* business. Since then he has continued to take out loans and has invested in his businesses. Raton is a hard-working man, so his businesses never make losses. Sometimes he makes only a minimal amount of profit. In 2000 Raton married Shorola and since then he has taken out loans in his wife's name rather than his mother. Raton states, 'I have some savings but I do not understand how to utilize it properly'. He also understood that he could not rely entirely on his *chira-muri* business, which he no longer enjoyed, if he wished to continue to be successful. Raton learnt to drive three-wheelers and in 2001 he asked his wife to apply for a TK 200,000 loan from GB to buy a three-wheeler. Raton handed over his homestead land deed and TK 60,000 as security for the loan. After taking out this loan, Raton bought a second-hand three-wheeler for TK 212,000, which he drove himself. He knew how to reap the benefits by running this three-wheeler business. He handled the three-wheeler cautiously and got used to his new profession. In early 2001 there were very few three-wheelers on the Shantigaon and Puja bazaar road so he earned a great deal. In 2003 Raton applied for a loan of TK 150,000 through his wife to buy another three-wheeler. As this sum was insufficient, he took out further loans from another microcredit organizations so that he could afford to buy a second-hand three-wheeler for TK 250,000. According to Raton, the NGO officials like him as he is able to repay the instalments on his loans without difficulty.

Raton does not like being idle. He is always seeking ways to expand his business. He hates poverty and does not want to be a burden on others. He starts work after breakfast early in the morning, returns home for lunch, and goes back to work until nightfall. His wife carries out all the household chores such as cooking, looking after the children and her mother-in-law. In 2009 Raton took out a loan of TK 200,000 from GB to finance a new three-wheeler. Now Raton drives the new three-wheeler and he has rented the two old three-wheelers to other people. As a result, he earns TK 800 daily from these two three-wheelers. Now Shorola's family pays TK 4,300 in weekly instalments and maintains a monthly and a weekly savings account at TK 100 and TK 50 respectively. The family also has insurance at TK 500 per month. The other microcredit borrowers in Shantigaon are very envious of the success of Shorola's family.

I talked to Shorola on the verandah of her house one morning. As I am a Muslim, I did not enter her house. The sun does not warm the house nor does the breeze cool it, because it is situated close to a two-storey primary school. Shorola's mother-in-law informed me that the family used to own the land that school is built on. Due to poverty and ignorance they sold the land to the government for building the primary school.

During my conversation with Shorola, her husband Raton entered the house after having completed his ablutions. He was wrapped in a piece of his wife's old *sari* and used a piece of ragged cloth as a towel. Shorola's mother-in-law also wore a very old sari. The family's attire did not match their economic prosperity. From the verandah, I peeped inside the house and saw that Shorola's husband had perhaps invested all the money from his business instead of more comfortable furniture for the house. Inside the house there are two wooden bed, a small work table for his sons and some *shikas* (string bags) in which the family keeps their clothes. While I talked to Shorola her husband quickly ate his breakfast before donning his uniform, which is provided by the three-wheeler association. He then left for work.

Shorola knew very little about her husband's three-wheeler business or microcredit investment. She is the facilitator who takes money from different microcredit organizations. Shorola claimed that her husband is more knowledgeable about the family matters and business. Raton did not consider microcredit to be the sole weapon in the fight against poverty. 'If you have no oil in your own body you cannot function by another's oil,' says Raton. According to him, people who have no capital, skills or business cannot progress despite financial help from a microcredit programme. He said, 'I have some money, so I can take the principal amount from GB and a little from BRAC, and invest the money properly to ensure a good living and an education for my children.' Moreover, he argued that without hard work, intelligence, self-discipline and austerity microcredit is of no use. Raton's assertion that Allah helps those who help themselves is interestingly matched with Weber's idea of the Protestant work ethic (M. Weber, 1991). Raton again referred to his elder brother Robi who has been involved in credit programmes but still faces difficulties in providing two meals a day. Raton told me that his oldest brother spends most of his time asleep and does not work so where will he get money from?

At the time, Raton's oldest son was seven years old and was in the second grade at a private kindergarten in Pujabzar, some six kilometres from Shantigaon. Each day Raton took his son to and from school. Raton was optimistic about his oldest son's future because he does well at school. His second son was five years old and attended the primary school next to his house. The other two children were too young to go to school. Raton's elderly mother also lives with him, because his brother Robi could not afford to keep her. 'Every week I need TK 1,500 to run my household. The quality of my family's food is very good. In addition, I have to spend some money on my sons' education', said Raton. Sometimes he found it difficult to pay the instalments if the three-wheelers broke down or during the rainy season when business is very slow. In such situations, he used his saving in the NGO banks to pay the instalments. When income is good again he saves the money in his bank account.

Raton planned to take out another loan to buy a new three-wheeler. His business is still going well and he is hopeful about his prospects. Interestingly, he has not yet bought any cultivable land or extended his homestead land. He considered land to be too expensive and said that he could not afford to buy any.

In the December of 2010 I visited Shantigaon again to meet my field assistants to inform them that I was leaving Sylhet at the end of the month. I went to the tea and grocery stall and met the owner of the shop, Mehedi. I spotted Raton in the shop looking depressed and unhappy. Mehedi told me that for the past month Raton's three-wheeler business had not been doing well. Four new three-wheelers had started operating and competing for business on the same road as Raton. As a result, the number of three-wheelers was higher in relation to the number of passengers and in consequence Raton's income had rapidly declined. Raton said, 'When I started this business on the Shantigaon and Puja bazaar road there were only four three-wheelers and I had the monopoly of this business in this road. Day by day the number of three-wheelers increased, and now there are 12. However, the number of passengers has remained about the same.' Mehedi informed me that at least two or three families have applied for loans to buy three-wheelers so they will add to the competition. Raton may be able to find another road on which to operate his business, but the rural market has already been saturated.

Discussion

Analysis of the data provided by these three cases suggests that with the exception of the third case the microcredit programmes have not brought about any noteworthy financial improvement to the borrowers' lives and their households. There is a plethora of borrowers who have procured small loans but who have no existing capital, nor a certain level of income or stable business to run, and who consequently are unable to achieve the expected economic outcomes of these microcredit programmes. More specifically, the above ethnographic example reveals that the borrowers who benefit from microcredit programmes have existing economic and social capital.

On the basis of membership and financial ability, I see two categories of microcredit borrowers in my research. The first segment (30.5 per cent) is in the same or promising situation as Raton (see the third case study) with his profitable business. In fact, this segment consists of those borrowers who are financially well off (such as school teachers, rural doctors, household members abroad, those who have lucrative businesss, or own a large amount of land), have maintained their membership for many years and paid instalments without interruption. The second group (69 per cent) comprises a large number of failed market entrepreneurs who are economically poor and who have been suffering from a vicious circle of indebtedness over the years. These households reflect the phenomenon that microcredit is simply an informal way to obtain subsistence and a temporary means to cope with financial difficulties as illustrated by the first and second case study. I should mention that there are some borrowers among the above-mentioned categories, i.e. both in the financially well off and poor families, who generally do not continuously maintain their memberships but maintain a savings account because it functions as security for taking credit when they might need it in the future.

The microcredit borrowers from Zelegaon village were in a comparatively fragile situation financially speaking. Of the 76 respondents the overwhelming majority were in a vulnerable situation financially despite the fact that many borrowers in this village have been using credit programmes for a decade or more. The microcredit borrowers from Nodigaon village were in a slightly better position than the borrowers in Zelegaon. The reason for this is that Nodigaon is adjacent to the urban area and is situated on the main road between Sylhet and Sunamgonj. Some households in this village gave up their previous occupations in fishing and the fish trade and have become involved in different occupations including driving three-wheelers, cart-pulling, rickshaw driving, and stationery shops. The microcredit borrowers from Shantigaon were in a better position in comparison to those living in Zelegaon and Nodigaon, because of the 38 borrowers in Shantigaon 20 households are involved in good professions (such as teaching, health care, pharmacy, grocery business, hair salon, stone crushing, three-wheeler driving and bamboo-cane crafts).

Although the borrowers have to show the money-lending organizations that they take out loans to improve their financial prospects, the first two case studies reveal that most borrowers cannot or do not use the total amount of credit for productive purposes. They frequently switch their full loan or part of a loan from one sector to another as they have little or no control over their lives. Thus it is difficult to work out the exact ways in which credit is used. To understand this would require a long-term observation which was not possible within this study.

However, most of the borrowers claim that they commonly use loans to buy food. With the exception of food expenses, the borrowers often also use their loans for paying off previous loans, buying housing materials and paying for medical treatment. Table 8.1 shows how my respondents used their loans.

Next I will discuss some economic indicators that may explain why most borrowers cannot achieve improvements through microcredit involvement. What are the prospects for the microcredit borrowers' households, like Suchona (first case study) or Nasibun (second case study), if they continue their membership for the next few years?

I have examined the issue of land ownership and access to arable land for the microcredit borrowers' households. Social hierarchy in rural Bangladesh is generally understood in terms of land ownership and access to cultivable land. Land is considered to be the most coveted of resources and an important means of production. Despite the fact that migration and education contribute to class stratification, most commentators on Bangladesh invariably assess rural class on the pre-eminence of land ownership (Jansen, 1987; Streefland *et al.*, 1986; Jahangir, 1979, 1982; van Schendel, 1981). Every major national survey has found sharp increases in landlessness in Bangladesh. De Vylder (1982 cited in White, 1992) estimated that 60 per cent of households in Bangladesh are effectively landless. The findings from the 1996 agricultural census of Bangladesh show that the absolute number of landless households, i.e. those who own less than 0.5 acres of land and can be treated as 'effectively landless households', increased from 3.7 million in 1983–84 to 6.4 million in 1996. Furthermore, landholdings are highly fragmented. Some

Table 8.1 Frequent uses of credit (with the exception of food expenses)

Activities	Frequency	%
Business and handicrafts	83	54.96
Agricultural activities	4	2.65
Poultry	2	1.32
Rickshaw	2	1.32
Lending money on interest	8	5.30
Sponsor for migration	3	1.99
Paying previous loan	22	14.60
Marriage expenses	4	2.65
Meet medical expenses	5	3.31
Three-wheeler	5	3.31
Land transaction	3	1.99
Housing	10	6.62
Total	151	100.00

Source: Author's survey of microcredit in Nodigaon, Shantigaon and Zelegaon villages.

researchers describe rural society in Bangladesh as increasingly polarized into rich and poor: the poor have great obstacles in improving their lot but the rich are becoming richer and more powerful (Jansen, 1987; Hartman and Boyce, 1983; Arens and Beurden, 1977; Jahangir, 1979). My ethnographic data obtained from the three villages also illustrates the same phenomenon and I argue that this process is likely to be continued.

The family size (see Chapter 4 in this volume), land ownership and the concurrent occupation structure of the respondent households were studied and were found to underpin the above conclusion. With the exception of one household, all the respondent households had homestead lands but the amount of land was negligible and varied between 3 and 15 decimals. With regard to agricultural land, most of the respondents studied have no cultivable land. Of 76 respondents from Zelegaon village only 7.9 per cent (six) of households and of 37 respondents from Nodigaon village only 5.4 per cent (two) of households have a small amount of cultivable land. However, of 38 respondents in Shantigaon 39.5 per cent (15) households have some agricultural land but a large portion of their land is low-lying marshland so the owners cannot cultivate the land properly.

The concurrent occupation structure of these households (the large majority were involved in the fishing business or were day labourers) and the education level of their children (most did not even complete secondary level education) indicated little potential to get lucrative jobs and to increase their land ownership in their local areas in future. Most homestead lands in Zelegaon village were jointly owned, so land disputes occurred frequently. Financial inequality was found to exist among the borrowers. Microcredit programmes tended to reinforce and increase the existing inequalities on a daily basis. If the current occupational structure and fertility trend remain the same in the study villages, I predict that poor people's marginalization in terms of land holdings, resources and income will continue in spite of their increased access to these credit programmes.

The inhabitants' vulnerability and the periods of scarcity are extensive in the villages studied. The economic crises have not been limited to a single household. The majority of the borrowers belong to deficit households in the sense that their incomes are less than their expenditure. They have little or no scope for maximizing their profits. I investigated the conventional notions of saving by asking borrowers whether they can accumulate an amount of money after their monthly expenditure, but they were hardly able to save at all. They can only save money if they cut consumption or delay consumption so as to pay the credit instalments. With regard to food consumption before and after microcredit involvement, we may not be able to reach a solid conclusion. Nonetheless, I was repeatedly informed by most borrowers that their expenditure exceeded their incomes: 'Our expenditure and income or profit never matched'.

Microcredit NGOs operate according to neoliberal principles of competition, profit and entrepreneurship but most of the study respondents were not in such a business environment and if they were, they could not run their respective businesses all year round. In Zelegaon most borrowers' households were involved in the fishing business but during the rainy season business was sluggish. In Shantigaon some borrowers' households are involved in making bamboo-cane products or day labour so they also face similar seasonal problems. Theirs is only subsistence business so during the lean period they have very little income which is insufficient to buy the food that they need. Consequently, they spend their capital or borrow money to eke out living. In order to restart a quiescent business during the business season cycle, they need loans from the NGOs. Therefore, according to Sen (1981) borrowing for *direct entitlement failure* and *trade entitlement failure* is ubiquitous in such villages. Most households are chronically in debt. Before microcredit programmes were established they took loans from local money-lenders or from relatives. Despite the fact the number is few, they do sometimes take small amounts of loans from relatives or neighbours but as a result of microcredit they no longer take loans from local money-lenders. They did not consider local money-lenders to be good people, and microcredit has relieved poor households from dependence on them.

This ethnographic study also indicates that microcredit programmes in an impoverished locality are unable to create the impulse to break the poverty threshold. A sector that is considered to be a major strategic facility to help the poor to break out of the vicious cycle of poverty paradoxically often traps them in a vicious cycle of debt. I found that the households who benefited from the microfinance loans shared similar characteristics – they had existing capital, established businesses and marketable skills (see also Karim, 2008). So what do most borrowers get from credit involvement? If we again examine our first two case studies we understand that microcredit in a poor locality can produce only minimal financial improvements to borrowers' lives. By participating in microcredit programmes these people can only subsist but cannot achieve a poverty-free life. They often explain their development thus: 'our main goal is to ensure two meagre meals of rice in a day'.

Microcredit programmes in the rural area of Bangladesh do not create any new income-generating opportunities nor do they offer any training through which rural people could effectively escape poverty. I am not against microcredit programmes per se, but their focus being purely on the cash (the credit-only approach) has emerged as an important point in understanding the problems. Microcredit is not a panacea for poverty alleviation. I concur with Baruah (2002) that instead of treating microcredit as a panacea, microcredit proponents could devise a specific agenda for helping poor borrowers to manage their day-to-day lives better than before. I also argue that if microcredit NGOs maintain credit as their only approach and run their operations through market rationality, the dream of a poverty-free society through microcredit will remain an illusion. Microcredit now works but it works as ready cash in rural areas. The heavy dependency on microcredit may limit other options and people's traditional survival strategies. Moreover, when something becomes too easily available, there is always a danger of it being misused. Some borrowers do not follow the rules of the credit agreement and exceed their limits or boundaries and use credit for different purposes such as a money-lending business, bearing the expenses of litigation.

Note

1 Muhammad Yunus, Nobel lecture, Oslo, 10 December 2006. Available at: http:// nobelprize.org/nobel_prizes/peace/laurates/ 2006/yunus-lecture-en.html.

9 Summary and conclusion

There is no doubt that over the past two decades or so the term microcredit has been widely used both in the discourse of mainstream development interventions and by development practitioners and actors in the field. Although the term microcredit is commonly used to refer to small loans given to poor women, the broader meaning of the concept indicates a particular kind of 'poverty lending approach' developed by GB, which focuses on poverty alleviation and social change (Robinson, 2002). *The Micro-politics of Microcredit* has contributed to the understanding of how the provision of microcredit relates to the everyday lives of borrowers in rural Bangladesh. Conceivably, the objective of this study has rotated around the question of the extent to which microcredit programmes, a product of neoliberalism and the capitalist world system, intersect and connect with local female borrowers to facilitate social capital, women's empowerment and poverty alleviation in rural Bangladesh. I have endeavoured to understand microcredit in the fields of Foucault's disciplinary power and governmentality against the background of neoliberalism.

As mentioned in the Introduction, the aim of governmentality is to shape human behaviour through calculated means of intervention. Governmentality, in Foucault's view, has two developmental aspects. One focuses on the welfare of the population, the improvement of its wealth, health, life expectancy and longevity. To achieve these purposes, governmentality operates by 'educating desires and configuring habits, aspirations and beliefs' (cf. Murray, 2007). Drawing attention to what microcredit NGOs aim to change, and the techniques which they employ, my scholarship has indicated that the NGOs' goals are motivated by a desire both to change conditions for the people and also to benefit their own capitalist interests. The book also offers an analysis of what microcredit initiatives fail to do: mobilize social capital, reconstruct gender relations, and alleviate poverty. I have argued that microcredit can be regarded as a form of governmentality that is exercised via a generalized control over people's behaviour and over their beliefs, and by spreading the values of entrepreneurship with the 'market' as the solver of all ills. While the much-lauded microcredit organizations push neoliberal ideologies onto rural borrowers, they have failed because many developmental subjects cannot yield sufficient profit and or use credit for the purpose for which it is intended. Therefore, ensuring a 'win-win' situation that microcredit originally promised has been failed. Microcredit organizations reinforce pre-existing kinship and gender structures and there has been a widespread 'mission creep' that has turned microcredit organizations into money-lending business organizations. Given the above arguments, let me summarize the major findings of the study.

Review of the major findings

In focusing on social capital in Chapter 2, this study has documented whether participation in microcredit programmes mobilizes women's social networks and civic engagement, facilitates norms of reciprocity and trust, and promotes collective identity and action in the villages where the study was conducted. Many researchers (Dowla, 2006; Larance, 1998; Jain, 1996; Ostrom, 1994) have hitherto demonstrated a direct association between organizational membership and building social capital. The findings of this study, however, suggest that the supposed association between microcredit membership and building a collective identity platform among female microcredit borrowers is much less clear-cut than has been frequently assumed. Meanwhile, the self-selected homogenous credit groups that originally were intended to boost social capital among women simply failed to function that way. The package of training, group meetings, norms and consciousness-raising lessons that originally accompanied the GB microcredit programme is now missing from their rural operations. Joining a group in most cases now functions as a means for the poor to access credit, and is not necessarily a sign of camaraderie among group members. The respondents unanimously stated that during last few years their organizations have failed to call any meetings at the centres. They often refer to the weekly meeting places as loan- or instalment-collecting centres. As a result, micro-lending NGOs have are now perceived as money-lending businesses, banks or instalment-collecting banks. This study rejects the Putnam-oriented approach to social capital, and argues that the 'quality and purpose' (cf. Kabeer *et al.*, 2012) of networks are much more important than the 'density of networks.'

It is assumed that the group lending technique through the collateral mechanism of micro-lending may create collectiveness or group inter-dependence among the members, which in turn helps to develop cooperation and construct common goals and trust between them. However, the study results demonstrate that there is no clear-cut example of joint-liability arrangements whereby group members take responsibility or help to resolve another member's repayment problems in the villages that were studied. Rather, collateral mechanism functions as disciplinary technology or govern-mentality which compels group members to comply with the NGOs' strict repayment policies or their market-based mechanisms, i.e. to pay weekly instalments on time. Owing to collateral mechanism, the guarantors and some active group members help to facilitate the work of the programmes by collecting instalments from defaulters and by disciplining the developmental subjects. This sometimes causes scuffles and cultivates isolation and alienation among the members. As a result, leadership roles are generally unpopular among the rural women, who do not want the 'headache' of chasing up loans from their neighbours.

Solidarity offers access to a valued resource flow such as loan money and cultivates dense networks among the members, i.e. what sociologists call social capital (Putnam, 1993a, 1995a; Coleman, 1990). However, it is not clear in what circumstances members of a group get involved in reciprocal relations. The overwhelming majority of the respondents in this study declared that they do not have the economic ability for reciprocity. An individual client is responsible for the success or failure of her own credit investments. The borrowers considered their debts to be private so each member was responsible for solving her own economic difficulties and her income generation or repayment problems. Through microcredit membership, in fact, borrowers are comprised as both the subjects and objects of development – or more precisely, 'subjects and subjected', as Elyachar expresses the issue, when describing the 'empowerment debt' as component of a new mode of governance 'in which the individual polices himself or herself' (2005: 193).

Microcredit has produced change to a certain extent in the social web so that people who have economic ability in the localities nowadays prefer not to lend money to the poor; instead, they suggest that they should take out loans from microcredit organizations. Consequently, people in many different economic situations get involved in the credit programmes. As this study shows, relatedness among the microcredit borrowers as well as between the organization and the borrowers was epitomized not only by trust but also by conflict, tensions and power-laden relationships. Conflicts, disunity, jealousy, expectations, competition and individualistic self-interest were an inherent part of normal family life for the poor, and currently these factors have been exacerbated by their view of economic weakness.

The microcredit borrowers in the villages studied agreed that trust is very important. Nonetheless, trust towards other borrowers is exceptionally low. This ethnographic account shows how poverty and insecurity erode the fabric of social trust in the rural areas. One positive sign revealed from the findings is that people are concerned about norms and criticize immoral activities. Trust towards people of other religions is also low, despite the seemingly good communal harmony prevailing among villagers. Only a few respondents declared that they trusted both Muslims and Hindus open-mindedly.

Organizational membership or network participation can increase members' awareness of social and political issues, and many earlier empirical studies (e.g. Stolle and Rochon, 1996; Almond and Verba, 1963; Billiet and Cambre, 1996; Olsen, 1972) have shown that members of associations and organizations are more politically active and more informed about politics and civic attitudes. The findings of my study show that the study respondents knew the names of their local representatives. This awareness is nonetheless poorly mirrored in their voting habits and direct participation in local politics. Female microcredit borrowers in the villages researched had been instructed who to vote for by the men of their families. A few female borrowers got involved in local politics. The study explores how women's political participation or active involvement is entangled with certain social capital including class, caste, kinship networks, the idea of relatedness and political patronage. The female microcredit borrowers are aware of the public good but they believed that because they are poor, their demands are ignored by the political leaders. Most of the respondents stated that the political leaders in the rural areas have no moral principles and they are too busy reaping benefits and filling their own pockets.

In Chapter 3 I explored whether the practice of giving dowries has strengthened as a result of microcredit programmes, and if dowry gifts strengthen social bonds and networks in the local areas. This study revealed that the microcredit programmes strongly fuel the practice of gift giving and dowry giving and marriage transactions in society. Unlike earlier studies (Khandker *et al.*, 1994; Rahman, 1986a), I found that dowry gifts or the giving of domestic items as a form of marriage gift is extensively practised among the clients. The microcredit borrowers, irrespective of class and caste, regard the giving of domestic items at a marriage ceremony is a social norm or local practice. Giving domestic items puts a hefty economic load on the parents of daughters but the parents interviewed in this study give domestic goods as marriage gifts trusting that they may ensure for their daughters' happy conjugal lives including a better standard of living and better treatment by their husbands and in-laws. I consider marriage gifts as 'symbolic capital' (Bourdieu, 2002), which, according to my findings, provides positive-self images including honour, esteem or recognition, and reconstructs new social and cultural identities for a bride in her marital home. Thus, gifts create and intensify the social bonds and networks between families connected by marriage. However, the way people use credit for giving dowry gifts limits their productive capacities. Credit is used for the payment of dowries, which reinforces the practice of dowry and the role of women as wives rather than their potential as productive individuals. It is an apparent ideological clash between the aspiration of/ideal of supposedly promoting women as independent economic agents and the praxis of their embeddedness in patriarchal gender relations.

Chapter 4 of my analysis revealed that most women in the study have taken out loans on behalf of their husbands or other male family members for investment. Credit channelled to women is frequently appropriated by male family members and is a strong and consistent criticism of microcredit's ability to empower women. Some studies (e.g. Goetz and Sen Gupta, 1996, Karim, 2008; Rahman, 1999) are frequently cited by critics of microfinance as proof of its failure to improve women's financial position within their families and societies. In sharp contrast to these findings, my study argues that such criticisms cannot be made so easily because credit is not regarded by female borrowers as individual property but rather as a family or collective resource that is used for the welfare of all household members. Unlike other researchers who view men's use of loans taken out by women as indicative of women's subordination, this study asserts that women do not have a high sense of entitlement to their loans. They think of the money as a collective resource and its use by men in the family is not an issue of conflict. Unlike other researchers who assumed that credit was taken from women through force and violence, the present study finds that an overwhelming majority of husbands take credit through mutual consensus or consultation with their wives. Indeed, the findings of the present study suggest that the benefits of credit need to be understood at the level of the household rather than at the level of the individual, and that women should be understood in the context of their roles as wives to their husbands. The benefits to husbands can also be reciprocated to wives, since they are part of the same economic unit. Consequently, the ethnocentric Euro-American notions of personal use and individual responsibility make it difficult to understand the ways in which credit is controlled and channelled in families in Bangladesh.

However, the household or the relationship between husband and wife is not simply a cooperative unit; rather, it often involves complicated negotiations, collective interest and episodes of discontents. Similarly to the existing published quantitative studies (Osmani, 1998; Hashemi *et al.*, 1996; Pitt and Khandker, 1995; Schuler and Hashemi, 1994; Mizan, 1994), the present ethnographic study does not show clearly that women's decision-making capacity, control over resources and social status have improved due to microcredit membership. However, I do not blieve that women's lack of self-interest is the main barrier to participation in household decision-making process. Rather, this study showed that most women have a clear understanding that they have little or no influence over household decision-making processes.

It is assumed that because microcredit intervention has reduced women's economic vulnerability, pulled them into the public space and exposed them the new ideas, it might influence fertility behaviour by promoting family planning norms. However, I did not find any connection between active membership of microcredit programmes and any modified reproductive behaviour or fertility control in the villages where the study was undertaken. For a few, the religious rules, norms and strictures are flexible and fluid but in most cases gender preferences, religious conviction, prohibition from husbands and in-laws effectively preclude the use of any method to limit the number of children born.

In Chapter 4 I paid particular attention to the question of how microcredit relates to women's exposure to violence in the household. Gender-based domestic violence, more specifically the abuse of wives, was common among the microcredit borrowers' families in the villages studied. While some critics have argued that GB micro-loans were associated with increased domestic violence against women, I did not find a link between microcredit loans and increased violence towards wives. Many of my respondents confirmed that their husbands often scolded them and that they were seldom physically assaulted by their husbands but this violence was not related to loan taking or credit repayment. The study described various reasons for the violence such as husbands' financial hardship and frustration, and disruptive children. However, one of the important causes that the respondents often mentioned is the inherent flaw of the men in society that does not stem from poverty. The husbands expressed their behavioural flaws through maleness, short-temperedness, and by exercising of power over their wives. The husbands often use filthy language with their wives and their in-laws (wives' parents) when scolded. Thus the husbands' roles and their attitudes are embodied in their language, thoughts and actions. They take advantage of their more powerful position in society socially and culturally and religious principles. When a wife challenges her husband's role it means she is challenging her husband's sense of masculinity and his position in the family structure. The women use 'the weapons of the weak', namely weeping, refusing to eat meals on one or two occasions, and not conversing with their husbands, but this is not indicative of a rebellious mentality of among wives.

Nevertheless, I found that some women used loans for self-managed enterprises, paid instalments from their own income and also met some family expenses. Within patriarchal structures of family and deeply embedded gender roles, these women have an input into household decision-making processes and are subject to little or no subordination. Their ability to earn incomes independently of their husbands gave them confidence in their own capabilities and a sense of self-worth, which also changed the general attitude of their neighbours to them. In this study such women were found to be constructing particular class categories in the local communities. They construct their freedom in terms of savings, control over household resources and the capacity to spend money themselves. However, what remains inflexible is husbands' control over land and house. In poverty-stricken families, I found that women who possess income-earning capacities help to strengthen the family bond between husbands and wives. Therefore, I argue that microcredit can improve the lives of some poor women in the rural setting, especially when credit is offered as part of the development of women's marketable skills and trading abilities.

In Chapter 5 the study examined the aspects of gender relations, both within the household and the wider community, that bar women from investing credit themselves. The study data showed that only a few women invest credit themselves. The women who invested credit themselves shared similar characteristics i.e. they had existing skills, or they were widowed, some of their husbands also did the same work, and some lived in their natal villages. In this part of this study, I argued that women do not invest credit themselves because there is a disjuncture between microcredit policy (i.e. neoliberal market ideology and practice) and the inherent structure of the studied localities. Most poor women are afraid to take out loans for their own investments owing to concerns about their inability to pay the weekly instalments. Sociocultural norms, gender-specific roles, lack of marketable productive skills and lack of access to a market make it extremely difficult for most women to invest on their own. NGO microcredit officials suggest that by organizing and providing financial assistance in the form of loans to women they can help to foster responsibility, earning potentiality, self-reliance and confidence. However, I found that the credit-only approach (providing loans, collecting instalments, and saving) is not nearly enough to prepare women to confront the challenges of credit investment in the rural areas of Bangladesh. Microcredit programmes have ignored or discounted the gendered practices, the reality of women's lives and the larger infrastructural conditions that impinge on the ability of women to invest credit in their rural localities.

As most women do not take credit to invest themselves, I return to the question of why credit is channelled through women. Is it to ensure covert regulatory practice? Credit through women is not an entirely noble mission in Bangladesh. Most of the respondents described the same characteristic that microcredit NGOs provide credit through women because of their restricted geographical mobility, their stereotypical docility and passivity (honour, shyness, shame, social modesty and submissiveness) in society. Shyness, shame, modesty and submissiveness are embedded in society as much as they are inculcated in rural women's bodies and thoughts. A few of these features may be flexible, but to a large extent all these characteristics of women in the rural areas fall within the arena of *doxa* (Bourdieu, 2002). Following the Foucaultian (1977) concepts of power, docile bodies and discipline, I suggest that such characteristics make it easier for NGOs to run their lending businesses and boost their capital. Therefore, microcredit-providing NGOs are not inevitably emancipators per se; rather, they increase the penetration of power over social and individual bodies in name of Third World women's empowerment and development.

Chapter 6 covered an ethnographic analysis of the consequences of multiple microcredit organizations offering credit simultaneously in the same locality. I explored the way in which microcredit organizations compete with each other for the same clients by appropriating neoliberal policies, and also deselect the poor and target richer clients for profit enhancement and to strengthen their own sustainability. The study indicates that targeting rural people as beneficiaries of microcredit loans has turned rural Bangladeshi people into assets of the microcredit programmes. The microcredit approach in Bangladesh is currently being run along financial sustainability lines. As microcredit organizations are adherents of the principles of market ideologies, the NGOs' field assistants do not give any advice about loan investment. Their duties include monitoring, providing credit, recruiting new members and recovering instalments on the due dates. It was evident from discussions that competition led to the microcredit NGOs being faced with a complicated lending environment and unprincipled competitive practices, which they had to reconcile with their original objectives. Obviously, competition has opened up diverse options for borrowers, but it has also led to people becoming multiple borrowers, which might be good for the financially well-off families, but for the poor it has meant that they have become mired in debt. Owing to the goals of financial sustainability micro-lending NGOs in the villages studied preferred to lend to the financially well-off families, i.e. the families who already have good businesses and steady incomes. Despite this practice, the majority of the NGOs' clients are still rural poor people.

In Chapter 7 I focused on credit arrangement, enforcement and resistance of microcredit borrowers in the villages studied. I examined the power relationships and implications of imposed institutional discipline and governmentality of microcredit organizations. Microcredit programmes had the potential to offer a 'win-win' (Morduch, 2000, 1999) situation, which ensures that NGOs and poor clients profit. In reality, programmes fail to a large extent to produce financial change for borrowers. Microcredit NGOs operate within neoliberal principles of competition, profit and entrepreneurship. They perpetuate the image of their borrowers as active economic agents, who should make profits and pay instalments one week after the disbursement of a loan. However, most of the market subjects are not in the position to put principle into practice. A commonly repeated statement was that there is a constant mismatch between the borrowers' incomes and expenditure, which contributes to borrowers being constantly under adverse conditions of tension, insomnia and under-nourishment. The power relations and implications of the imposed institutional discipline of microcredit organizations were discussed. It was argued that the governmentality techniques of microcredit NGOs to a large extent ensure that borrowers behave in a manner consistent with market rationality and achieve the micro-lending NGOs' profits at the expense of any profit made by poor clients. The borrowers in this study were obliged to demonstrate their allegiance to the NGOs' governmentality, rules and regulations. Otherwise they would face fines, harassment and possibly lost the chance to get future loans.

Microcredit borrowers are not always the passive victims of programme rules and regulations. Following Scott's notion of hidden resistance (1985) and weapons of the week' (1990), the focus of this study turned to the way in which microcredit borrowers widely criticized microcredit programme rules and procedures but these were only expressed in the absence or without the knowledge of the NGO officials. Some members manipulated the rules of the NGOs to their own advantage. Some members also emerged as informal money-lenders, who diverted their own loans to other people at a higher interest rate. Therefore, micro-loans have emerged as a mechanism not for only the NGOs but for also some participants to improve their own situations. Nevertheless, the relationship between the microcredit borrowers and the officials is not built on equality of power. Instead, the nature of the lender-borrower relationship is hierarchical and built on an unequal division of power: the creditors and the debtors. The microcredit borrowers do not overtly challenge the system because they have no alternative options to circumvent this strong capitalist system. Neither do they have any alternative detailed ideas for improving microcredit programmes. Moreover, the usual question asked by the borrowers was: 'who else will lend money to us?' However, the poor developed covert forms of resistance, which include not only speeches of protest but also a range of practices and alternative social spaces where they can express their dissidence. Some examples showed how the microcredit borrowers criticized microcredit policies and procedures (such as the *kabuliwala*, and the 'bloodsuckers') without coming into direct confrontation with NGOs or their staff. I contend that through their criticism they have created the first condition of open resistance even if open resistance has not yet materialized.

Finally, in Chapter 8 I examined why people take credit year after year despite the many disadvantages it has for them. Microcredit that follows the GB model is not a 'magic bullet' or the best anti-poverty strategy. By concentrating on the concepts of insecurity and vulnerability, and the entitlement approach (Sen, 1999, 1981), it was shown why poor people take credit year after year and become permanently indebted. The analyses of study data showed that both direct entitlement failure and trade entitlement failure (ibid., 1981) are ubiquitous in the villages studied. Before microcredit programmes became established, the poor took loans from local money-lenders or from relatives. Nowadays, with a few exceptions, the poor do not take loans from local money-lenders. In this sense, microcredit intervention has relieved local people from the tyranny of traditional local money-lenders. However, a significant number of the study respondents described the main benefit of microcredit: 'our main goal is to ensure two meagre meals of rice each day'. These 'failed market subjects' used credit as a survival mechanism, to meet everyday needs, and to overcome unanticipated economic events and difficulties. More specifically, these households reflect the phenomenon that microcredit is simply an informal way to obtain subsistence and a temporary means to cope with economic difficulties.

Poor people who take out loans but who are then unable to repay their instalments also maintain multiple memberships of different NGOs to fulfil their repayment commitments. They take out new loans in order to be able to pay outstanding dues. Consequently, they fall into a vicious cycle of indebtedness. The borrowers who do benefit from microcredit loans are not from the poorest segment of the population. More specifically, the borrowers who benefited from microfinance loans shared similar characteristics: they possessed existing capital, skills and either a business or the knowledge to run a business. In particular, this study indicates that microcredit programmes in poor localities are unlikely to help poor borrowers to be released from poverty. By participating in microcredit programmes these people can sustain their lives, therefore without microcredit these people could not think of alternative options. This study also explored how poverty, scarcity of work and competition over limited resources among the poor microcredit borrowers are omnipresent, and the situation is likely to worsen. More specifically, it was argued that poor people's marginalization in terms of landlessness, lack of resources and income is likely to continue in spite of their increased access to credit programmes.

The way ahead

As mentioned previously, Bangladesh has one of the largest NGO sectors in the world. The sector began its activities in war relief and rehabilitation soon after Bangladesh became independent in 1971. During the early years of independence NGOs mainly gave attention to the mainstream development programmes following a community-based approach. However, they soon realized the limitations of the community-based approach and implemented the target group approach. They started highlighting the fact that the main cause of poverty was structural and that they themselves were catalyst organizations working towards altering the power structure (Siddiqui, 2002). During the 1980s and 1990s the NGO sector in Bangladesh witnessed rapid growth under the framework of neoliberal policies. Now the World Bank, the Asian Development Bank and Western donor agencies often emphasize better government-NGO relations in all sectors of the economy (Karim, 2011). At present, the NGOs in Bangladesh provide various types of services including health care, family planning, voters' education programme, legal aid, non-formal primary education and so on, but the most important service that has attracted international community and has contributed to the building of a positive global image of Bangladesh is the delivery of microcredit.

Yet the present study demonstrates that microcredit does not lead to certain types of positive development regardless of the social and cultural context. Microcredit is socially and culturally appropriated so that it gets tied in with local processes, which were already underway. Rural people in their everyday life obtain loans for their immediate consumption during periods of scarcity or to overcome unavoidable economic circumstances. Some widows, divorced or abandoned women earned their living from their credit investments. Owing to microcredit some women and their family members were able to pay for small indulgences: small pieces of jewellery, occasionally good clothes and food, home improvements, kitchen utensils, house repair or construction. These loans eased many of their temporary sufferings but their impact was not as positive or as drastic as described by much of the earlier scholarship on the subject.

Taking a out loan from the government or private banks is difficult for the poor. They do not have the necessary papers or documents, which private and government banks often demand for sanctioning a loan. Informational asymmetries, adverse incentives, contract enforcement problems and political intervention are some of the major features of the formal financial market in Bangladesh. However, rural people still expect government support and intervention. Although poverty elimination is a national priority in Bangladesh, where over half of the population lives below the poverty line, it is unrealistic to expect the government to give rural people the help that they need. A broadly democratic system based merely on elections is not enough to improve the condition of the poor, particularly in a society that has such strong clientele or patronage relationships, widespread rent-seeking, corruption, and little or no accountability (Wood, 1994; Sobhan, 1998).

However, there is an alternative approach that can be applied to micro-credit in Bangladesh. It is not my intention to provide policy directions but my study contains a number of suggestions with direct policy relevance. Microcredit is a specific policy intervention and a means of bringing financial capital to the local people in Bangladesh. However, one of the main short-comings of current microfinance policy is that it is not a poor-friendly system. Muhammad Yunus has often argued that credit is a human right. I believe that credit can never be a solution on its own. Strategic planning efforts and rigorous assessments are needed to improve the system. I have argued in this study that microcredit programmes can change the lives of the poor, if they abolish their credit-only approach which involves merely disbursing loans, recovering instalments and collecting savings. In addition to providing credit, it is necessary to create new income-generating opportunities, offer training in marketable skills and to facilitate the trade of women's products. Training could be offered in more lucrative fields such as solar technology, ICT and mobile telephony for greater future potential. Monitoring and client dis-ciplining are now tightly intertwined with credit repayment, but there is a need for the redirection of effort towards the guidance of the borrowers in making profitable investment of credit. The preparation period of paying instalments could be extended. Reducing the rate of interest could ensure a broader goal of poverty alleviation. Independent access to credit for both men and women should be introduced. Critical conscience, gender-awareness and strong family planning policies ensuring reproductive rights should be integrated into all credit programmes.

Appendix

Both GB and BRAC share some unique features that make them stand out from other organizations and explain their success (see Table A.1 and Table A.2).

Table A.1 Striking features of GB and BRAC

Programme feature	Grameen Bank	BRAC
Membership criteria	Maximum landholding of half an acre of land. Only one member allowed per household. From the outset largest segment of members are female. Initially attention given both to men and women; since 2009: 97% women.	Maximum landholding of half an acre of land. At least one household member must work for wages. One household member may earn daily wages. Since 1992 only one member allowed per household. Initially almost as many men as women; since 2009: 98% women.
Goals	Combating poverty and emancipation of poor women.	Combating poverty and emancipation of poor women.
Group features	Five members form a group. Five to eight groups form a centre. Separate groups and centres for men and women. Weekly meetings of groups.	30–40 members constitute a village organization (VO). Each VO is divided into solidarity groups of 5–7 members. Separate groups for men and women. Each group of men has a counterpart women's group. Weekly meetings of solidarity groups.

Programme feature	Grameen Bank	BRAC
Savings mobilization	TK 1 per week. 5% of each loan (non-refundable) goes to group fund. 0.5% of each loan used for group insurance. Option to buy shares worth TK 100 per member.	TK 2 per week. 4% of each loan (non-refundable) goes to group fund. 1 % of each loan used for group insurance.
Credit delivery mechanism	No collateral but group liability. Loans to be repaid in 46-week instalments. Interest at the end of loan cycle. 20% interest rate for general loan. 8% for housing loan. Maximum loan TK 10,000. Repayment above 90% for female members.	No collateral but group liability. Loans to be repaid in 46-week instalments. Interest at the end of loan cycle. 20% interest rate for production loans. Maximum loan TK 10,000. Repayment above 90% for female members
Social development	Training duration 15–30 days. Review of code of conduct at centre meetings. Minimal skills-based training.	Training duration 3–6 months. Review of code of conduct at village organization meetings. Substantial skills-based training.

Source: Khandker (1998); Chowdhury and Alam (1997); Grameen Bank (2009); BRAC (2009).

Table A.2 Decisions and promises of GB and BRAC

Grameen Bank's 16 decisions	*BRAC's 17 promises*
1 We shall follow and advance the four principles of Grameen Bank – Discipline, Unity, Courage and Hard Work – in all walks of our lives.	1 We shall not do malpractice or injustice.
2 We shall bring prosperity to our families.	2 We will work hard and bring prosperity to our family.
3 We shall not live in dilapidated houses. We shall repair our houses and work towards constructing new houses.	3 We will send our children to school.
4 We shall grow vegetables all the year round. We shall eat plenty of them and sell the surplus.	4 We will adopt family planning and keep our family size small.
5 During the planting season, we shall plant as many seedlings as possible.	5 We will try to be clean and keep our house tidy.
6 We shall plan to keep our families small. We shall minimize our expenditure. We shall look after our health.	6 We will always drink pure water.
7 We shall educate our children and ensure that we can earn to pay for their education.	7 We will not keep our food uncovered and will wash our hands and face before we take our meal.
8 We shall always keep our children and the environment clean.	8 We will construct latrines and will not leave our stool where it doesn't belong.
9 We shall build and use pit-latrines.	9 We will cultivate vegetables and trees in and around our house.
10 We shall drink water from the tube wells. If it is not available, we shall boil water or use alum.	10 We will try to help each other under all circumstances.
11 We shall not take any dowry at our sons' weddings, nor shall we give any dowry at our daughters' weddings. We shall keep the centre free from the curse of dowry. We shall not practise child marriage.	11 We will fight against polygamy and injustices to our wives and all women.
12 We shall not inflict any injustice on anyone, nor shall we allow anyone to do so.	12 We will be loyal to the organization and abide by its rules and regulations.
13 We shall collectively undertake bigger investments for higher incomes.	13 We will not sign anything without having a good understanding of what it means (we will look carefully before we act).
14 We shall always be ready to help each other. If anyone is in difficulty, we shall all help him or her.	14 We will attend weekly meetings regularly and on time.
15 If we come to know of any breach of discipline in any centre, we shall all go there and help to restore discipline.	15 We will always abide by the decisions of the weekly group meeting.
16 We shall introduce physical exercise at our centres. We shall take part in all social activities collectively.	16 We will regularly deposit our weekly savings.
	17 If we receive a loan we will repay it on time.

References

Abdullah, T. and Zeidenstein, S. A. (1982) *Village Women of Bangladesh: Prospects for Change*. Oxford: Pergamon Press.

Abecasis, D. (1990) *Identity, Islam and Human Development in Rural Bangladesh*. Dhaka: The University Press.

Abu-Lughud, L. (1986) *Veiled Sentiments: Honor and Poetry in a Beduin Society*. Berkeley, CA: University of California Press.

Ackerly, B. (1997) What's in a Design? The Effects of NGO Programme Delivery Choices on Women's Empowerment in Bangladesh. In A. M. Goetz (ed.), *Getting the Institutions Right for Women in Development*. New York: Zed Books, pp. 140–160.

Adams, D. and Vogel, R. (1986) Rural Financial Markets in Low-income Countries: Recent Controversies and Lessons. *World Development* 14: 477–488.

Adams, D. W., Graham D. H. and von Pischke, J. D. (1984). *Undermining Rural Development with Cheap Credit*. Boulder, CO: Westview Press.

Afsar, H. (ed.) (1998) *Women and Empowerment: Illustration from the Third World*. Basingstoke: Macmillan.

Agarwal, B. (1994) *A Field of One's Own: Gender and Land Rights in South Asia*. Cambridge: Cambridge University Press.

Agarwal, B. (1997) Bargaining and Gender Relations: Within and Beyond the Household. *Feminist Economics* 3(1): 1–51.

Ahmad, M. M. (2002) Who Cares? The Personal and Professional Problems of NGO Field Workers in Bangladesh. *Development in Practice* 12(2):177–191.

Ahmad, M. M. (2003) Distant Voices: The Views of the Field Workers of NGOs in Bangladesh on Microcredit. *The Geographical Journal* 169(1): 65–74.

Ahmad, Q. K. (ed.) (2007) *Socio-Economic and Indebtedness: Related Impact of Micro-credit in Bangladesh*. Dhaka: The University Press.

Ahmed, M. (1985) *Status, Perception, Awareness and Marital Adjustment of Rural Women: The Role of Grameen Bank*. Grameen Bank Paper No. 31, Dhaka: Grameen Bank.

Ahmed, S. M. (2005) Intimate Partner Violence against Women: Experiences from a Women-focused Development Programme in Matlab. *Bangladesh Journal of Health, Population and Nutrition* 23(1): 95–101.

Ahmed, R. and Naher, M. S. (1987) *Brides and the Demand System in Bangladesh*. Dhaka: Centre for Social Studies, Dhaka University.

Ahmed, S. H., Petzold M., Kabir, Z. N. and Tomson, G. (2006) Targeted Intervention for the Ultra Poor in Bangladesh: Does It Make any Difference in their Health-seeking Behavior? *Social Science and Medicine* 63(11): 2899–2911.

Ali, I. and Hatta, Z. A. (2012) Women's Empowerment or Disempowerment through Microfinance: Evidence from Bangladesh. *Asian Social Work and Policy Review* 6 (2): 111–121.

Almond, G. A. and Verba, S. (1963) *The Civic Culture*. Princeton, NJ: Princeton University. Press.

Amin, S. and Cain, M. (1997) The Rise of Dowry in Bangladesh. In G. W. Jones, Robert Douglas, John C. Caldwell and Rennie d'Souza (eds), *The Continuing Demographic Transition*. Oxford: Clarendon Press, pp. 290–306.

Amin, S. and Pebley, A. (1994) Gender Inequality within Households: The Impact of a Women's Development Programme in 36 Bangladeshi Villages. *Bangladesh Development Studies* 22(2–3): 121–153.

Amin, R., Ahmed, A. U., Chowdhury, J. and Ahmed, M. (1994) Poor Women's Participation in Income-Generating Projects and their Fertility Regulation in Rural Bangladesh: Evidence from a Recent Survey. *World Development* 22(4): 555–564.

Angelusz, R. and Tardos, R. (2001) Change and Stability in Social Network Resources: The Case of Hungary under Transformation. In N. Lin, K. Cook and R. S. Burt (eds), *Social Capital: Theory and Research*. New York: Aldine de Gruyter: 297–323.

Anthony, D. (2005) Cooperation in Microcredit Borrowing Groups: Identity, Sanctions, and Reciprocity in the Production of Collective Goods. *American Sociological Review* 70: 495–515.

Arefeen, H. K. S. (1982) Muslim Stratification Patterns in Bangladesh: An Attempt to Build a Theory. *Journal of Social Studies* 16. Dhaka: Centre for Social Studies, Dhaka University.

Arens, J. and Van Beurden, J. (1977) *Jhagrapur: Poor Peasants and Women in a Village in Bangladesh*. New Delhi: Orient Longman.

Armendáriz de Aghion, B. and Morduch, J. (2005) *The Economics of Microfinance*. Cambridge, MA: MIT Press.

Ashrafun, L. and Uddin, M. J. (2010) Fertility Practices: A Qualitative Study of a Slum in Sylhet, Bangladesh. *IUB Journal of Social Sciences and Humanities* 8(1): 113–130.

Augsburg, B. and Fouillet, C. (2010) The Microfinance Institution's Mission Drift. *Perspectives on Global Development Technology* 9: 327–355.

Aziz, K. M. A. and Maloney, C. (1985) *Why Does Bangladesh Remain So Poor? Part 1: The Situation and Efforts to Change it*. University Field Staff International Reports No. 29 (CM-1-85).

Bähre, E. (2007a). *Money and Violence: Financial Self-Help Groups in a South African Township*. Leiden: Brill.

Bähre, E. (2007b). Reluctant Solidarity: Death, Urban Ppoverty and Neighbourly Assistance in South Africa, *Ethnography* 8: 33–59.

Bailey, F. G. ([1969] 1990) *Stratagems and Spoils: A Social Anthropology of Politics*. Oxford: Blackwell.

Bangladesh Bureau of Statistics (BBS) (2011) Planning Division, Ministry of Planning. Dhaka.

Bangladesh Demographic and Health Survey (BDHS) (2007) March, NIPORT, Mitra & Associates, Dhaka, and USAID. Available at: www.unicef.org/bangladesh/BDHS2007_Final.pdf.

Bangladesh Institute of Development Studies (BIDS) (2004) *Baseline Survey For Assessing Attitudes and Practices of Male and Female Members and In-laws Towards Gender-Based Violence (Final Report)*. Dhaka: United Nations Population Fund.

Bangladesh Rural Advancement Committee (BRAC) (2009) *Annual Report*. Available at: www.brac.net/oldsite/useruploads/files/brac-ar-2009.pdf.

Baruah, B. (2002) In the Field – Women and Microcredit Worldwide: A Spectrum of Possibilities. *Women and Environments* (spring).

Baruah, B. (2010) *Women and Property in Urban India*. Vancouver: University of British Columbia Press.

Bateman, M. (2010) *Why Doesn't Microfinance Work? The Destructive Rise of Local Neoliberalism*. London: Zed Books.

Bates, Lisa M., Schuler, S. R., Islam, F. and Islam, M. K. (2004) Socio-economic Factors and Processes Associated with Domestic Violence in Rural Bangladesh. *International Family Planning Perspectives* 30(4): 190–199.

Beck, U. (2000) *What is Globalization?* Cambridge: Polity Press.

Bernasek, A. (2003) Banking on Social Change: Grameen Bank Lending to Women. *International Journal of Politics, Culture and Society* 16(3): 369–385.

Bertocci, P. (1970) *Elusive Villages: Social Structure and Community Organization in Rural East Pakistan*. PhD dissertation, Michigan State University.

Bertocci, P. J. (1974). Rural Communities in Bangladesh: Hajipur and Tinpara. In C. Mahoney (ed.), *South Asia: Seven Community Profiles*. New York: Holt, Rinehart, and Winston.

Besley, T., Coate, S., and Loury, G. (1993) The Economics of Rotating Savings and Credit Associations. *American Economic Review* 83(4): 792–810.

Besley, T. (2002) Social Education and Mental Hygiene: Foucault, Disciplinary Technologies and the Moral Constitution of Youth. *Educational Philosophy and Theory* 34(4): 419–433.

Bhatt, E. (1995) Women and Development Alternatives: Micro and Small-Scale Enterprise in India. In L. Dignard and J. Havet (eds), *Women in Micro and Small-scale Enterprise Development*. Boulder, CO: Westview, pp. 86–100.

Bhuiya, A., Sharmin, T. and Hanifi, S. (2003) Nature of Domestic Violence against Women in a Rural Area of Bangladesh: Implication for Preventive Interventions. *Journal of Health, Population and Nutrition* 2: 48–54.

Biekhart, K. (1996) European NGOs and Democratization in Central America: Assessing Performance in Light of Changing Priorities. In M. Edwards and D. Hulme (eds), *Beyond the Magic Bullet: NGO Performance and Accountability in the Post-Cold War World*. West Hartford, CT: Kumarian Press, pp. 80–91.

Billiet, J. and Cambre, B. (1996) *Social Capital, Active Membership in Voluntary Associations and Some Aspects of Political Participation: A Case Study*. Paper presented at conference on Social Capital and Democracy. Milan, 3–6 October.

Binswanger, Hans P. and Landell-Mills, P. (1995) *The World Bank's Strategy for Reducing Poverty and Hunger: A Report to the Development Community*. Environmentally Sustainable Development Studies Monograph 4. Washington, DC: World Bank.

Blanchet, T. (1984) *Women, Pollution and Marginality. Meanings and Rituals of Birth in Rural Bangladesh*. Dhaka: The University Press.

Blood, R. O. and Wolfe, D. N. (1960) *Husbands and Wives: The Dynamic of Married Living*. Glencoe, IL: The Free Press.

Bohle, H. G., Downing, T. E. and Watts, M. (1994) Climate Change and Social Vulnerability: Toward a Sociology and Geography of Food Insecurity. *Global Environmental Change* 4(1): 37–48.

Bongaarts, J. and Amin, S. (1997) *Prospects of Fertility Decline and Implications for population growth in South Asia*. Working Paper No. 94. Population Council, Policy Research Division.

Boserup, E. (1970) *Women's Role in Economic Development*. New York: St. Martin's Press.

Bourdieu, P. ([1977] 2002) *Outline of a Theory of Practice*. Cambridge: Cambridge University Press.

Bourdieu, P. (1986) The Forms of Capital. In J. G. Richardson (ed.), *Handbook of Theory and Research for the Sociology of Education*. New York: Greenwood, pp. 241–258.

Bourdieu, P. (1990) La domination masculine. *Actes de la recherché en sciences socials* 84(September): 2–31.

Bourdieu, P. (1992) *An Invitation to Reflexive Sociology*. Cambridge: Polity Press.

Bourdieu, P. and Wacquant, L. (2001) Neo-Liberal Speak: Notes on the New Planetary Vulgate. *Radical Philosophy* 105: 2–5.

Burt, R. S. (1989) *Basic Version of Structure's Assistant*. New York: Center for Social Science, Columbia University.

Cain, M. (1977a). *Economic Class, Economic Mobility, and the Development Cycle of Households: A Case Study in Rural Bangladesh*. Village Fertility Study, Report No. 4. Dhaka: Bangladesh Institute of Development Studies.

Cain, M. (1977b). The Economic Activities of Children in a Bangladesh Village. *Population and Development Review* 3(3): 201–227.

Cain, M. (1980) Risk, Fertility and Family Planning in a Bangladesh Village. *Studies in Family Planning* 11(6): 219–223.

Cain, M. (1981) Risk and Insurance: Perspectives on Fertility and Agrarian Change in India and Bangladesh. *Population and Development Review* 7(3): 435–474.

Cain, M. (1983) Fertility as an Adjustment to Risk. *Population and Development Review* 9(4): 688–702.

Cain, M., Khanam, S. and Nahar, S. (1979) Class, Patriarchy and the Structure of Women's Work in Bangladesh. *Population and Development Review* 5(3): 405–438.

Cantile, A. (1984) *The Assamese*. London: Curzon Press.

Casini, P. (2008) *Competition and Altruism in Microcredit Markets*. ECARES Working Paper, 2008_037.

Chaudhury, Iftekar A. and Matin, Imran (2002) Dimensions and Dynamics of Microfinance Membership Overlap–A Micro Study from Bangladesh. *Journal of Small Enterprise Development* 13(2).

Consultative Group for Assistance to the Poorest (CGAP) (1996) *Microcredit Interest Rates*. CGAP Occasional Paper, No. 1, August.

Consultative Group for Assistance to the Poorest (CGAP) (2002) *Microfinance Consensus Guidelines: Guiding Principles on Regulation and Supervision of Microfinance*. Washington, DC: Consultative Group to Assist the Poor/The World Bank Group.

Chambers, R. (1989) Editorial Introduction: Vulnerability, Coping and Policy. *IDS Bulletin* 2(2): 1–7.

Chamlee-Wright, E. (2005) Fostering Sustainable Complexity in the Microfinance Industry: Which Way Forward? *Institute of Economic Affairs*: 5–11.

Charitonenko, S., Campion, A. and Fernando, N. (2004) *Commercialization of Microfinance Perspectives from South and Southeast Asia.* Asian Development Bank, Regional Report, Manila.

Chattopadhay, S. (2007) *Interrogating Violence, Uncovering Silences: Investing Marital Violence in India.* Unpublished PhD dissertation, Dept of Anthropology at Brown University, Providence, Rhode Island.

Chaudhury, R. and Ahmed, N. (1980) *Female Status in Bangladesh.* Dhaka: Bangladesh Institute of Development Studies.

Chen, M. and Mahmud, S. (1995) *Assessing Change in Women's Lives: A Conceptual Framework.* Working Paper No. 2, BRAC-ICDDR, B, Joint Research Project, Matlab, Dhaka.

Chowdhury, N. (2002) Bangladesh's Experience: Dependence and Marginality in Politics. In *The Implementation of Quotas: Asian Experiences.* Jakarta, Indonesia, 25 September. Quota Workshops Report Series. International IDEA. Stockholm.

Chowdhury, A. M. R. and Alam, M. A. (1997) BRAC's Poverty Alleviation Programme: What it Is and What it Achieved. In G. D. Wood and I. Sharif (eds), *Who Needs Credit? Poverty and Finance in Bangladesh.* Dhaka: The University Press, pp. 171–190.

Chowdhury, A. and Bhuiya, A. (2001) Do Poverty Alleviation Programmes Reduce Inequalities in Health? The Bangladesh Experience. In D. Leon and G. Walt (eds), *Poverty, Inequality, and Health: An International Perspective.* Oxford: Oxford University Press.

Christen, R. and Darke, D. (2002) Commercialization: The New Reality of Microfinance. In D. Darke and E. Rhyne (eds), *The Commercialization of Microfinance: Blanching Business and Development.* Bloomfield, CT: Kumarian Press, pp. 2–22.

Cleland, J. C., Phillips, J. F., Amin, S. and Kamal, G. M. (1994) *The Determinants of Reproductive Change in Bangladesh: Success in a Challenging Environment.* Washington, DC: World Bank.

Coleman, J. S. (1988) Social Capital in the Creation of Human Capital. *American Journal of Sociology*, 94: S95–S120.

Coleman, J. S. (1990) *Foundations of Social Theory.* Cambridge, MA: Harvard University Press.

Collier, P. (2007) *Bottom Billion: Why the Poorest Countries Are Failing and What Can Be Done About it.* New York: Cambridge University Press.

Copestake, J. (2002) Inequality and the Polarizing Impact of Microcredit: Evidence from Zambia's Copperbelt. *Journal of International Development* 14: 743–755.

Cosgrove, S. (2002) Levels of Empowerment: Markets and Microenterprise-Lending NGOs in Apopa and Nejapa, El Salvador. *Latin American Perspectives* 29(5): 48–65.

Cross, J. and Street, A. (2009) Anthropology at the Bottom of the Pyramid. *Anthropology Today* 25(4): 4–9.

Centre for Policy Dialogue (CPD). (2000) *Political Participation of Women in Bangladesh: The Issue of Constitutional Representation.* Report No. 37. Dhaka, Bangladesh.

Cruikshank, B. (1999) *The Will to Empower: Democratic Citizens and Other Subjects.* Ithaca, NY: Cornell University Press.

Daniel, E. V. (1984) *Fluid Signs: Being a Person the Tamil Way.* Berkeley, CA: University of California.

Datta, S. K. and Neugent, J. B. (1984) Are Old Age Security and the Utility of Children in Rural India Really Unimportant? *Population Studies* 38: 507–509.

Davis, M. (1983) *Rank and Rivalry: The Politics of Inequality in Rural West Bengal.* Cambridge: Cambridge University Press.

de Soto, H. (2003) *The Mystery of Capital: Why Capitalism Triumphs in the West and Fails Everywhere Else.* New York: Basic Books.

de Stuers, V. (1968) *Parda: A Study of Muslim Women's Life in Northern India.* Assen: Van Gorcum.

De Vylder, S. (1982) *Agriculture in Chains: Bangladesh.* London: Zed Press.

Department for International Development (DFID) (2000) *Poverty Elimination and the Empower of Women.* London: DFID, September. Available at: www.albacharia. ma/xmlui/bitstream/handle/123456789/31733/1577Target_Strategy_Paper_Povertyeli mination_and_the_empowerment_of_women%5B2000%5Dr.pdf?sequence=1.

Devine, J. (2003) The Paradox of Sustainability: Reflections on NGOs in Bangladesh. *The Annals of the American Academy of Political and Social Sciences* 590: 227–242.

Dichter, T. W. and Harper, M. (2007) What's Wrong with Microfinance? In T. W. Dichter and M. Harper (eds), *What's Wrong with Microfinance.* Essex: Practical Action Publishing.

Dilley, M. and Boudreau, T. E. (2001) Coming to Terms with Vulnerability: A Critique of the Food Security Definition. *Food Policy* 26(3): 229–247.

Dixon, R., Ritchie, J. and Siwale, J. (2007) Loan Officers and Loan 'Delinquency' in Microfinance: A Zambian Case. *Accounting Forum* 31(1): 47–71.

Dobkin, M. (1967) Social Ranking in the Women's World of Purdah: A Turkish Example. *Anthropological Quarterly* 40: 65–72.

Dowla, A. (2006) In Credit We Trust: Building Social Capital by Grameen Bank in Bangladesh. *Journal of Socio-Economics* 35: 102–122.

Dreyfus, R., and Rabinow, P. (1982) *Michel Foucault: Beyond Structuralism and Hermeneutics.* Chicago, IL: Chicago University Press.

Dreze, J. and Sen, A. (1995) *India, Economic Development and Social Opportunity.* Oxford: Oxford University Press.

Dryburgh, A. and Fortin, S. (2010) Weighing In on Surveillance: Perception of the Impact of Surveillance on Female Ballet Dancers' Health. *Research in Dance Education* 11(2): 95–108.

Edwards, M. and Hulme, D. (eds). (1996) *Beyond the Magic Bullet: NGO Performance and Accountability in the Post-Cold War World.* West Hartford, CT: Kumarian Press.

Ehlers, T. B. and Main, K. (1998) Women and the False Promise of Microenterprise. *Gender and Society* 12(4): 424–440.

Elyachar, J. (2002) Empowerment Money: The World Bank, Non-Goverental Organizations, and the Value of Culture in Egypt. *Public Culture* 14(3): 493–513.

Elyachar, J. (2005) *Markets of Dispossession: NGOs, Economic Development, and the State in Cairo.* Durham, NC and London: Duke University Press.

Enarson, E. and Chakrabarti, P. G. D. (eds) (2009) *Women, Gender and Disaster: Global Issues and Inititatives.* New Delhi: Sage.

Escobar, A. (1995) *Encountering Development: The Making and Unmaking of the Third World.* Princeton, NJ: Princeton University Press.

Evans, P. (1996) Government Action, Social Capital and Development: Reviewing the Evidence on Synergy. *World Development* 24(6): 1119–1132.

Feldman, S. and McCarthy, F. (1983) Purdah and Changing Patterns of Social Control among Rural Women in Bangladesh. *Journal of Marriage and the Family* 45(4): 949–957.

Fernando, J. L. (1997) Nongovernmental Organizations, Microcredit, and Empowerment of Women. *Annals of the American Academy of Political and Social Science* 554: 150–177.

Fernando, J. L. (2007) Introduction: Microcredit and the Empowerment of Women: Blurring the Boundaries between Development and Capitalism. In J. L. Fernando (ed.), *Micro-Finance: Perils and Prospects.* New York: Routledge, pp. 1–36.

Fisher, W. F. (1997) Doing Good? The Politics and Antipolitics of NGO Practices. *Annual Review of Anthropology* 26: 439–464.

Flora, J. L. (1998) Social Capital and Communities of Place. *Rural Sociology* 63(4): 481–506.

Foucault, M. (1977) *Discipline and Punish: The Birth of the Prison.* London: Penguin Books.

Foucault, M. (1978) *The History of Sexuality: An Introduction.* Vol. 1, trans. Robert Hurley. New York: Vintage Books.

Foucault, M. (1979) Governmentality. *Ideology and Consciousness* 6: 5–29

Foucault, M. (1980) *Power/Knowledge: Selected Interviews and Other Writings 1972–1977.* Colin Gordon (ed.). Brighton: Harvester Press.

Foucault, M. (1988) The Ethic of Care for the Self as a Practice of Freedom. In J. Bernauer and D. Rasmussen (eds), *The Final Foucault.* Cambridge, MA: MIT Press.

Foucault, M. (1991) Governmentality. In G. Burchell, C. Gordon and P. Miller (eds), *The Foucault Effect: Studies in Governmentality.* London: Harvester Wheatsheaf.

Franklin, J. (ed.) (2004) *Politics, Trust and Networks: Social Capital in Critical Perspective.* Families and Social Capital, ESRC Research Group, Working Paper No. 7.

Friedman, M. (1962) *Capitalism and Freedom.* Chicago, IL: University of Chiacgo Press.

Fruzzetti, L. (1990 [1982]) *The Gift of a Virgin: Women, Marriage, and Ritual in a Bengali Society.* New Delhi: Oxford University Press.

Fruzzetti, L. and Ostor, A. (1976) Seed and Earth: A Cultural Analysis of Kinship in a Bengali Town. *Contribution to Indian Sociology,* 10(1): 97–130.

Fruzzetti, L. and Tenhunen, S. (2006) Introduction. In L. Fruzzetti and S. Tenhunen (eds), *Culture, Power, and Agency: Gender in Indian Ethnography.* Kolkata: Stree, pp. vi–xxiii.

Fuglesang, A. and Chandler, D. (1993) *Participation as a Process: Process as Growth: What We Can Learn from Grameen Bank of Bangladesh.* Dhaka: Grameen Trust.

Fukuyama, F. (1995) *Trust: The Social Virtues and the Creation of Prosperity.* New York: The Free Press.

Gambetta, D. (1988) Can We Trust Trust? In D. Gambetta (ed.), *Trust Making and Breaking Cooperative Relations.* New York: Basil Blackwell.

Gambetta, D. (1993) *The Sicilian Mafia: The Business of Private Protection.* Cambridge, MA: Harvard University Press.

Gardner, K. (1992) Migration and the Rural Context in Sylhet. *New Community* 18(4): 579–590.

Gardner, K. (1995) *Global Migrants, Local Lives: Travel and Transformation in Rural Bangladesh.* Oxford: Clarendon Press.

Gardner, K. (1998) Women and Islamic Revivalism in a Bangladeshi Community. In P. Jeffery and A. Basu (eds), *Appropriating Gender: Women's Activism and Politicized Religion in South Asia.* New York and London: Routledge, pp. 203–220.

Gardner, K. (2012) *The Discordant Development: Global Capitalism and the Struggle for Connection in Bangladesh.* London: Pluto Press.

Geirbo, H. C. and Imam, N. (2006) *The Motivations Behind Giving and Taking Dowry.* Research Monograph Series No. 28. Dhaka, Bangladesh: BRAC, Research and Evaluation Division.

Ghai, D. (1984) *An Evaluation of the Impact of the Grameen Bank Project.* Dhaka: Grameen Bank.

Giddens, A. (1984) *The Constitution of Society: Outline of The Theory of Structuration.* Cambridge: Polity.

Goetz, A. M. and Sen Gupta, R. (1996) Who Takes the Credit? Gender, Power, and Control over Loan Use in Rural Credit Programmes in Bangladesh. *World Development* 24(1): 45–63.

Goffman, E. (1975) *Asylums.* Harmondsworth: Penguin Books.

Goffman, E. (1977) The Arrangement between the Sexes. *Theory and Society* 4: 301–331.

Goody, J. (1973) Bride Wealth and Dowry in Africa and Eurasia. In J. Goody and S. J. Tambiah (eds), *Bride Wealth and Dowry.* Cambridge Papers in Social Anthropology, No. 7. Cambridge: Cambridge University Press, pp. 1–58.

Goody, J. (1976) *Production and Reproduction: A Comparative Study of the Domestic Domain.* Cambridge Studies in Social Anthropology. Cambridge: Cambridge University Press.

Gordon, C. (1991) Governmental Rationality: An Introduction. In G. C. Burchell and P. Miller (eds), *The Foucault Effect: Studies in Governmentality.* Chicago, IL: University of Chicago Press, pp. 1–51.

Gramsci, A. (1971) *Selections from the Prison Notebooks.* Ed. and trans. Q. Hoare and G. Nowell-Smith. New York: International Publishers.

Grameen Bank (2009). *Annual Report.* Available at:www.grameen.com/index.php?option=com_content&task=view&id=786&Itemid=756.

Gregory, J. (1984) The Myth of the Male Ethnographer and Women's World. *American Anthropologist* 86(2): 31–27.

Guerin, I. (2006) Women and Money: Lessons from Senegal. *Development and Change* 37: 549–570.

Gugliotta, G. (1993) Harvesting a Living from Seeds of Credit: Anti-poverty Strategy Called Microenterprise Is Growing in U.S. *Washington Post*, 6 May.

Hadi, A. (2005) Women's Productive Role and Marital Violence in Bangladesh. *Journal of Family Violence* 20(3): 181–189.

Hanifan, L. J. (1916) The Rural Community Center. *Annals of the American Academy of Political and Social Science* 67: 130–138.

Haque, M. S. and Yamao, M. (2009) Can Microcredit Alleviate Poverty? A Case Study of Bangladesh. *International Journal of Human and Social Sciences* 4(13): 929–937.

Hardin, R. (1995) *One for All: The Logic of Group Conflict.* Princeton, NJ: Princeton University Press.

Hardin, R. (1999) Do We Want Trust in Government? In M. E. Warren (ed.), *Democracy and Trust.* New York: Cambridge University Press, pp. 22–41.

Harford, T. (2008) The Battle for the Soul of Microfinance. *Financial Times*, 6 December.

Harper, M. (2002) Self-Help Groups and Grameen Bank Groups: What are the Differences? In T. Fisher and M. S. Sriram (eds), *Beyond Microcredit: Putting Development Back into Microfinance*, New Delhi: Sage: 169–198.

Hartman, B. (1987) *Reproductive Rights and Wrongs: The Global Policies of Population Control and Contraceptive Choice*. New York: Harper & Row.

Hartman, B. and Boyce, J. K. (1983) *A Quiet Violence: View from Bangladesh Village*. San Francisco, CA: Institute for Food and Development Policy.

Harvey, D. (2005) *A Brief History of Neoliberalism*. Oxford: Oxford University Press.

Hashmi, T. (2000) *Women and Islam in Bangladesh: Beyond Subjection and Tyranny*. New York: St Martin's Press.

Hashemi, S. M., Schuler, S. R. and Riley, A. (1996) Rural Credit Programmes and Women's Empowerment in Bangladesh. *World Development* 24(4): 635–653.

Helms, B. (2006) *Access for All: Building Inclusive Financial Systems*. Washington, DC: World Bank.

Hietalathi, J. and Nygren, A. (2011) Microcredit as a Socio-political Institution in South Africa: The Complexity of Rules, Logic and Power Relations. In F. Hossain, C. Rees and T. Knight Millar (eds), *Microcredit and International Development: Contexts, Achievements and Challenges*. Abingdon: Routledge, pp. 21–51.

Hoff, K. and Stiglitz, J. E. (1990) Introduction: Imperfect Information and Rural Credit Market: Puzzles and Policy Perspectives. *The World Bank Economic Review* 4(3): 235–251.

Hofferth, S. L., Boisjoly, J. and Duncan, G. J. (1999) The Development of Social Capital. *Rationality and Society* 11(1): 79–110.

Hoffman, L., DeHart, M. and Collier, S. (2006) Notes on the Anthropology of Neoliberalism. *Anthropology News* 47: 9–10.

Holcombe, S. H. (1999) *Managing to Empower: The Grameen Bank's Experience of Poverty Alleviation*. Zed Books: London and New York.

Holt, S. L. and Ribe, H. (1991) *Developing Financial Institutions for the Poor and Reducing Barriers to Access for Women*. World Bank Discussion Papers No. 117. Washington, DC.

Hossain, M. (1984) *The Impact of Grameen Bank on Women's Involvement in Productive Activities*. Paper presented in the seminar on Bank Credit For Landless Women: A Study Tour of Grameen Bank organized by the Economic and Social Commission for Asia and Pacific, Dhaka (November). Bangladesh: Working Paper No. 4. Dhaka: Bangladesh Institute of Development Studies.

Hossain, M. (1988) *Credit for Alleviation of Rural Poverty: The Grameen Bank in Bangladesh*. Research Report No. 65. Washington, DC: International Food Policy Research Institute.

Huda, S. and Mahmud, S. (1998) *Women's Control over Productive Assets: The Role of Credit-based Development Interventions*. Working Paper No. 28, BRAC-ICDDR, B, Joint Research Project, Matlab, Dhaka.

Hulme, D. (2000) Is Micro-debt Good for Poor People? A Note on the Dark Side of Microfinance. *Small Enterprise Development* 11(1): 26–28.

Hulme, D. and Mosley, P. (1996) *Finance against Poverty*. London: Routledge.

Hulterström, K. (1995) The Dilemma of Personal and Public Social Capital: A Study on the Creation of Social Capital in Bangladesh. Unpublished MA thesis, Uppsala University, Sweden.

Inhorn, M. (1996) *Infertility and Patriarchy: The Cultural Politics of Gender and Family Life in Egypt*. Philadephia, PA: University of Pennsylvania Press.

Islam-Rahman, R. (1986) *Impact of the Grameen Bank on the Situation of Poor Rural Women*. Grameen Bank Evaluation Project Working Paper No. 1. Dhaka: Bangladesh Institute of Development Studies.

Ito, S. (1999) *The Grameen Bank: Rhetoric and Reality.* Unpublished thesis, University of Sussex.

Ito, S. (2003) Microfinance and Social Capital: Does Social Capital Help Create Good Practice? *Development in Practice* 13(4): 322–332.

Jackson, C. (1996) Rescuing Gender from the Poverty Trap. *World Development* 24(3): 489–504.

Jacobs, J. (1961) *The Life and Death of Great American Cities.* New York: Random House.

Jahangir, B. K. (1979) *Differentiation, Polarisation and Confrontation in Rural Bangladesh.* Dhaka: Centre for Social Studies, University of Dhaka.

Jahangir, B. K. (1982) *Rural Society, Power Structure and Class Practice.* Dhaka: Centre for Social Studies, University of Dhaka.

Jain, P. S. (1996) Managing Credit for the Rural Poor: Lessons from the Grameen Bank. *World Development* 24(1): 79–89.

Jansen, A. (1999) *The Limits of Microfinance as an Economic Development Tool.* Paper presented at the Association of Collegiate Schools of Planning Conference. Pasadena, CA.

Jansen, E. (1987) *Rural Bangladesh: Competition for Scarce Resources.* Dhaka: The University Press.

Jeffery, P. (1979) *Frogs in a Well: Indian Women in Purdah.* London: Zed Books.

Jeffery, P. and Jeffery, R. (1996) Delayed Periods and Falling Babies: The Enthnophysiology and Politics of Pregnancy Loss in Rural India. In R. Cecil (ed.), *The Anthropology of Pregnancy Loss: Comparative Studies in Miscarriage, Stillbirth and Neonatal Death.* Oxford: Berg.

Jeffery, P., Jeffery, R. and Lyon, A. (1989) *Labour Pains, Labour Power: Women and Childbearing in India.* London: Zed Books and New Delhi: Manohar.

Jelin, E. (1998) Toward a Culture of Participation and Citizenship: Challenges for a More Equitable World. In S. E. Alvarez, E. Dagnino and A. Escobar (eds), *Culture of Politics, Politics of Culture: Re-Visioning Latin American Social Movements.* Boulder, CO: Westview, A Member of the Perseus Books Group, pp. 405–414.

Johnson, S. and Kidder, T. (1999) Globalization and Gender: Dilemmas for Microfinance Organizations. *Small Enterprise Development* 10(3): 4–15.

Johnson, S. (2005) Gender Relations, Empowerment and Microcredit: Moving on from a Lost Decade. *European Journal of Development Research* 17(2): 224–248.

Kabeer, N. (1994) *Reversed Realities: Gender Hierarchies in Development Thought.* New Delhi: Kali for Women.

Kabeer, N. (1996) Agency, Well-being and Inequality: Reflections on the Gender Dimensions of Poverty. *IDS Bulletin* 27(1): 11–21.

Kabeer, N. (1998) *Money Can't Buy Me Love? Re-evaluating Gender, Credit and Empowerment in Rural Bangladesh.* IDS Discussion Paper No. 363. Institute of Development Studies, Sussex.

Kabeer, N. (1999) *The Conditions and Consequences of Choice: Reflections on the Measurement of Women's Empowerment.* UNRISD Discussion Paper DP108. Geneva: United Nations Research Institute for Social Development.

Kabeer, N. (2001) Conflicts over Credit: Re-Evaluating the Empowerment Potential of Loans to Women in Rural Bangladesh. *World Development* 29(1): 63–84.

Kabeer, N., Mahmud, S. and Castro, J. G. I. (2012) NGOs and the Political Empowerment of Poor People in Rural Bangladesh: Cultivating the Habits of Democracy? *World Development*, 40(10): 2044–2062.

Kabir, M., Amin, R., Ahmed, A. U. and Chowdhury, J. (1994) Factors Affecting Desired Family-Size in Bangladesh. *Journal of Biological Science* 26(3): 369–375.

Kamal, F. M. (1998) *Impact of Credit-plus Paradigm of Development on Gender Inequality, Women's Empowerment and Reproductive Behaviour in Rural Bangladesh.* Unpublished paper. Dhaka: BRAC.

Kandiyoti, D. (1988) Bargaining with Patriarchy. *Gender and Society* 2(3).

Karim, L. (2004) Democratizing Bangladesh: State, NGOs, and Militant Islam. *Cultural Dynamics* 16(2/3): 291–318.

Karim, L. (2008) Demystifying Micro-credit: The Grameen Bank, NGOs, and Neoliberalism in Bangladesh. *Cultural Dynamics* 20(1): 5–29.

Karim, L. (2011) *Microfinance and Its Discontents: Women in Debt in Bangladesh.* Minneapolis, MN: University of Minnesota Press.

Keating, C., Rasmussen, C. and Rishi, P. (2010) The Rationality of Empowerment: Microcredit, Accumulation, and the Gendered Economy. *Journal of Women in Culture and Society* 36(1): 153–176.

Khan, M. E., Rob, U. and Hossain, S. M. I. (2001) Violence against Women and its Impact on Women's Lives: Some Observations from Bangladesh. *Journal of Family Welfare* 46(2): 12–24.

Khandker, S. R. (1998) *Fighting Poverty with Microcredit: Examples in Bangladesh.* New York: Oxford University Press.

Khandker, S. R. (2003) *Microfinance and Poverty: Evidence Using Panel Data from Bangladesh.* Working Paper No. 2945, World Bank Policy Research. Washington, DC: World Bank, 31 January.

Khandker, S. R. and Chowdhury, O. H. (1995) *Targeted Credit Programmes and Rural Poverty in Bangladesh.* Washington, DC: World Bank,.

Khandker, S. R. and Latif, M. A. (1995) *The Role of Family Planning and Targeted Credit Programmes in Demographic Change in Bangladesh.* Workshop: Credit Programmes and the Poor, 19–22 March. Dhaka: Education and Social Policy Department, World Bank, and Bangladesh Institute of Development Studies (BIDS).

Khandker, S., Khalily, B. and Khan, Z. (1994) *Grameen Bank Performance and Sustainability.* World Bank Discussion Paper No. 306. Washington, DC: World Bank.

Kishwar, M. (1986) Dowry: To Ensure her Happiness or to Disinherit Her? *Manushi* 34(May–June): 2–13.

Koenig, M., Ahmed, S., Hossain, M. and Mozumder, A. (2003) Women's Status and Domestic Violence in Rural Bangladesh: Individual and Community-led Effects. *Demography* 40: 269–288.

Kotalova, J. (1993) *Belonging to Others: Cultural Construction of Womenhood among Muslims in Village in Bangladesh.* Uppsala: Almqvist & Wiksell.

Krishna, A. and Shrader, E. (1999) *Social Capital Assessment.* Paper for the Conference on Social Capital and Poverty Reduction. Washington, DC: World Bank, 22–24 June.

Larance L. Y. (1998) *Building Social Capital from the Centre: A Village-level Investigation of Bangladesh's Grameen Bank.* Centre for Social Development, Working Paper No. 98(4). St. Louis, MO: Washington University in St. Louis.

Lerner, D. (1972) Modernization Social Aspects. In D. Sills (ed.), *International Encyclopedia of the Social Sciences*, Vol. 9. New York: Collier Macmillan.

Leach, F. and Sitram, S. (2002) Microfinance and Women's Empowerment: A Lesson from India. *Development in Practice* 12(5): 575–588.

Lin, N. (1999) *Building a Network Theory of Social Capital.* Paper presented at the International Sunbelt Social Network Conference, Charleston, South Carolina, 18–21 February.

McDermott, P. (2001) Globalization, Women and Development: Microfinance and Factory Work in Perspective. *Journal of Public Affairs* 13: 65–79.

McDonald, J. H. (1999) The Neoliberal Project and Governmentality in Rural Mexico: Emergent Farm Organization in the Michoacan Highlands. *Human Organization* 62(2): 100–111.

McGregor, J. A. (1988) Credit and the Rural Poor: The Changing Policy Environment in Bangladesh. *Public Administration and Development* 8: 467–482.

McIntosh, C. and Wydick, B. (2005) Competition and Microfinance. *Journal of Development Economics* 78: 271–298.

Maclean, K. (2010) Capitalizing on Women's Social Capital? Women-targeted Microfinance in Bolivia. *Development and Change* 43(3): 495–515.

McNay, L. (1992) *Foucault and Feminism: Power, Gender and the Self.* Cambridge: Polity Press.

McNay, L. (1999) Gender, Habitus and the Field: Pierre Bourdieu and the Limits of Reflexivity. *Theory, Culture and Society* 16(1): 95–117.

Madan, T. N. (1975) Structural Implications of Marriage in North India: Wife-givers and Wife-takers among the Pandits of Kashmir. *Contribution to Indian Sociology* 9 (2): 218–243.

Madan, T. N. (1989) *Family and Kinship: A Study of the Pandits of Rural Kashmir.* Delhi: Oxford University Press.

Maes J. P. and Reed, L. R. (2012) *State of the Microcredit Summit Campaign Report 2012,*Washington, DC: Microcredit Summit Campaign. Available at: www.micro creditsummit.org/pubs/reports/socr/2012/WEB_SOCR-2012_English.pdf.

Mahmud, S. (2003) Actually how Empowering Is Microcredit? *Development and Change* 34(4): 577–605.

Maloney, C., Aziz, K. M. A. and Sarkar, P. (1981) *Beliefs and Fertility in Bangladesh.* Dacca: International Cholera Research Laboratory Bangladesh.

Mamdani, M. (1972) *The Myth of Population Control: Family, Caste and Class in an Indian Village.* New York: Monthly Review Press.

Mandelbaum, D. G. (1988) *Women's Seclusion and Men's Honor: Sex Roles in North India, Bangladesh and Pakistan.* Tuscon, AZ: University of Arizona Press.

Mann, M. (1986) A Crisis in Stratification Theory? Persons, Households/Families/ Lineages, Genders, Classes, and Nations. In R. Crompton and M. Mann (eds), *Gender and Stratification.* London: Polity Press.

Mari Bhat, P. N., and Halli, S. S. (1999) Demography of Brideprice and Dowry: Causes and Consequences of the Indian Marriage Squeeze. *Population Studies* 53 (2): 129–148.

Matin, I. (1998) *Rapid Credit Deepening and the Joint Liability Credit Contract: A Study of Grameen Bank Borrowers in Madhupur.* Doctoral dissertation, University of Sussex.

Matin, I. and Hulme, D. (2003) Programmes for the Poorest: Learning from the IGVGD Program in Bangladesh. *World Development* 31(3): 647–665.

Mayoux, L. (1995) *From Vicious to Vicious to Virtuous Circles? Gender and Micro-enterprise Development.* UNRISD, Occasional Paper No. 30.

Mayoux, L. (1999). Questioning Virtuous Spirals: Micro-Finance and Women's Empowerment in Africa. *Journal of International Development* 11: 957–984.

Mayoux, L. (2000) *Micro-Finance for Women's Empowerment: A Participatory Learning, Management and Action Approach*. Paper presented at the Asia Regional Micro-credit Summit, New Delhi, India, February.

Mayoux, L. (2001a). Tackling the Downside: Social Capital, Women's Empowerment and Micro-finance in Cameroon. *Development and Change* 32: 421–450.

Mayoux, L. (2001b). Women's Empowerment Versus Sustainability? Towards a New Paradigm in Micro-finance Programmes. In B. Lemire, R. Pearson and G. Campbell (eds), *Women and Credit. Researching the Past, Refiguring the Future*. New York: Berg: 245–269.

Mayoux, L. (2002a). Microfinance and Women's Empowerment: Rethinking 'Best Practice'. *Development Bulletin* 57: 76–80.

Mayoux, L. (2002b). *Empowerment or Feminisation of Debt: Towards a New Agenda in African Microfinance*. Report based on One World Action Conference, March, London.

Mayoux, L. (2006) *Women's Empowerment through Sustainable Microfinance: Rethinking Best Practice*. Discussion Paper. Available at: www.genfinance.info/documents/Mayoux Background paper.pdf.

Meier, G. M. (1984) *Emerging From Poverty: The Economics That Really Matters*. New York: Oxford University Press.

Ministry of Health and Population Control (MHPC). (1978) *Bangladesh Fertility Survey 1975: First Country Report*. Dhaka: Bangladesh.

Miles, M. and Huberman, A. M. (1984) *Qualitative Data Analysis: A Source Book of New Methods*. Thousand Oaks, CA: Sage.

Milgram, B. L. (2001) Operationalizing Microfinance: Women and Craftwork in Ifugao, Upland Philippines. *Human Organization* 60(3): 212–224.

Miller, B. (1981) *The Endangered Sex*. Ithaca, NY: Cornell University Press.

Miraftab, F. (2004) Making Neo-Liberal Governance: The Disempowering Work of Employment. *International Planning Studies* 9: 239–259.

Mizan, A. N. (1994) *In Quest of Empowerment: The Grameen Bank Impact on Women's Power and Status*. Dhaka: The University Press.

Moghadam, V. M. (1990) *Gender, Development, and Policy: Toward Equity and Empowerment*. Helskini: World Institute for Development Economics Research of the United Nations.

Mohanthy, C. T. (1991) Under Western Eyes: Feminist Scholarship and Colonial Discourses. In C. T. Mohanthy, Ann Russo and Lourdes Torres (eds), *Third World Women and Politics of Feminism*. Bloomington, IN: Indiana University Press.

Molyneux, M. (2002) Gender and the Silences of Social Capital: Lessons from Latin America. *Development and Change* 33: 167–188.

Monsoor, T. (2003) Dower and Dowry: Its Effect on the Empowerment of Muslim Women. *Star Law Analysis, The Daily Star*, 27 July.

Montgomery, R. (1995) Disciplining or Protecting the Poor? Avoiding the Social Costs of Peer Pressure in Solidarity Group Microcredit Schemes. Paper presented at the conference on Finance against Poverty, 27–28 March. University of Reading.

Montgomery, R. (1996) Disciplining or Protecting the Poor? Avoiding Social Costs of Peer Pressure in Micro-Credit Schemes. *Journal of International Development* 8(20): 289–305.

Montgomery, H. and Weiss, J. (2005) Great Expectations: Microfinance and Poverty Reduction in Asia and Latin America. *Oxford Development Studies* 33(3–4): 391–416.

Montgomery, H. and Weiss, J. (2011) Can Commercially-oriented Microfinance Help Meet the Millennium Development Goals? Evidence from Pakistan. *World Development* 39(1): 87–109.

Montgomery, R., Bhattacharya, D. and Hulme, D. (1996) Credit for the Poor in Bangladesh: The BRAC Rural Development Programme and Employment Programme. In D. Hulme and P. Mosley (eds), *Finance against Poverty*, Vol. 2. London: Routledge.

Moodie, M. (2008) Enter Microcredit: A New Culture of Women's Empowerment in Rajasthan? *American Ethnologist* 35(3): 454–465.

Moore, H. L. (1988) *Feminism and Anthropology*. London: Polity Press.

Moore, H. L. (1991) Households and Gender Relations: The Modelling of the Economy (draft paper). Department of Anthropology, London School of Economics.

Moore, H. L. (1994) *A Passion for Difference. Essays in Anthropology and Gender*. Cambridge: Polity Press.

Morduch, J. (1998) Does Microfinance Really Help the Poor? New Evidence from Flagship Programmes in Bangladesh (draft paper). Department of Economics and HIID, Harvard University and Hoover Institution, Stanford University, July.

Morduch, J. (1999) The Microfinance Promise. *Journal of Economic Literature* 37(4): 1569–1614.

Morduch, J. (2000) The Microfinance Schism. *World Development* 28(4): 617–629.

Morgan, B. (2001) Empowering NGOs: The Microcredit Movement through Foucault's Notion of Dispositif. *Alternatives: Global, Local, Political* 26(3): 233–258.

Morgan, B. (2006) Discipling the Developmental Subject: Neoliberal Power and Governance through Microcredit. In Jule Fernando (ed.), *Micro-Finance: Perils and Prospects*. New York: Routledge, pp. 64–88.

Murray, T. (2007) *The Will to Improve: Governmentality, Development, and Practice of Politics*. Durham, NC: Duke University Press.

Nag, M. (1976) *Factors Affecting Human Fertility in Nonindustrial Societies: A Cross Cultural Study*. Yale University Publications in Anthropology, No. 66.

Nag, M. (1991) *Sex Preferences in Bangladesh, India and Pakistan and its Effect on Fertility*. New York: Population Council. WP 27.

Nanivadekar, M. (2003) *Women's Quota in Urban Local Government: A Cross-national Comparison*. Paper presented at an international seminar organized by the French Embassy's Center for Social Sciences in New Delhi, 6–7 February.

Narayan, D. and Cassidy, M. F. (2001) A Dimensional Approach to Measuring Social Capital: Development and Validation of a Social Capital Inventory. *Current Sociology* 49(2): 59–102.

Offe, C. and Fuchs, S. (2002) A Decline of Social Capital? The German Case. In R. Putnam (ed.), *Democracies in Flux: The Evolution of Social Capital in Contemporary Society*. New York: Oxford University Press, pp.188–243.

Oldenburg, V. T. (2003) *Dowry Murder: The Imperial Origins of a Cultural Crime*. Delhi: Oxford University Press.

Olsen, M. (1972) Social Participation and Voting Turnout. *American Sociological Review* 37: 317–333.

Ong, A. (2006) *Neoliberalism as Exception: Mutations in Citizenship and Sovereignty*. Durham, NC: Duke University Press.

Osmani, L. N. (1998) The Grameen Bank Experiment: Empowerment of Women through Credit. In H. Afsar (ed.), *Women and Empowerment: Illustrations from the Third World*. Basingstoke: Macmillan.

Ostrom, E. (1994) Constructing Social Capital and Collective Action. *Journal of Theoretical Politics* 6(4): 527–562.

Papanek, H. (1964) The Women Field Worker in Purdah Society. *Human Organization* 23(2): 126–166.

Papanek, H. (1973) Purdah: Separate Worlds and Symbolic Shelter. *Comparative Studies in Society and History* 15: 289–325.

Papanek, H. (1990) To Each Less than She Needs, From Each More than She Can Do: Allocations, Entitlements, and Value. In I. Tinker (ed.), *Persistent Inequalities: Women and World Development*. Oxford: Oxford University Press.

Parmar, A. (2003) Micro-credit, Empowerment and Agency: Re-evaluating the Discourse. *Canadian Journal of Development Studies* 24(3): 461–476.

Parry, J. P. (1979) *Caste and Kinship in Kangra*. London: Routledge and Kegan Paul.

Peck, J. and Tickell, A. (2002) Neoliberalizing Space. *Antipode* 34: 380–404.

Peterson, S. (2005) How (the Meaning of) Gender Matters in Political Economy. *New Political Economy* 10(4): 499–521.

Petras, J. (1997) Imperialism and NGOs in Latin America. *Monthly Review* 49 (7):10–33.

Pitt, M. and Khandker, S. R. (1995) *Households and Intrahousehold Impacts of the Grameen Bank and Similar Targeted Credit Programmes in Bangladesh*. Paper presented at workshop on Credit Programmes for the Poor: Household and Intrahousehold Impacts and Program Sustainability by the Education and Social Policy Department, Washington, DC and Bangladesh Institute of Development Studies.

Pitt, M. and Khandker, S. R. (1998) The Impact of Group-Based Credit Programmes on Poor Households in Bangladesh: Does the Gender of Participants Matter? *Journal of Political Economy* 106: 958–996.

Pitt-Rivers, J. (1977) *The Fate of Shechem: On the Politics of Sex*. Cambridge: Cambridge University Press.

Portes, A. (1998) Social Capital: Its Origins and Applications in Modern Sociology. *Annual Review of Sociology* 24: 1–24.

Portes, A. and Landolt, P. (2000) The Downside of Social Capital. *The American Prospect* 26: 18–21.

Portes, A. and Sensenbrenner, J. (1993) Embeddednes and Immigration: Notes on the Social Determinants of Economic Action. *American Journal of Sociology* 98: 1320–1350.

Putnam, R. (1993a). *Making Democracy Work: Civic Traditions in Modern Italy*. Princeton, NJ: Princeton University Press.

Putnam, R. (1993b). The Prosperous Community: Social Capital and Public Life. *American Prospect* (spring): 35–42.

Putnam, R. (1995a). Bowling Alone: America's Declining Social Capital. *Journal of Democracy* 6(1).

Putnam, R. (1995b). Tuning In, Tuning Out: The Strange Disappearance of Social Capital in America. *PS: Political Science and Politics* 28: 664–683.

Putnam, R. (1996) The Strange Disappearance of Civic America. *American Prospect* (winter): 34–48.

Putnam, R. (1998) Foreword. *Housing Policy Debate* 9(1): v–viii.

Putnam, R. (2000) *Bowling Alone: The Collapse and Revival of American Community*, New York: Touchstone.

Rahman, A. (1986a). *Impact of the Grameen Bank Intervention on Rural Power Structure*. Working Paper No. 2. Dhaka: Bangladesh Institute of Development Studies.

Rahman, A. (1986b). *Consciousness Raising Efforts of Grameen Bank*. Working Paper No. 3. Dhaka: Bangladesh Institute of Development Studies.

Rahman, H. Z. (ed.) (1991) *Rethinking Poverty: Dimensions, Process, Options. Poverty Trends Study*. Dhaka: Bangladesh Institute of Development Studies.

Rahman, A. (1999) Micro-Credit Initiatives for Equitable and Sustainable Development: Who Pays? *World Development* 27(1): 67–82.

Rahman, A. (2001) *Women and Microcredit in Rural Bangladesh: An Anthropological Study of Grameen Bank Lending*. Boulder, CO: Westview.

Rahman, M. and Da Vanzo, J. (1993) Gender Preference and Birth Spacing in Matlab, Bangladesh. *Demography* 30(3): 315–332.

Rahman, A. and Khandker, S. R. (1994) Role of Targeted Credit Programmes in promoting Employment and Productivity of the Poor in Bangladesh. *Bangladesh Development Studies* 22(2–3): 49–92.

Rankin, K. N. (2001) Governing Development: Neoliberalism, Microcredit, and Rational Economic Women. *Economy and Society* 30(1): 18–37.

Rankin, K. N. (2002) Social Capital, Microfinance, and the Politics of Development. *Feminist Economics* 8(1): 1–24.

Razavi, S. (1997) Fitting Gender into Development Institutions. *World Development* 25(7): 1111–1125.

Rhyne, E. (1998) The Yin and Yang of Microfinance: Reaching the Poor and Sustainability. *Micro Banking Bulletin* 2: 6–9.

Robinson, M. S. (2002) *The Microfinance Revolution. Vol. 2: Lessons from Indonesia*, Washington, DC: World Bank.

Rodman, H. (1972) Marital Power and the Theory of Resources in Cultural Context. *Journal of Comparative Family Studies* 3 (spring): 50–70.

Roodman, D. and Morduch, J. (2009) *The Impact of Microcredit on the Poor in Bangladesh: Revisiting the Evidence*. Working Paper, Washington, DC: Centre for Global Development, p. 174.

Roy, A. (2010) *Poverty Capital: Microfinance and the Making of Development*. New York: Routledge.

Rozario, S. (1992) *Women and Social Change in a Bangladeshi Village*. London: Zed Books.

Rozario, S. (1998) The Dai and the Doctor: Discourses on Women's Reproductive Health in Rural Bangladesh. In R. Kalpana and J. Margaret (eds), *Maternities and Modernities: Colonial and Postcolonial Experiences in Asia and the Pacific*. Melbourne, New York and Cambridge: Cambridge University Press.

Rozario, S. (2001) *Purity and Communal Boundaries: Women and Social Change in a Bangladeshi Village*. Dhaka: The University Press.

Rowlands, Jo. (1997) *Questioning Empowerment: Working with Women in Honduras*. Oxford: Oxfam.

Rudner, D. W. (1994) *Caste and Capitalism in Colonial India: The Nattukottai Chettiars*. Berkeley, CA: University of California Press.

Säävälä, M. (1997) *Child as Hope: Contextualizing Fertility Transition in Rural South India*. PhD Thesis, Helsinki University Press.

Säävälä, M. (2006) Sterilized Mothers: Women's Personhood and Family Planning in Rural South India. In L. Fruzzetti and S. Tenhunen (eds), *Culture, Power, and Agency in Indian ethnography*. Kolkata: Stree, pp. 135–170.

Säävälä, M. (2010) *Middle-Class Moralities: Everyday Struggle over Belonging and Prestige in India*. Hyderabad: Orient BlackSwan.

Sahlins, M. (1994) Goodbye to Tristes Tropes: Ethnography in the Context of Modern World History. In R. Borofsky (ed.), *Assessing Cultural Anthropology*. New York: McGraw-Hill.

Scheufele, D. and Shah, D. V. (2000) Personality Strength and Social Capital. *Communication Research* 27(2): 107–131.

Schneider, D. (1984) *A Critique of the Study of Kinship*. Ann Arbor, MI: University of Michigan Press.

Schneider, J. (1971) Of Vigilance and Virgins: Honour, Shame, and Access to Resources in Mediterranean Societies. *Ethnology* 10(1): 1–24.

Schuler, S. R. and Hashemi, S. M. (1994) Credit Programmes, Women's Empowerment, and Contraceptive Use in Rural Bangladesh. *Studies in Family Planning* 25 (2): 65–76.

Schuler, S. R., Hashemi, S. M. and Badal, S. (1998) Men's Violence against Women in Rural Bangladesh: Undermined or Exacerbated by Microcredit Progrmmes? *Development in Practice*, 8: 148–157.

Schuler, S. R., Hashemi, S. M. and Riley, A. P. (1997a). *Men's Violence against Women in Rural Bangladesh: Undermined or Exacerbated by Micro-Credit Pro-grammes?* Paper presented at the Population Association of America Annual Meetings, Washington, DC.

Schuler, S. R., Hashemi, S. M. and Riley, A. P. (1997b). The Influence of Women's Changing Roles and Status in Bangladesh's Fertility Transition: Evidence from a Study of Credit Programmes and Contraceptive Use. *World Development* 25(4): 563–575.

Schuler, S. R., Hashemi, S. M., Riley, A. P. and Akhter, S. (1996) Credit Programes, Patriarchy and Men's Violence against Women in Rural Bangladesh. *Social Science and Medicine* 43(12): 1729–1742.

Scott, J. (1972) Patron-Client Politics and Political Change in Southeast Asia. *American Political Science Review* 66(1): 91–113.

Scott, J. (1976) *The Moral Economy of the Peasant: Rebellion and Subsistence in Southeast Asia*. New Haven, CT and London: Yale University Press.

Scott, J. (1985) *Weapons of the Weak: Everyday Forms of Peasant Resistance*. New Haven, CT: Yale University Press.

Scott, J. W. (1988) *Gender and the Politics of History*. New York: Columbia University Press.

Scott, J. (1990) *Domination and the Arts of Resistance: Hidden Transcripts*. New Haven, CT and London: Yale University Press.

Sen, A. K. (1981) *Poverty and Famines: An Essay on Entitlement and Deprivation*. Delhi: Oxford University Press.

Sen, A. K. (1982) Food Battles: Conflict in the Access to Food. Coromandel Lecture, New Delhi, 13 December; republished in *Mainstream*, 8 January 1983.

Sen, A. K. (1987) *Hunger and Entitlement*. Helsinki: World Institute for Development Economics Research.

Sen, A. K. (1990) Gender and Cooperative Conflicts. In Irene Tinker (ed.), *Persistent Inequalities: Women and World Development*. New York: Oxford University Press.

Sen, A. K. (1992) *Inequality Reexamined*. Oxford: Clarendon Press.

Sen, A. K. (1999) *Development as Freedom*. Oxford: Oxford University Press.

Serageldin, I. and Grootaert, C. (2000) Defining Social Capital: An Integrating View. In P. Dasgupta and I. Serageldin (eds), *Social Capital: A Multifaceted Perspective*. Washington, DC: World Bank.

Shaheed, F. (1998) The Other Side of the Discourse: Women's Experiences of Identity, Religion, and Activism in Pakistan. In P. Jeffery and A. Basu (eds), *Appropriating Gender- Women's Activism and Politicized Religion in South Asia*. New York and London: Routledge, pp. 143–166.

Sharif, I. (1997) Poverty and Finance in Bangladesh: A New Policy Agenda. In G. D. Wood and I. Sharif (eds), *Who Needs Credit? Poverty and Finance in Bangladesh*. Dhaka: The University Press, pp. 61–81.

Sharma, U. (1978) Women and Their Affines: The Veil as a Symbol of Separation. *Man* 13: 13–33.

Sharma, U. (1980) *Women, Work and Property in North West India*. London: Tavistock.

Sharma, U. (1984) Dowry in North India: Its Consequences for Women. In R. Hirschon (ed.), *Women and Property, Women as Property*. London: Croom Helm and New York: St. Martin's Press, pp. 62–74.

Siddiqui, T. (2002) NGOs in Bangladesh: Challenges on the Threshold of the New Millennium. In A. M. Chowdhury and F. Alam (eds), *Bangladesh: On the Threshold of the Twenty-First Century*. Dhaka: Asiatic Society of Bangladesh.

Smith, P. and Thurman, E. (2007) *A Billion Bootstraps: Microcredit, Barefoot Banking, and the Business solution for Ending Poverty*. New York: McGraw Hill.

Sobhan, R. (1997) The Political Economy of Micro-Credit. In G. D. Wood and I. Sharif (eds), *Who Needs Credit? Poverty and Finance in Bangladesh*. Dhaka, The University Press, pp. 131–141.

Sobhan, R. (1998) *How Bad Governance Impedes Poverty Alleviation in Bangladesh*. OECD Development Centre, Working Paper No. 143.

Sorensen, G. (1993) Strategies and Structures of Development: The New Dogma and the Limits to its Promises. In M. von Troil (ed.), *Changing Paradigms in Development: South, East and West*. Uppsala: The Scandinavian Institute of African Studies.

Spivak, G. C. (1996 [1985]) Discussion. Subaltern Studies: Deconstructing Historiography. In R. Guha (ed.), *Subaltern Studies IV: Writings on South Asian History and Society*. Delhi: Oxford University Press.

Srinivas, M. N. (1966) *Social Change in Modern India*. Berkeley, CA: University of California Press.

Stake, R. E. (1994) Case Studies. In N. K. Denzin and Y. S. Lincoln (eds), *Handbook of Qualitative Research*. Thousand Oaks, CA: Sage, pp. 1–17.

Stake, R. E. (2000) Case Studies. In N. K. Denzin and Y. S. Lincoln (eds), *Handbook of Qualitative Research*. Thousand Oaks, CA: Sage, pp. 435–454.

Steele, F., Amin, S. and Naved, R. T. (1998) *The Impact of a Micro-credit Programme on Women's Empowerment and Fertility Behavior in Rural Bangladesh*. Policy Research Division Working Paper 115. New York: Population Council.

Stenman, O. J., Mahmud, M. and Martinsson, P. (2004) *Trust and Religion: Experimental Evidence from Bangladesh*. Working Paper 167. Department of Economics, Göteborg University, Sweden.

Stiglitz, J. E. (1990) Peer Monitoring and Credit Markets. *The World Bank Economic Review* 4(3): 351–366.

Stolle, D. and Rochon, T. R. (1996) *Social Capital, but How? Associations and the Creation of Social Capital.* Paper presented at the Conference for Europeanists, Chicago, March.

Streefland, P., Ahmed, H., Nafisa, M., Barman, D. C. and Arefeen, H. K. (1986) *Different Ways to Support the Rural Poor: Effects of Two Development Approaches in Bangladesh.* Dhaka: The Centre for Social Studies, University of Dhaka, Bangladesh.

Swedberg, R. (1987) Economic Sociology: Past and Present. *Current Sociology* 35(1): 1–25.

Tambiah, S. J. (1973) Dowry and Bridewealth and the Property Rights of Women in South Asia. In J. Goody and S. J. Tambiah (eds), *Bridewealth and Dowry.* Cambridge Papers in Social Anthropology, No: 7. Cambridge: Cambridge University Press, pp. 51–169.

Tambiah, S. J. (1989) Bridewealth and Dowry Revisited: The Position of Women in sub- Saharan Africa and North India. *Current Anthropology* 30(4): 412–435.

Teachman, J. D. and Paesch, K. (1997) Social Capital and the Generation of Human Capital. *Social Forces* 75(4): 1343–1359.

Tedlock, B. (2000) Ethnography and Ethnographic Representation. In N. K. Denzin and Y. S. Lincoln (eds), *Handbook of Qualitative Research.* London: Sage, pp. 455–486.

Tenhunen, S. (2009) *Means of Awakening: Gender, Politics and Practice in Rural India.* Kolkata: Stree.

Todd, H. (1996) *Women at the Centre: Grameen Bank Borrowers after One Decade*: Dhaka: The University Press.

Townley, B. (1993) Foucault, Power/Knowledge, and its Relevance for Human Resources Management. *Academy of Management Review* 18(3): 518–545.

Townsend, J., Gina, P. and Emma M. (2004) Creating Spaces of Resistance: Development NGOs and their Clients in Ghana, India and Mexico. *Antipode* 35(5): 871–889.

Trawick, M. (1990 [1996]) *Notes on Love in a Tamil Family.* Berkeley, CA: University of California Press.

Uberoi, P. (1997 [1993]) Marriage, Alliance, and Affinal Transactions. In P. Uberoi (ed.), *Family, Kinship and Marriage in India.* Delhi, Oxford University Press, pp. 225–236.

UNICEF (2007) *The State of the World's Children 2007. Women and Children: The Double Divided of Gender Equality, UNICEF Annual Report.* Available at: www. unicef.org/publications/files/The_State_of_the_Worlds__Children__2007_e.pdf.

United Nations Development Fund for Women (UNFPA) (2010) Available at: www. unfpa-bangladesh.org/php/about_ bangladesh.php.

United Nations Development Program (UNDP) (1995) *Human Development Report 1995.* New York: UNDP.

Uusikylä, H. (2000) *The Other Half of My Body: Coming into Being in Rural Bangladesh.* Research Reports No. 236, Department of Sociology, University of Helsinki: Helsinki University Printing House.

van Bastelaer, T. (1999) Does Social Capital Facilitate the Poor's Access to Credit?A Review of the Microeconomic Literature. Social Capital Initiative Working Paper No. 8, Washington, DC: IRIS and World Bank. Available at: http://128.8.56.16/docs/docs/SCI-WPS-08.pdf.

van Bastelaer, T. (2000) *Imperfect Information, Social Capital, and the Poor's Access to Credit*, IRIS Center Working Paper No. 234, University of Maryland, Center for Institutional Reform and the Informal Sector (IRIS).

van Schendel, W. (1981) *Peasant Mobility: The Odds of Peasant Life in Bangladesh.* Assen: Van Gorcum.

Vatuk, S. (1975) Gifts and Affines in North India. *Contribution to Indian Sociology* 9 (2): 155–195 (New Series).

Vatuk, S. (2006) Domestic Violence and Marital Breakdown in India: A View from the Family Courts. In L. Fruzzetti and S. Tenhunen (eds), *Culture, Power, and Agency: Gender in Indian Ethnography.* Stree: Kolkata, pp. 204–226.

Vogelgesang, U. (2003) Microfinance in Times of Crisis: The Effects of Competition, Raising Indebtedness, and Economic Crisis on Repayment Behaviour. *World Development Elsevier* 31(12): 2085–2114.

Wadley, S. S. (1993) Family Composition Strategies in Rural North India. *Social Science and Medicine* 37: 1367–1376.

Weber, H. (2002) The Imposition of a Global Development Architecture: The Example of Microcredit. *Review of International Studies* 28: 537–555.

Weber, H. (2004) The New Economy and Social Risk: Banking on the Poor? *Review of International Political Economy* 11(3): 356–386.

Weber, M. (1991 [1922]) *The Protestant Ethic and the Spirit of Capitalism.* Trans. T. Parsons. London: Routledge.

Westergaard, K. (1983) *Pauperization and Rural Women in Bangladesh: A Case Study.* Comilla: Bangladesh Academy for Rural Development.

White, S. C. (1991) *Evaluating the Impact of NGOs in Rural Poverty Alleviation.* Bangladesh Country Study, ODI Working Paper, No. 50. London: Overseas Development Institute.

White, S. C. (1992) *Arguing with the Crocodile: Gender and Class in Bangladesh.* Dhaka: The University Press.

White, S. C. (2010) Domains of Contestation: Women's Empowerment and Islam in Bangladesh. *Women's Studies International Forum* 33: 334–344.

Wolfensohn, J. D. (1996) *The Microcredit Summit: 2–4 February 1997: Declaration and Plan of Action.* Available at: www.microcreditsummit.org/declaration.

Woller, G. M. (2002) The Promise and Peril of Microfinance Commercialization. *Small Enterprise Development* 13(4): 12–21.

Woller, G. M., Dunford, C. and Woodworth, W. (1999) Where to Microfinance? *International Journal of Economic Development* 13(4): 12–21.

Wood, G. D. (1994) *Bangladesh: Whose Ideas, Whose Interests?* Dhaka: The University Press.

Wood, G. D. (2000) Financing Poverty Eradication: Towards New Frontiers. In I. Sharif and G. Wood (eds), *Challenges for Second Generation Microfinance: Regulation, Supervision and Resource Mobilization.* Dhaka: The University Press.

Wood, G. D. and Sharif, I. (1997) Introduction. In G. D. Wood and I. Sharif (eds), *Who Needs Credit? Poverty and Finance in Bangladesh.* Dhaka: The University Press, pp. 27–58.

Woodworth, W. P. (2008) Reciprocal Dynamics: Social Capital and Microcredit. *ESR Review* 10(2): 36–42.

Woolcock, M. J. V. (1998a). *Social Theory, Development Policy, and Poverty Alleviation: A Comparative-Historical Analysis of Group-Based Banking in Developing*

Economies. PhD dissertation, Department of Sociology, Brown University, Providence, Rhode Island.

Woolcock, M. J. V. (1998b). Social Capital and Economic Development: Towards a Theoretical Synthesis and Policy Framework. *Theory and Society* 27: 151–208.

World Bank (1989) *World Development Report: Financial Systems and Development*. New York: Oxford University Press.

World Bank (1994) *Enhancing Women's Participation in Economic Development: A World Bank Policy Paper*. Washington, DC: World Bank.

Wright, G. A. N., Hossain, M. and Rutherford, S. (1997) Savings: Flexible Financial Services for the Poor and not just the Implementing Organization. In G. D. Wood and I. Sharif (eds), *Who Needs Credit? Poverty and Finance in Bangladesh*. Dhaka: The University Press.

Wright, K. (2007) The Darker Side to Microfinance: Evidence from Cajamarca, Peru. In J. L. Fernando (ed.), *Microfinance Perils and Prospects*. New York: Routledge, pp. 154–171.

Yaron, J. (1991) *Successful Rural Financial Institutions*. Washington, DC: World Bank.

Yaron, J. (1994) What Makes Rural Finance Institutions Successful? *The World Bank Research Observer* 9(1).

Yunus, M. (1984) *On Reaching the Poor*. Paper presented at the IFAD Project Implementation Workshop, New Delhi, April.

Yunus, M. (1989) Credit for Self-Employment, A Fundamental Human Right. In D. S. Gibbons (ed.) *The Grameen Reader* (revised 1994). Dhaka: Grameen Bank.

Yunus, M. (1994) *Grameen Bank as I See It*. Dhaka: Grameen Bank.

Yunus, M. (1997) The Grameen Bank Story: Rural Credit in Bangladesh. In A. Krishna, N. Uphoff and M. J. Esman (eds), *Reasons for Hope*. London: Kumarian Press.

Yunus, M. (2003) *Banker to the Poor: Micro-lending and the Battle against World Poverty*. New York: Public Affairs.

Yunus, M. and Jolis, A. (1998) *Banker to the Poor: Micro-Lending and the Battle against World Poverty*. Dhaka: The University Press.

Zaman, H. (1996): Microcredit Programs: Who Participates and to what Extent? BRAC-ICDDR, B Joint Research Project Working Paper 12, Dhaka.

Index

Entries in *italics* denote figures; entries in **bold** denote tables.

participation in instalment
meetings 36; political awareness of 58–
60; relations between 185; relatives of
47; repayment rating of 151;
resistance to NGO rules 146, 160,
162–4, 182, 190; training in use of
credit 123, 157, 193; transferring credit
115, 160–1, 172; use of real names 28;
using loans for dowries *see* microcredit, used for dowries; women as 124
Bourdieu, Pierre 15; on neoliberalism 7;
on social capital 34; on symbolic
domination 129–30
boycotts 23, 162
BRAC (Bangladesh Rural Advancement
Committee): 17 promises of **196**;
attitudes to research 23–4; and
competition 133; conversations with
officials of 27; on dowries 16, 66, 73;
GB borrowers and 22; and group-
lending mechanism 2, 37; growth of
131, 134; interest charges of 147–8;
and joint liability 65n14; lack of training for clients 157; lending
policies of 124, 129, 137; operations in
Nodigaon 25, 29, 133; operations in
Shantigaon 26, 55; operations in Zelegaon 29, 170; repayment policies of
149; research on 10; size of 18n3; staff
relations of 135; striking features of
194–5; working conditions of
staff 151
Brahmin caste 31, 61, 68
branch managers 20–1, 23–4, 46, 132–3,
151–3
Bretton Woods institutions 3
brides, cultural identity of 186
bride wealth 71, 83
British colonial rule 57, 71
burqa 39, 121–2

camaraderie 7, 184
capital: pre-existing 177, 181; types of
34–5, 64n4
capital accumulation 11, 13, 37, 138
capitalism, integrating poor into 154
case studies, in qualitative research 26–7
cash, as dowry 70, 72, 75–7, 79
caste: in rural Bangladesh 31; in
Shantigaon 68; weaver community
within 50
centre chiefs 38, 40, 57
Chaudhuri title 30–1
child marriage 67, 196

child mortality 3, 108, 110–11
children: disruptive 104, 188; as old age
security 109
chira-muri 50, 175
Chittagong district, research in 5
chores *see* household work
chotolok status 117, 119
chotomanush 30
civic engagement 61, 63, 184
class categories: and marriage practices
70; and women's self-managed
enterprise 95, 188
clergy 39
cognitive empowerment 15
Coleman, James 15; on forms of capital
65n5; on social capital 34–5
collateral: for individual applicants 40;
microcredit-specific form of 2, 37
collateral mechanism: as governmentality
13, 52, 184–5; and market principle
43–4; social 13, 15–16, 33
collective identity: and collateral
mechanism 33; and microcredit
membership 16, 42, 52, 184; and social
capital 37, 52
colour televisions 94, 132, 170
commercial banks 146
communities, social capital of 7, 35
community mobilization 63, 157
competitiveness 11, 47, 51
confidence 16
conflict negotiation capacities 16, 84
conjugal relationships: as collective unit
88; cooperation and conflict in 85–7,
104, 187; decision-making in 16, 84
(*see also* intra-household decision-
making); unsatisfactory 101–2; and
violence 82 (*see also* domestic
violence)
connections, in social capital 34
contraception: attitudes to 111–12;
side-effects of 113; use in Bangladesh
105–6; willingness to discuss 28; and
women's empowerment 14, 114n1
corruption 1, 193
credit: access to 12, 134, 137; as
collective property 85, 186–7; demand
for 132; as human right 193; from
state institutions 1; subsidized 1, 11;
who benefits from 6, 16–17; *see also*
microcredit
credit groups: dysfunction of 52, 184;
formation of 33, 37–40; leaders of *see*
group leaders

land disputes 168, 172, 180
landlessness 32, 168, 179, 192
land ownership: and exchange
 entitlement 167; and microcredit 90,
 179; questions about 26; and social
 class 30, 32n3, 180; women's
 entitlement to 80
La Reproduction (Bourdieu) 34, 64n3
legal trouble, microcredit used for 161–2
loan collectors: avoiding 126; and credit
 recovery 150; and family disputes 48;
 at instalment meetings 41; meetings
 with 20–1; on religious differences 56
loans: inability to repay 7; vicious cycle
 of 106; *see also* credit
lojjasharam 60, 97, 127; *see also* modesty
love marriages 70, 101

mahajan 133, 147; *see also* money-lenders
maimol 30, 43, 68, 70
malaun 56
male children 81, 108–10
marketable skills 95, 116, 122–3, 181,
 188, 193
market economy, integrating the poor
 into 10–11
market place, women excluded from 116,
 121–3
market principles 11, 43, 132, 139
market rationality: microcredit
 conducted through 181; neoliberalism
 encouraging 8; NGO loans enforcing
 146
market subjects: active 150; failed 191
marriage gifts 67; borrowing for 83;
 bride's opinions on 78–9; ownership of
 80; as symbolic capital 186; *see also*
 khat-maal
marriage negotiations 67, 75, 78
marriage practices 16, 66–70
marriage transactions 70, 72, 75, 186; *see
 also* dowries
material empowerment 15
mawlana 39, 100
MDGs (Millennium Development
 Goals), and microcredit 3
microcredit: claims and research about
 3–6; commercialization of 11–12, 131–
 3, 136, 138, 156–8; as covert regulation 123; economic impact of 165;
 financial sustainability of 12;
 globalization of 3; governance
 and power relations in 10; as
 governmentality 9–10, 130, 183, 190;

and household decision-making 95;
 impact on women 84, 87, 126;
 investment of 86–7 (*see also*
 investment, by women); and microfinance 17n2; and pre-existing
 inequalities 176, 180, 183–4, 192; qualitative research into 27; rates of interest in 146–7; and self-worth 104; use
 of term 2, 183; uses of *see* uses of
 credit; and women's income 89
microcredit organizations: borrower
 criticism of 13, 17, 149, 161, 163;
 capitalist interests of 115; competition
 among 16–17, 131, 133–7, 144, 170,
 189–90; encouraging borrowing 39,
 150; goals of 183; governance of 17;
 lending policies of 124–6, 130, 142;
 obtaining research permissions from
 19; opposition to dowries 71, 78;
 patronage relationships of 62–3, 136;
 repayment policies of 149–51, 156;
 replacing traditional lenders 133; use
 of women's honour and shame 124,
 189; working conditions of staff 151–3
microcredit programmes: and birth rate
 105–6; criteria for access to 44, 52;
 drift and diffusion of 17; exclusion of
 the poorest from 139–40; generalizability of 27; group-based 2, 33, 36;
 group-meeting norms in 41; impact on
 economic pressure 104, 177–8; impact
 on solidarity 47, 52; initiative to join
 85, *86*; leaving 94, 150; and local
 gender norms 123; membership in 37,
 39–40, 53, 63–4; memberships in multiple *see* borrowers, multiple; negative
 aspects of 147; power relations in 28,
 146, 149, 152, 158, 190–1; reasons for
 joining 166–7, 169, 173; repayment
 schedules of 122 (*see also* credit
 repayments); social capital in 36–7;
 suggested reforms to 193;
 surveillance in 126, 154
Microcredit Summits 3
microenterprises *see* self-managed
 enterprises
microfinance, use of term 17n2
micro-savings 17n2, 44, 155–6, 159, 177
midwifery 157
Miraftab, Faranak 37
mission drift 138, 156, 184
Mizan, Ainon Nahar 5
mobile phones 22, 63, 70, 123
modernization theorists 1

For Product Safety Concerns and Information please contact our EU
representative GPSR@taylorandfrancis.com
Taylor & Francis Verlag GmbH, Kaufingerstraße 24, 80331 München, Germany

www.ingramcontent.com/pod-product-compliance
Ingram Content Group UK Ltd.
Pitfield, Milton Keynes, MK11 3LW, UK
UKHW021615240425
457818UK00018B/567